THE RUNAWAY HEART

Reb Sanderson was wakened at first light by a gentle tapping on his door. He opened it to find Pilar standing there, so young and vulnerable in her boyish buckskins.

Wordlessly, she stepped across the threshold and flung herself into Reb's arms, sobbing uncontrollably.

"What happened?" he said.

"Manuel . . ." she murmured, struggling to speak.

"You must tell me," he said, tightening his arms about her.

"He twisted my arm behind and forced me into the library." Now the words came in a torrent. "He pushed me onto the couch. He accused me of being your lover. He called me filthy names and said he wouldn't marry me unless I could prove to him that I was still a . . ."

She broke off—the taboo was so strong for this aristocratic Spanish girl-child, that she could speak no further . . .

Reb Sanderson knew inside him that what happened between him and Pilar in the next hour would set the course of his life and the Sanderson destiny.

The Making of America Series

THE
GOLDEN
STATERS

Lee Davis Willoughby

A DELL/BRYANS BOOK

Published by
Dell Publishing Co., Inc.
1 Dag Hammarskjold Plaza
New York, New York 10017

Dell ® TM 681510, Dell Publishing Co., Inc.

ISBN: 0-440-03020-X

Printed in the United States of America

First printing—December 1980

HORIZONS WEST

LEM SANDERSON was dying. Inflammation in the pleura of the left lung had not lessened with extensive treatment. Age had decided against him and there was nothing more the local doctor could do, his son Robert reflected as he sat on the front porch of the white frame house in the stifling Virginia dusk. A darkly handsome twenty-three, Robert brooded in thoughtful silence beside his young brother John, a fair-haired twenty-two.

Robert's and John's mother, the quiet and retiring Caroline, was indoors at the father's bedside, where she had stayed for the past twenty-four hours, keeping a faithful but futile vigil. Before the night was out the old man would probably die, Robert judged, at final peace after his long illness. He was sad that his father must suffer so. Lem had been such a good man always, a kind and helpful parent, a teacher who had spent his life's energy in dispensing the Greek and Latin classics and raising his two sons with respect for everyone and infinite tolerance for human foibles.

If Lem Sanderson had not been the kind of man he was, Robert might not have made the long and grueling summer journey up to Falls Church, Virginia from Knoxville, Tennessee, where he owned a thriving drygoods business and was engaged to be married. It was pure chance that he had been able to get home in time to be of some comfort, and that his father had remained alive this long. He might well have arrived to find Lem dead and already buried.

Beside Robert, John stirred in the porch rocker in the brooding twilight and cleared his throat. Slimmer and less robust than Robert, John was the literary one of the family once containing six siblings, of whom only John and Robert had survived. John wrote religious verse, had visions of a life through God that Robert had never been able to comprehend, and which, in fact, made him vaguely uncomfortable. All the same, Robert loved John, a decent man, and at this particular moment—for John was taking his father's dying hard—felt an empathy for his brother just as strong as he did for his wan, exhausted mother.

"Why don't you go on to bed?" John told Robert. "I'm not tired. I'll keep watch with mother, and wake you if there's any change."

For the past year John had longed to go West, first to Illinois, then to follow the Mormon prophet of Zion into the desert wilderness to a new life, his own words. But Lem's poor health and his mother's desperate need for companionship, with Robert away, had bound him to Falls Church.

"I think *you* ought to go to bed," Robert replied. "That nap I had this afternoon took the edge off my journey. I'm not weary at all."

John glanced at his brother's strong profile. "You actually like Knoxville, don't you?" he said.

"Yes. It suits my sense of adventure for the time being," Robert said. "The money's good, and there's Sarah."

Sarah Calder was the daughter of a local banker, in love with Robert, as he was with her, a big, full-busted, red-haired beauty who wanted him as much as he wanted her. Robert considered himself a lucky man. Not religious, as both John and his Sarah were, but very fortunate. He would be marrying Sarah in the spring if all continued to go well with his business, and there was no foreseeable reason why it would not.

"It's a difficult time to think of making a family in the States," John observed.

"Why now especially?"

"Well, President Polk's declared war on Mexico. Sooner or later you may have to go, if you stay in the States."

Robert shrugged indifferently. Talk of war didn't ruffle him. "It'll be over in a few months. The Mexicans don't have a chance of winning," Robert declared firmly. "They're disorganized, they don't even know where their loyalties lie."

"You may have a point. Anyway, I'll be out of it," said John.

"You really do aim to join those people in Illinois and go West with them," said Robert, finding it hard to believe that John could be so utterly possessed by the teachings of Joseph Smith, who was considered a religious heretic at best, a pariah at worst, someone to be shunned, not followed.

"God has to be my life," John said with gentle determination, "just as much as yours is business."

"You can always join me if you feel like it. *Sanderson Brothers* in gold letters would make a handsome sign on the roof of the store. In a year or two we'd have another outlet. In ten years we'd be represented in all the major capitals of the South. The work's challenging and rewarding. Come on, John, join with me. Don't drift off into hostile country. You might never come back."

"I can't, I'm committed," John told Robert. "But I'm grateful for the offer because I know you mean it." During the week, John worked as a law clerk for a Washington, D.C. attorney across the Potomac, coming home to spend Sundays with Caroline. "I admire Brigham Young and his leadership, although I've never met him. Plans are to migrate next year. I'll be going to join the party when the call comes."

"Well," Robert remarked, "I suppose you must do what you feel is right. I'll miss you, John. It'll be a very long time between visits."

"Yes, it will be," John agreed, thinking that perhaps this time of their father's dying would be the last reunion they might ever have.

"Remember one thing," said Robert, "you'll always be close to me. And if fate should manage to keep us apart, we'll always be close in spirit as brothers."

"In our minds," John agreed, "we'll never lose touch. The blood tie is strong."

"Always," Robert said emotionally, reaching his big, knotty hand out to touch the slim, cold fingers that clenched the rocker's arm, pressing them briefly.

After that the two men lapsed into silence, listening to the crickets in the dense woods to the right of the house, seeing the faint, flickering lights of fireflies dancing above the broad sweep of the lawn. The silence lasted only a short time, suddenly broken by a piercing shriek. The sound issued from the upper floor of the house, from their father's bedroom. It was their mother Caroline's voice.

The brothers were instantly on their feet. Nearest the door, Robert entered the hallway with quick strides and started up the staircase.

Caroline stood at the top of the stairs, her white dress a blur in the light of the landing's oil lamp. Her arms were flung out in despair.

"He's gone," she wailed to her sons. "Your father is dead."

She collapsed in a heap on the upper landing. Their black housekeeper Hattie knelt beside Caroline's limp form.

Lem Sanderson's funeral was held the next day at mid-afternoon in the local cemetery, according to Lem's instructions, for he belonged to no church. A good share of the townspeople turned out, for Lem was much-loved by ex-pupils as well as peers. Several mourners had come all the way from Washington, D. C. to pay last respects.

After the gruelling ordeal of the minister's interminable eulogy, well-intentioned but dismal, the funeral was concluded with prayers, and then the main body of mourners moved to the Sanderson home for refreshments. In a suffocating black dress with a high neck, Caroline insisted on presiding over the lemonade and cakes, accepting with a mild, restrained resignation the condolences offered to her by one and all. She did this against the wishes of her boys who wanted her to sit quietly to one side and let Hattie and some lady volunteers do the serving.

The minister, Reverend Whitmore, drew Robert away from the bulk of guests to the far end of the wide front porch. Well-meaning but arrogant and a confirmed busybody, Whitmore got right to his point.

"Now it's none of my business, Robert, but Miss Caroline won't last out the year if you and John leave her alone at a time like this. She's holding together just fine for the moment, but I know her moods. I've seen them more than you have these past few months. She'll die on the vine if you and John desert her now."

Robert controlled his irritation. He'd never cared much for Whitmore. The man was, to Robert's knowledge, a hypocritical meddler with a hearty taste for pretty octoroon ladies from the whorehouses of Washington, D. C., whenever he could get away from his wife and their large brood of noisy children.

"Reverend," Robert said with cool reserve, "I have a lucrative business in Knoxville. I'm engaged to be married. This is no time to offer a home to my mother. Once my wife-to-be and I have built a house, then will be the proper time to see if mother wants to come down and live with us. And I doubt very much that she will."

Whitmore considered this for a moment. "I'm speaking only to you, Robert," he said. "I know that John is deserting his family faith for distant heathen fields." Whitmore's lip curled on the final phrase.

"My mother, Mr. Whitmore, is a pragmatic woman with courage and self-sufficiency. Her normally cheerful and optimistic nature will soon reassert itself. She isn't one to malinger, not even over my father's death. There's my Aunt Cissie in Washington, and mother may even teach at her sister's private day school. We've talked of her going there when it's time to close the Falls Church house down. She has many friends in the capital. Besides, she doesn't want to come south with me, she's said so."

"Well, Robert, it's your responsibility," Whitmore pointed out. "Her future is on your shoulders, as the eldest son."

"Which means letting her do as she wants," Robert replied. "And now if you'll excuse me, Reverend, there are some people I must see before they leave."

With a curt nod of his dark head, Robert turned away from the minister and put long steps between them, nearly bumping into John as he strode into the foyer.

"Something wrong?" John asked. "You look like a thundercloud."

"It's the godly one, Whitmore," Robert said. "What a two-faced bastard!"

John smiled his fair blond smile. "He cornered me earlier. At least he means well. He admires mother."

"I'm not as charitable as you are toward people," Robert said, glancing into the crowded sitting room. "Where's mother now?"

"With Aunt Cissie, already making plans."

"Good. That means she'll rally fast."

"It's not as though father wasn't ill for a long time," John pointed out. "She's already done her mourning. When will you be starting back?"

"In the morning, I think."

"I'm going to miss you," John said. "You're my closest friend, and always will be."

Robert drew John toward the entry door beneath the broad staircase. He opened it and the two men moved along the aromatic passageway that led past Hattie's kitchen to the deep back porch. They sat on the kitchen steps, as they'd done as boys.

"I wish you'd change your mind and come with me," Robert urged his brother. "I'd love it, I really would. I'm not just saying it to make you feel good."

"I know, but it's not possible, Rob, no more than you'd come with me to Illinois. We're already in very different worlds, dear brother, and we both know it. No use fooling ourselves."

"But, good God," Robert said abruptly, overcome by a sentiment that threatened to bring tears to his eyes, tears he hadn't been able to shed for his father, "we might not ever see each other again."

"That's true," John conceded, "we might not. But I have faith that we will. Now let's go back inside. Mother needs our presence. We should be visible."

The brothers walked through the kitchen and into the foyer. The memorial gathering appeared to be breaking up. Robert saw a florid woman in a frilly bonnet bearing down on them, accompanied by a young woman.

"Oh, oh," he groaned under his breath to John, "here comes that old Fowler gorgon with her daughter in tow."

"I'll see you when the guests have gone," John said quickly, and hurried off, leaving Robert to deal with the effusive Mrs. Fowler. Gushy, primped and perfumed, her cheeks bright with actress's rouge, Mrs. Fowler held a parasol in one hand and her daughter's arm in the other. Poor Agatha! Robert remembered her as a little girl; she didn't stand a chance against her mother's determination. It was almost as if Mrs. Fowler might suddenly thrust the shy, flat-chested creature into his arms and demand that he marry her, since she was certainly old enough, perhaps twenty.

"Robert, dear boy!" Mrs. Fowler cawed at him. "You know my sweet little Agatha, don't you?"

Robert nodded. "Of course, ma'am," he said. "But we haven't seen one another in several years."

Mrs. Fowler essayed a trilly laugh. "And whose fault is that, may I ask? Agatha's been past the age of consent for years."

Agatha flushed in deep embarrassment, her expression pained. "Mother, please—" she begged, obviously wanting to break away but knowing if she did her mother would cause a scene.

"Young, eligible, charming, and handsome," Mrs. Fowler cooed at Robert, gazing up into his hazel eyes. "Young man, you hold all the proper cards. I think it's a downright shame that you're buried alive down there in that horrid Knoxville, of all the uncivilized spots."

"It's a very pleasant place," Robert informed Mrs. Fowler, "and it's going to be my life. I'm marrying soon."

Mrs. Fowler's face fell. "To a Knoxville woman?" she nearly shrieked, so that a stout matron just passing cast her a frigid glance of disdain.

"That's right, ma'am."

"Well, dear boy, I hope you're marrying money."

Robert glanced at Agatha whose eyes were downcast as she pursed her lips in discomfort.

"I'm marrying for love," Robert told Mrs. Fowler, adding a wide grin to soften the remark.

Mrs. Fowler tossed her head. "I once made that mistake myself, first time around. *Au revoir*, Robert! Come, Agatha," she said, leading her daughter away, not releasing her grip on Agatha's arm until they were descending the porch steps. The old woman, Robert realized, hadn't uttered even one small platitude to his father's memory.

An hour later the guests had departed. Caroline sat stiffly on the porch in the gentle evening breeze that drifted down from the dense woods. A quick, light shower had permeated the air with damp earth smells.

Robert was keeping his mother company, proud that she hadn't broken down during the funeral or reception.

"It won't be easy for you," he said at length. "You and father lived twenty-five years together in this house."

A rush of guilt for leaving her claimed him. He must have straightened up in his chair without knowing it, for Caroline sensed his concentration, turned and looked at him in the deepening twilight.

"Darling Robert, you mustn't worry so about me. I'll be just wonderful, I promise. I'm well, Doctor Morton says, and I'll enjoy being a part of Cissie's Washington atmosphere. I assure you I won't become a professional widow. Once a year we'll go up to New York for a shopping tour. Every August we'll take a house at Rappahannock on the Cheapeake and have a lovely time. In the winter there'll be concerts in Washington and some theatre. Why, in many ways my life will be freer and more varied than it ever was with your father. You must accept and believe that, son."

"I'll certainly try, mother. I'd feel better if John weren't going away too."

"That's sheer nonsense, darling. You and John will both be back. Goodness, you make it sound as permanent as . . . your father's going. Robert, you have great strengths. They'll never desert you, they're from your father. John has my characteristics, not Lem's. I wish he wouldn't go off with those, those fanatics, but I'd never say so to him. I hope you haven't. If there's one thing your father and I always tried to do, it was to give you boys the independence of judgment that would mature you early."

Robert chuckled. "I hope it's worked. At least I'm doing what I want to with my life, and so is John."

Caroline sighed. "But that sect of his. I've heard lurid stories about them which I'd rather not believe."

So had Robert. Joseph Smith's doctrine of plural marriage, supposedly divined in a vision from God, was abhorrent to most Christians. He still didn't see how John could find satisfaction in such a way of life.

"I think the stories are exaggerated, mother," he said. "I wouldn't worry about John. He's level-headed, even if he does dream a lot."

"I wish he'd go to Knoxville with you, not to the ends of the earth. Oh dear, I almost forgot. Mrs. Henley wants us to come for tea tomorrow afternoon. Will you take me?"

He hadn't told her about his departure. "Mother, I'm planning to leave early tomorrow morning."

"Oh no! I thought you'd stay on a few more days."

"I can't, mother. I put Sarah in charge; I can't leave her alone too long. She hasn't had that much experience with the business."

Caroline's hands fluttered to her face. In the failing light Robert saw that the news of his departure had opened the floodgates of her grief. Quietly, steadily, she began to weep.

He got up from his chair and knelt beside his mother. In moments her weeping subsided.

"Listen to me," he said gently. "Let yourself

go, but listen. I want to promise you something. You long for grandchildren, don't you?"

Caroline lowered her hands to her lap, and nodded. "You know it's my dream," she whispered.

"You want the Sanderson line to go on, isn't that right?"

"More than anything. It's what dear Lem would want if he were still with us."

"Well then, you'll have a grandchild within a year of my marriage to Sarah. But you must promise me something."

"What is that?"

"You must come and see it, wherever the child is born. Will you do that?"

Caroline said, "You know I will." Then abruptly she surrendered to her grief and began crying again. He held her as best he could until the darkness was complete.

John came out a half hour later. "Hattie's laid out a cold supper for us," he told them. "Come inside."

They ate without conversation. Halfway through the meal Caroline excused herself and went upstairs to bed.

"She'll be all right," Robert said.

"She'll be fine, in due time."

"I dislike leaving the details of father's estate to you."

"Everything's in good legal order; it's no problem."

"I feel I'm letting you down," said Robert.

"Don't be silly. You have a business. I'm free to remain on as long as I need to."

Robert rose from the table. "I'm going for a walk," he said. "I'm too restless to eat more."

"As you wish," John said. "I'll see you in the morning."

Robert walked through the village where he had been raised, past the schoolhouse where his father had taught generations of children. A light was burning in the Fowler house. Maybe the old lady was up and prowling, he thought. As he passed the front gate, Agatha called out softly to him from the porch. He stopped; she came down the steps and the walk and joined him.

"I thought you'd be asleep," she said.

"I should be. I'm leaving early tomorrow. I guess I'm too restless to sleep."

"So am I," Agatha responded, slipping eagerly through the gate and latching it quietly behind her.

"Care for a walk?" she asked.

"I don't mind."

Agatha moved close to Robert; he could smell her lilac-scented flesh. He had always thought her a pleasant enough girl, rather thin, not particularly attractive. Or was it the intimidating image of Gertie Fowler that had distorted his view, put him and others off? So long as that old fire-breathing monster was standing stage-center in Agatha's life, the unfortunate young woman would never get a husband.

"Let's go down by the creek," Agatha suggested. "There's a new gazebo at my Uncle William's place. We can sit there and watch the moon come up."

"Won't we be intruding?" asked Robert.

"Uncle William goes to bed with the chickens. It's all right."

They strolled in the cooling night air, talking in low voices of inconsequentials. Agatha had recently returned from the spring season in Washington where she had visited a cousin.

"I had a marvelous time. I vowed I'd never come back here to stay," she told Robert. "And yet, here I am again, as dismal as ever."

Just how does a young woman who can't snare a husband get away from an ogre like Gertie Fowler? Robert wondered. Find a job, if possible, or sell herself?

"I met lots of charming men in the capital," Agatha admitted. "There are plenty around. But they're not marrying *me* this season."

"Maybe you should try New York."

"Don't mock me, hear?" Agatha said sharply, grabbing his forearm. "How would I survive in New York? I don't have any relatives there. I'm not trained for anything special. And for sure, Mama wouldn't give me the money. She wants me right here in Falls Church, or no further away than Washington. You saw how she drives everybody off with her manner, like today, embarrassing me. I'll never have a decent life, never!" she complained.

The gazebo's filigreed profile loomed up ahead of them, a sliver of new moon rising behind it. They sat down on a wide bench under the wooden pagoda roof.

"I was so sorry about your father, Robert," Agatha said when they were settled. "He was a very nice man, so good and kind." She moved close to him, placing a slim hand on his knee, making her intent quite clear. "I don't even remember my own daddy—Mama's seen to that!" She sighed. "But you don't want to hear about my troubles. Tell me about your life in Knoxville. It must be exciting."

"It's routine," Robert said. "I'm up before dawn and seldom close before dark. Then I stay on doing the books, ordering. I eat, drink and sleep business."

"Who's handling things while you're away?"

"My fiancée's taking care of everything."

"Is she pretty?"

Sarah? Much more than that, Robert thought. Strong, clear-eyed, level-headed, passionately devoted to him. He could hardly wait to get married. For months he'd held himself in check against the torrent of Sarah's desire. Despite a staunch faith in God, she would have allowed him to make love to her if he'd pressed the issue, which he hadn't. He didn't want her to have any regrets about their knowing each other intimately before marriage. But the self-enforced abstinence was gnawing now at his groin. And this flighty, excitable girl-woman wasn't doing anything to ease his distress, as she drummed her fingers on his knee.

"She'll do," he said of Sarah, smiling at the understatement.

"But she's far away," Agatha whispered, snuggling against him, "and I'm right here. Won't I do for now?" She ran restless fingertips up his inner thigh.

"You're a charming young lady," Robert said, and put his arms around her. This was all the encouragement Agatha needed. She flung her arms around his neck and kissed him fiercely on the mouth. He realized that she had been drinking.

Agatha took his hand and thrust it inside the

bodice of her dress against her small, warm breast. Suddenly Robert's restraint dissolved. He embraced Agatha strongly, squeezing the breath out of her. Then he stretched her out full-length on the gazebo's bench and lowered his weight on top of her. She pushed him off, saying, "No, not that, I'm afraid!" and sat up.

"This!" she murmured huskily, reaching for his trouser buttons, opening them and running her hand inside, finding him ready, drawing him out. With her mouth to his, she slowly manipulated him until he shuddered and climaxed.

Immediately Agatha was on her feet, anxious to be gone. Arranging himself, angry at what he'd done, slightly humiliated, he accompanied Agatha to her front gate in silence. He opened the gate, she turned and whispered, "Don't think harshly of me, Robert. I'm not a bad person really!" Then she fled up the path to her house in the clear moonlight.

He hoped she would find someone soon, poor lonely soul. He felt sorry for her. He walked the short distance to the Sanderson house, relieved that he was leaving early and wouldn't have to see Agatha tomorrow. Making love wasn't nasty, it was sweet and natural. But fumbling in the dark like clumsy school-children wasn't his idea of fulfillment.

The house was dark when he got to it. He felt heavy with the melancholy of loss as he realized that his father was no longer sleeping out his final hours in the upstairs front bedroom. He worried about Caroline; but she was such a determined woman, she would survive.

He went up to his room overlooking the

woods and undressed in the dark. He had a
strong premonition as he drifted off to sleep
that this was the last night he would ever spend
in Virginia.

Knoxville in 1846 was a pretty town of neat
homes, churches and businesses, named for
General Henry Knox and surrounded by the
Appalachians, ornamented with lakes of limpid
beauty. Knoxville had had the distinction of
being the capital of the South Ohio River Territory during the 1790s. By the time Robert Sanderson decided to open a business in the town,
it was already a thriving freshwater port on the
Tennessee River, a busy commercial center.
Marble was quarried locally, coal was mined,
and tobacco grown.

Rail lines and canals developed and touched
the settlement. Immigrants arrived, predomi-
nantly of Irish and German stock. After the
Cherokee and Chickasaw Indians were pushed
westward, the town became a small city. By
1846 it was a hive of industry, a small cotton
kingdom that brought quick riches to many of
its more enterprising inhabitants. The notion
that money breeds money was Knoxville's unofficial *modus vivendi.*

Robert Sanderson had arrived in Knoxville
with a cash legacy from his Uncle Eli Sanderson, Lem's brother. The estate was split equally
between Lem and his two sons. John placed
his money in government bonds in Washington,
D. C., while Robert took his west, finally settling in Knoxville because he loved the countryside and liked the people.

At first Robert lodged with an Irish family

named O'Malley, sharing a room with Brian
O'Malley, close to his own age. Robert wasn't
in town twenty-four hours before he had met
Henry Calder at the latter's bank, where he
went to open an account and deposit his cash.

The elderly Calder was impressed by this
reserved, soft-spoken Virginian whose clothes
were subdued yet gentlemanly, and whose conversation was obviously the result of an educated background. He was surprised, therefore,
when Robert divulged his plans: not to teach
school or tutor privately the young children of
local gentry, but to find himself a modest store-
front and open a drygoods business.

"Why do you want to become a merchant,"
Calder asked Robert, "when you could easily
become a success in banking, or some other
profession? I don't understand why you want
to be the proprietor of a market."

Robert smiled. His father had asked him the
same question.

"Sir, I've been around classically educated
people all my life, at Falls Church and in Washington. I feel the need of a change. I want to
test my strengths in the world of commerce."

Calder accepted this with a nod. "Sound
enough, I suppose. Obviously you have your
reasons. And you've certainly come to the right
place to start a new business. Knoxville can
only continue to develop."

A Sunday dinner invitation to the Calder
house put Robert in touch with Sarah Calder
for the first time.

A widower with a sharp eye on the future of
his only child, Calder liked Robert well enough
to want to see how he would conduct himself

with Sarah, who played hostess for her father,
did some occasional cooking, supervised the
running of the household.

It wasn't long before Robert and Sarah were
seeing a lot of one another, which pleased
Calder, who wanted his daughter to marry
someone she admired, not merely someone he
might choose for her. Besides, he wanted grandchildren, and Robert was as good a candidate
for that function as any he'd found in Knoxville.
The effete sons of some of his wealthy clients
often cast ardent glances at Sarah, but they
hadn't pleased her any more than they had
pleased Calder. Robert was a different matter
altogether.

Robert's store, supported at the beginning
by Henry Calder's occasional loans, always paid
back promptly, soon began to make a name for
itself in Knoxville by carrying specialty lines
unavailable elsewhere. Robert had a talent for
anticipating customer needs. Sarah augmented
his acumen with her own; she had a knack for
choosing textiles and home goods that were
snatched up immediately by eager Knoxville
matrons the moment they went on display. In
fact, Sarah enjoyed the merchandising aspect of
the store almost as much as Robert did.

After six months' association, Robert and
Sarah decided on marriage. It wasn't a question
of Robert's proposing formally and Sarah sub-
missively accepting. The agreement was arrived
at by both parties simultaneously. All that remained was to secure Henry Calder's approval,
which he gave them happily as soon as they
asked for it, along with his blessing. Calder had
by this time reassessed his evaluation of Rob-

ert's career choice, for it seemed now to be
clearly the wisest decision. Calder liked the way
the store was operating and had no criticism to
make of the quiet-spoken, serious young man
he expected would soon join the Calder family
circle.

When Robert received word from his brother
John that Lem Sanderson was dying, he went
to Virginia reluctantly, not happy about leaving
Sarah. She insisted on managing the store in
his absence, which meant that she would be
fully occupied and, with her father's guidance,
well looked-after until his return.

Robert returned to Knoxville on the early
morning train, at a time when there were no
familiar faces abroad on the streets. He went
directly to the O'Malley house to leave his suit-
case before going to the store. He was greeted
from the kitchen by Mrs. O'Malley. The old
woman looked as if she'd seen a ghost when he
entered, and immediately burst into tears,
dropped her frying pan with a clatter on top of
the wood stove and rushed to embrace him.

"There now," said Robert, "I haven't been
away that long." But Mrs. O'Malley continued
to weep until Robert finally held her at arm's
length. "What's wrong?" he asked.

Mrs. O'Malley managed to get herself under
control. "You ain't heard anything?"

"Heard what?"

"The store! Your business burnt down last
night."

"My God! How?"

"They think it was a lamp . . ." Mrs. O'Malley
started to sob again. "And that ain't all. Sarah—"
She couldn't go on.

"Sarah?" Robert began to feel a small core of horror flowering in his gut, prickling his flesh. "Was Sarah in the store?"

Mrs. O'Malley nodded.

"Oh no!" he shouted. Thrusting Mrs. O'Malley aside he ran out of the house, down the three blocks to the Calder residence. He banged frantically on the oaken door. Moments later Henry Calder answered. One look at Calder's haggard, ashen features and red-rimmed eyes and Robert knew that Mrs. O'Malley's story was true.

Calder stepped forward, his arms outstretched. He drew Robert into the sitting room and pressed him into a chair, then proceeded to tell him the story of the fire.

"The way we think it happened," Calder explained, "was that Sarah fell asleep working late. She went back after supper to fill out some new orders. I was to pick her up at ten and walk her home. When I got to the store it was already too late. She must have fallen asleep at the desk and awakened with a start, knocking over the oil lamp. She went for water but the fire was out of control. It was smoke asphyxiation, Robert. Our darling was dead when they carried her out."

"Where is she?" Robert asked.

"At the Steinman Funeral Home."

"I want to see her."

"Son, you should rest," Calder said gently. "You've been travelling quite a while. After you've rested we'll go together to Steinman's."

"I want to see her now, sir. I must!"

"It won't bring her back, son."

"I'm going," said Robert. Seeing Sarah was

necessary to register the fact of her death. He would never accept the reality, but he must have the facts. He left the mourning Calder and walked through the dawn-tinted streets of Knoxville to the funeral parlor where Sarah lay in death.

Robert's second funeral within a week was held the following afternoon. He didn't weep openly over Sarah's death, but his grieving bitterness was profound. At one point he wondered if he weren't being paid back by an angry God for his nasty little episode with the neurotic Agatha. But he quickly put the thought aside; he wasn't religious, he saw no reason to add guilt to the agony he was enduring over the loss of his beloved Sarah.

Henry Calder had a long, explorative talk with him after the funeral.

"You're like a son to me," the bereft old banker told Robert. "I want you to come and live at my house, be my heir. We'll rebuild the store on the same site; it'll be a memorial to our Sarah. I want to leave all my worldly goods to you, Robert. You won't lose by staying here."

"Sir, I appreciate your consideration," Robert responded, "but I can't bear to stay in Knoxville. My memories are too powerful; they'd haunt me always."

For a moment Calder stiffened, looking pained; then he sighed, nodded his head. "I understand. Where will you go?"

"I don't know yet. West, I think. That was what Sarah and I dreamed of doing someday. There's no reason why I can't do it now."

"I'll miss you terribly, Robert. You know that."

"I know, sir, and I shall miss you."

"You don't have any cash to take with you."

"A little, sir, not much."

"What will you need?"

"A few hundred dollars will do."

"It's yours," Calder said promptly.

"Only as a loan, sir. I'll pay you back."

"I forbid it. Let this be your legacy."

"As you wish, sir. With it I'll do something Sarah would have liked."

Calder sighed again. "Very well, son. I'm sorry that nothing I can say will change your mind about staying on."

"I'm deeply grateful to you, sir, but it's best this way," Robert said. He felt saddened that he couldn't accommodate the lonely old man whose life was irreparably shattered by Sarah's death. The elderly Calder was much too old to walk away to a new life elsewhere.

"You'll still be my heir," Calder reminded him. "You have something to come back for."

"As you wish, sir."

The Sanderson line would have to begin in another place, Robert thought, and perhaps with John. He doubted that he would want a son by anyone other than Sarah.

That night Brian O'Malley produced a bottle of whiskey and he and Robert got drunk after dinner in the large O'Malley kitchen, after the old woman had retired.

The talk came around to the Mexican War as O'Malley tried to distract Robert from his grief. At that point, General Zachary Taylor had oc-

cupied Point Isabel, a town on the Gulf of
Mexico at the mouth of the Rio Grande. Mexican and American troops had first clashed two
months earlier. In May, President Polk had declared war on Mexico.

"Since you're movin' on, Rob," O'Malley observed after the whiskey had loosened his
tongue, "you might as well go all the way. Have
an adventure! It's something to think about."
O'Malley swigged from the bottle, wiped its
neck with his palm, handed it across the table
to Robert. "You're a free agent now, you can go
anywhere you like."

"You mean join up with Old Zack, Old Rough-
and-Ready?"

"Not necessarily, nor even with the Tennessee
Regiment. One of mom's cousins is related to
Colonel Kearny by marriage."

"What good would that do me?" Robert
asked. "Kearny's probably left Fort Leavenworth by now for Mexico."

"You could join them by headin' south."

"Kearny will have all the recruits he needs,"
Robert theorized. "Striplings, experienced fron-
tiersmen who speak the Indian languages and
Spanish, and know the terrain."

"Kearny's forces are called the Army of the
West. Think, man, of the excitement, if you
join up with Stephen Kearny! I met him once. A
small man, all brisk and businesslike. You could
do worse for a commander."

"*If* I were interested in wars," Robert said,
and took a deep draught of whiskey. "I'll think
about it."

"Now you'll have to do more than just think,

lad. You'll have to act. And soon. You can't stay around here moping. You know it as well as I. Memories will eat you up."

"You're right, Brian," Robert agreed. "But going to war isn't a child's game."

"Hell no," said O'Malley, "it's a challenge to manhood. Why, there isn't a lad in Knoxville who won't be envious of you going into the unknown like that."

Robert had a vague concept of the responsibilities that enlistment would involve. He knew that he had romanticized what might turn into his death, or at least permanent injury, imprisonment and torture by the enemy. But in joining up he could be certain of one thing; his fateful future would be out of his hands. It was one way of forgetting the tragedy that had just happened, and perhaps the only way. If he didn't come back from the war, what did that matter? He had nothing to come back to anyway.

"If you feel so strongly," said Robert, "why not join me? We'll go together."

"How I wish I could," O'Malley sighed with sincere ardor. "To march in triumph through the halls of Montezuma, to see Mexico's silver mines, its deserts, the señoritas. I envy you, Rob. I'm stuck with me mother.'"

Next morning, slightly befuddled still from liquor he seldom drank in such quantity, he went down to the Army recruiting depot and secured the information he would need to rendezvous with Kearny's force of some three thousand men, presently on the long march from Fort Leavenworth, Kansas to New Mexico. If he left Knoxville at once, Robert could probably time it right so he'd catch up with Kearny somewhere in the Texans panhandle near Amarillo (so the information went) where the colonel would probably bivouac for a while, taking a break to replenish his supplies and morale before heading south.

"Why run off to Texas?" the recruiting sergeant asked Robert. "You can't be sure Kearny will even want you. The Tennessee Regiment sure as hell does."

"I just want to go," Robert said, not realizing until much later that he was instinctively hoping to get to California.

"Ah well, man, if you're that damn-fool stubborn, maybe you better go." The sergeant shrugged him off disinterestedly, having enough experience to know when he'd lost fish.

Mrs. O'Malley wrote a letter to Stephen Watts Kearny introducing Robert. As she presented him with the envelope she said, misty-eyed at his departure, "I hope it'll get you what you want, son. Although God knows all you need except our dear Sarah's right here in Knoxville." She embraced him as if he were one of her own. Brian, with an arm around Robert's shoulder, walked him to the Calder house.

After an emotional farewell with Henry Calder that reduced the old man to tears, and giving his solemn promise to keep in touch, Robert put Knoxville behind him. He headed across Arkansas and Oklahoma, into the Texas Panhandle, and thence up into Colorado. With strong mounts and light supplies, Robert made much better time than Kearny's forces moving south to Bent's Fort. He would not return to

Knoxville to stand before the white marble
shaft that Henry Calder raised over Sarah's
grave, but he'd never forget the first love of his
life.

THE LONG MARCH

WHEN THE BULK of Colonel Kearny's Army of the West marched southwest toward Santa Fe from Fort Leavenworth, Kansas, in July of 1846, with them marched a battalion of some five hundred Mormons. These men were enlisted by Brigham Young and their salaries paid to the Mormon Church to help underwrite the westward migration of the sect from Illinois to Great Salt Lake in Utah Territory. Also moving with the army was a large wagon train of traders and artisans—wagoners, blacksmiths, carpenters, and men of other crafts. All were eager to visit New Mexico to sell their goods and skills. All were apparently undaunted by the hazards that their affiliation with an army approaching battle might bring them. They were a rough, tough group, drinking and brawling constantly among themselves. Kearny wisely kept a half-mile between them and his army, for every time the two groups met there was trouble; and yet Kearny needed the wagon train's services, tolerating its men despite the conflict they brought.

Robert caught up with Kearny's troops while they rested at Bent's Fort on the Upper Arkansas River in Colorado territory, about a hundred miles north of New Mexico. He delivered his letter to Colonel Kearny in person and found that the commander was indeed a small man, around fifty, with pale piercing eyes and grey hair. About him hovered an air of quiet calm that seemed inconsistent with his position as leader of a Polk-sponsored expedition.

Kearny read the letter, then thanked him courteously for it, asking after Mary O'Malley.

"As you can see," said the colonel, "we're a raggle-taggle outfit with more fighters than we can comfortably support. We can't take on more recruits at this time."

"Sir, I've come all the way on my own from Knoxville," Robert explained. "I've criss-crossed the countryside trying to catch up with you." It was all Robert could do to mask his bitter disappointment at being rejected. "I want more than anything to be a part of your company, sir. And besides, I can't turn back. I've nowhere to go."

Kearny regarded him intently for a moment. "You're without funds?" he asked.

"Well no, sir, I've a little money. It won't take me far," Robert hedged. "I was counting on recruitment." He would never tell Colonel Kearny that he had a considerable amount of cash with him.

"Very well," Kearny replied, "there is an alternative to joining my brigade. The traders who follow us need men. They've had desertions, a score or more's run off, and a good pair of hands will be highly appreciated. You may not be part of the conflict, Sanderson, but you can be an observer and serve the armed forces as a supplier. Here—" The colonel scribbled a hasty note on the back of Mary O'Malley's letter and handed it to Robert. "Give this to Ethan Drew, master of the wagon train. He'll put you to work."

"Thank you, sir."

Kearny gave Robert a wintry smile. "You may not thank me after you've settled in. But good luck anyway."

"Thank you, sir," Robert said again, and went in search of the wagon master.

Ethan Drew was a stocky man with heavy, beetle-black eyebrows, almost as short as Kearny. Yet he possessed a powerful physique with rippling steel for muscles, and looked to Robert as though he could wrestle the strongest opponent to earth and hold him there until he cried for mercy. In his late thirties, Drew had a rumbling bass voice, as deep as any Robert had ever heard. His hair was kinky, his color *café-au-lait*. Robert wondered what Drew's racial origins were, contenting himself with speculation.

Drew was pleased to see him. He grinned briefly as they shook hands and immediately asked, "Are you any good with horses? You'd better be."

"I rode mine all the way from Knoxville, sir," Robert said modestly. "I know how to woo them and spare them."

Drew grinned widely this time, revealing stubby teeth. "Spare them, eh? Now if you'd said 'use' instead of 'woo' I'd have had no place for you . . . Robert Sanderson," he read from Kearny's scribble. "What's your age, religion, education, things like that?"

"I'm twenty-three years old, sir, and—"

Drew held up his large hand. "No more sirs, if you please. They're a waste of time. Call me Ethan, everybody does, and I'll call you Bob. Now, go on—"

"I'm an agnostic, Ethan." And Robert told the wagon master about his family background in Virginia, that his father had recently died and his brother would soon go to Illinois to join the Mormons. He said nothing about Sarah, for the subject was as yet too painful for him to discuss with strangers.

Ethan frowned at the mention of Mormons. "Your brother's making a serious choice," he observed. "He could have come along with you and done his joining right here. They hold regular prayer services, all of them."

"Would I be working with you?" Robert asked.

"If you're worth your salt you can become my right hand," Ethan said. "And if you're worthless, we'll find that out soon enough and you'll be on your way. Come, time to meet some of the merchants in this motley caravan. It takes all kinds to make a world, as you'll soon enough find out."

The supply train consisted of some two hundred wagons, all loaded with drygoods for sale, a veritable general store on wheels, carrying mainly items that would sell quickly in New

Mexico. Robert's duties were to carry out the orders that Ethan gave his men, to see that the wagon train's horses were properly fed and watered, and that all was made ready for the advance into Mexico. The pay for his duties was board and whatever extra Drew felt like giving him from time to time.

Robert adjusted immediately to his new responsibilities, finding Ethan brusque sometimes, and downright short with everyone, but honest, direct, expecting no more than he himself would give. The wagon train personnel were another matter altogether, some of them as mean and cantankerous as diamond-back rattlers. They drank and gambled constantly, got into fights among themselves, while Robert and Ethan moved among them trying to keep law and order. It was forbidden for soldiers to come into the wagon train camp where liquor and cards were available twenty-four hours a day. Robert's efficient policing of the camp, his organization and patient disposition pleased Ethan from the start, for the older man tended to fly off the handle whenever his authority was challenged, bashing heads together instead of using tact.

Everyone was anxious to move on, which caused powerful tensions. Kearny, however, was a deliberate man who was determined to capitalize fully on his singular, presidentially backed position as commander of the Army of the West. He expected his subordinates and the wagon train to accept his authority. The soldiers had no choice, so they buckled under; however, the wagoneers were not as compliant. Kearny didn't intend to jeopardize his one chance to make a name in history for himself by moving on before he judged it prudent. Zachary Taylor might operate outside of President Polk's wishes, but not Kearny. And the commander depended upon Ethan, his new assistant, Robert, and the wagoneers themselves to support him in all decisions.

As the colonel and his staff sat around analyzing reports that some three thousand Mexican troops were marching from Chihuahua to defend New Mexico from the Americans, something happened in the wagon train camp to bind Ethan Drew and Robert together as closely as brothers.

Generally Ethan and Robert made their evening rounds through the camp together before settling in for the night, but this evening Robert made them alone. Ethan had gone to bed early with indigestion. Robert was on his way to the lower end of the wagon campsite when a wagoneer ran up to him to complain about a noisy game in progress in an isolated tent at the camp's edge. Bets could run high in these games, including whole wagons of rich goods that Robert knew represented the entire holdings of some wagoneers. Soldiers often stole over from Kearny's camp to try their luck, and sometimes won. Kearny was severe with any soldier caught in the wagon train area after taps, and everyone knew it. This, however, didn't deter the inveterate gamblers.

Robert strode up to the lighted tent and threw back the flap. A quartet of players was grouped around a blanket covered with currency. Already drunk, one soldier and three civilians were betting wildly, cursing each other, passing whiskey around, set for a long night's play.

"Gentlemen, time to break up the game," Robert advised. "Curfew, taps." He ignored the soldier, drunkest of the four, hoping he would have the sense to withdraw quickly.

"Mind your own goddamn business!" one of the wagoneers snarled at Robert, doubtless emboldened by Ethan's absence.

"Gentlemen," Robert warned, "either shut down the game or suffer consequences," which meant a report to Kearny.

Another player said, "Tell that gorilla you work for to go wipe his ass. I can smell it from here."

Robert started to get angry. "Tell that to *me*," he said evenly. "I'm on my own tonight."

"Listen to the *gentleman* talk!" the soldier scoffed. "You can always tell a sissy by his tone of voice." And with that, the soldier threw a nearly empty whiskey bottle at Robert. It struck his shoulder and fell to the ground at his feet.

Robert's anger exploded. He stepped into the tent, pulled the man to his feet, swept him outside and slammed him against a nearby wagon, knocking the wind from him. The man grunted, sagged forward and lapsed into unconsciousness.

As Robert was wondering what to do next, he felt a sharp painful thrust through the muscles of his upper right arm. He released the soldier's limp weight and turned in time to see the glittering knife held by one of the wagon train players; it was raised high to guide another thrust into him. He put up his hands to ward off the second thrust, which never came; the knife was stopped in mid-air by Ethan, who had appeared from nowhere.

Ethan twisted the knife from the wagoneer's hands and sent him sprawling in the dust with one well-aimed blow to his chest. Then he turned to the tent, ripped its canvas flap off and ordered the two remaining players to come out, which they did at once, docile as lambs, all weak grins and apologies. An armed soldier stepped forward to guard them.

Ethan led Robert back to his wagon, settled him gently in the wagon bed, pulled off his shirt and swabbed the wound with a clean handkerchief, then bound it with a strip of cotton.

"You rest," Ethan said. "I'm going back to sort out that situation. You all right?"

"I'm fine," said Robert, "it's not deep."

"Why did you go to answer a complaint alone? You should have roused me."

"You weren't feeling well."

"That's beside the point," said Ethan. "Don't ever do anything like that again. A minute or two later and you could have been a goner. Those four would bury their mother if she interfered with their fun."

"Thanks for coming to my aid. How did you know I was in trouble?"

"I wasn't asleep when you left," Ethan said. "I followed you. Wanted to see how you'd do on your own."

"You saw."

"Don't do anything like that again, Bob. I can't afford to lose you."

Robert grinned, despite his discomfort. "So I'm valuable?"

Ethan grunted. "Hell yes, of course you are."

"I'm relieved. You haven't given me any indication up till now."

"I was observing. I don't usually spell out my sentiments until I'm sure of a man," Ethan declared.

"Are you sure now?"

Ethan nodded. "You're my partner."

"Then I've passed my term of trial."

"We're a team."

"Full brothers, as the saying goes."

Ethan frowned. "We probably couldn't be that. You don't know much about me."

"I think I've guessed," Robert said mildly.

Ethan stared at him. "What?" he demanded.

"It's not important."

"It is to some. I'm a quadroon, Bob. Being from Virginia, it wasn't so hard for you to figure, was it?"

"It doesn't matter, Ethan. My father never owned a slave, if that'll make you feel any better. Anyway, what a man comes from isn't the test, it's what he does with himself."

"Well said," Ethan told him. "Now get some sleep. I've got to turn those miscreants over to the stockade."

While Kearny was reconnoitering at Bent's Fort, Governor Manuel Armijo was in his palace at the capital of Santa Fe, New Mexico, fully aware of the American enemy to his north. Armijo had good reason to be fearful. His own forces were mainly raw recruits with a strong antipathy to fighting a war. The regulars under the Governor's command were a mere two hundred men.

Governor Armijo might have won a contest against the Americans had he taken full advantage of his unique geographical position. For with a little strategy, Armijo might easily have held off the Americans in the narrow defile of Apache Canyon through which Kearny had to pass to reach Santa Fe. By penning in his enemy, Armijo could have forced an American surrender through hunger and thirst. But instead, incredibly enough, he made no stand at all, thanks to the shrewdness of one James Magoffin, a Santa Fe trader. Magoffin returned to town ahead of Kearny's military advance to talk with the governor while Kearny was still bivouacked at Bent's Fort.

Magoffin was a clever manipulator, a young man who saw the inevitable absorption of New Mexico into the body politic of the United States. For his own private ends and for humanitarian reasons, he wanted this event to happen with as little bloodshed as possible. Armijo was not a subtle man, Magoffin had heard. His audience with the governor proved it.

"Excellency," Magoffin told Armijo in his elegant Santa Fe offices, "there is no holding off the Americans. They mean to take us and they're invincible."

Pale with fear the Governor said, "It's a terrifying concept."

"Only if you mount a defense."

"We'll be driven out of the country," Armijo moaned. "We'll lose everything."

"On the contrary, you yourself may actually

gain by declaring Santa Fe an open town and letting the Americans walk in. You'll be remembered in history as a great pacificist."

"How can I manage that?" Armijo asked eagerly.

Magoffin lifted the heavy valise he had brought with him and placed it on the Governor's polished desk top. He pushed it toward the Governor.

"Go ahead, open it," he told Armijo. The governor unlocked the metal clasp and stared inside.

"Gold," he murmured in awe.

"And all yours," Magoffin declared, "by simply opening up Santa Fe and thereby averting bloodshed and the loss of countless innocent lives. Everyone will recognize you as a man of peace."

"I shall only be accepting what is inevitable," mused the Governor. "I think, Señor Magoffin, that your suggestion can be followed . . ."

As a result of Magoffin's interview with Armijo, the American army marched south without meeting resistance and passed safely through Apache Canyon in mid-August of 1846. The following day Santa Fe officially surrendered itself quietly to American hands without either army so much as firing a single shot.

Once in charge of Santa Fe, Kearny guaranteed the New Mexicans their land titles, freedom of religion and full American citizenship. A civil government was organized, with Charles Bent the appointed governor. After the chiefs from the leading New Mexican pueblos had come to Santa Fe to swear official allegiance to the United States under President Polk, there was no reason for Kearny to remain in the area any longer.

Kearny's next move was to divide the Army of the West into various units. One group of soldiers would remain in New Mexico, as an army of occupation, under the command of Colonel Sterling Price. A second portion, the Missouri Volunteers, went south under Colonel Doniphan, to a brief encounter with the Navajo Indians, then further south down the Rio Grande to the town of El Paso, thence across the desert to Chihuahua, moving upward to join Zachary Taylor.

The third portion of the army was ordered to California, under the command of the newly promoted General Kearny. This unit consisted of three hundred dragoons and a supporting wagon train, led by Ethan Drew. The Mormon Battalion under Lt. Colonel Cooke was to follow from Santa Fe to California and open a passable wagon route for settlers.

Kearny set off from Santa Fe on September 25th. He marched down the Rio Grande to Socorro, turning west toward the Gila River Valley. With the small army was a caravan of supply wagons. Ethan Drew was in charge and Robert was his assistant. Robert was jubilant to be going to California, thankful to have seen no action so far, hopeful that the future would be as pacific.

Just east of Socorro, Kearny met up with the fabled scout, Kit Carson. In 1842 Carson had met General Frémont while returning to St. Louis up the Missouri by boat. Frémont hired Carson as a guide for his Western expeditions from 1842 through 1845. He became famous throughout the Western hemisphere for his skill and courage. Carson was returning from California with official dispatches from Frémont to Washington, D. C. These concerned the Pacific Coast's war involvement. The guide was optimistic about the subjugation of California by America and described some of the complex events taking place.

"It's my belief," Carson told the general, "that the war in the West is virtually over. Los Angeles is under martial law, for example, and carrying firearms is forbidden. Other key territorial points are also under American control."

On the basis of this good news from California, Kearny decided that he could return two hundred of his dragoons to Santa Fe to become part of the occupation army there.

After talking with Kearny, Carson rode down along the wagon train to visit with Ethan Drew. Carson had known Ethan years earlier when both worked as teamster, cook and guide on expeditions. Robert was deeply impressed with the respect that this peppery, weather-worn figure had for Ethan, and pleased that Carson would take a meal with them.

Dinner, however, was interrupted by Kearny's orderly, summoning Carson back to the general's quarters. Annoyed, Carson entered the general's tent wondering what in hell was so damned important. Once again, as was Kearny's habit, the general was deliberating his next move. It remained for him to persuade Carson to accept the plan.

"What would you say, Kit, to returning to California?" the general asked bluntly, and Carson replied "Why, sir? I've just left the territory and I've dispatches to carry East. And besides, sir, I have personal matters to look after."

"What personal matters?" Kearny probed.

"My wife's at Taos; my home is there. I've been away a long time."

"Yes," Kearny agreed, "that situation is regrettable. We've all been deprived while performing our duty. However, I would still like to recruit you for an important responsibility."

"And what might that be, sir?"

"I am empowered to travel from New Mexico to California to act as the new military governor."

This was surprising news to Carson, who was Frémont's staunch supporter in California. Carson did not wish to discuss with Kearny the struggle for leadership that was now going on in the territory. Kearny would soon enough find out for himself. Meanwhile, in order to see that Frémont got a fair shake, perhaps he should do Kearny's bidding.

"There are some who will question your authority to act as governor, sir," Carson observed.

"And who would they be?" Kearny demanded.

"Frémont, Commodore Stockton."

"All the more reason why I want you to lead us through the desert to the Pacific. Haste is imperative," Kearny said, "if I'm to carry out my orders."

"Well, sir, I can lay out the route for you," Carson said. "That would be almost the same as guiding you in person."

"Nothing will be as effective as your presence," Kearny said. "I want *you* to ride with us, Carson. If need be, I could force you to go."

"As a prisoner, sir?"

"No, no, of course not," Kearny protested. "All the same, I think that your presence with us is every bit as important as the dispatches you carry."

Carson paused, studying the small man before him, who was finding out that luck and a fanatic's devotion to all his military problems were a sure way to achieve a successful command. Carson could respect pragmatic decisions; his life had hung in balance many times, depending purely on quick action. Going to California with Kearny would postpone his visit to Taos indefinitely, but he knew that Kearny meant business, and that there would be trouble with Frémont. Trapped, he saw no way of refusing the General other than sneaking off in the middle of the night, which wasn't his way of solving personal crises.

"All right, sir. If we can arrange for the dispatches to be sent East via Santa Fe with your returning troops, I'll agree to guide you."

"Excellent! Everything will be arranged," Kearny agreed, and the interview was over. Carson returned to his dinner.

En route to California, the military expedition first encountered roving bands of Apaches. They were peaceful enough but not friendly, and followed the progress of the expedition with scouts. Carson could get no agreement from the sullen Indians. They hung on the army's tracks but refused to furnish them even a bare minimum of needed supplies.

In central Arizona the army passed through Pima country, where the Indians were quite

amiable. Kit Carson, Ethan and Robert went in
a party to bargain with the Pimas for provisions.
Under Carson's skilled blandishments, using
barter items from the wagon train's supplies, the
Pimas gladly gave them what they needed.
They refused to sell bread, however, but gave
it free, saying it was only to eat.

Near the banks of the Colorado River, Kearny
captured four Mexican herders. Under Carson's
interrogation they reported that the Los Angeles
victory had been nullified; there had been an
uprising against the American takeover.

Beside himself with frustrated anger, Kearny
drove his small army deep into the desert inferno beyond the Colorado. It was the worst
time of the year to be traversing that awesome
wasteland, and even with full supplies the passage would have been difficult. Under the circumstances, faced with broiling heat, severely
rationed water and very little food, many soldiers and wagoneers died, and the entire expedition suffered almost inhuman hardships.

Without Ethan, Robert might have expired;
many others did. By some miraculous manipu-
lation of supplies, Ethan could always produce
a full canteen of water, though warm and
brackish, while some had none. He managed dry
rations as well, having built a false bottom beneath the wagon floor where he kept jerky,
dried fruits, biscuits, packets of sugar, tea and
coffee.

Once Robert asked how Carson could function as well as he did, on the advance trail each
torrid day, for Ethan had offered the scout none
of their supplies.

"Don't you worry about Kit," Ethan said. "He

has his right hand in the general's pocket. Don't take either one for a novice or a fool. The old man knows Kit's value and caters to him. Without Kit we'd all be dead."

"Kearny's a damned slave driver," Robert observed one night when they lounged in the wagon barely able to breathe in the steamy night air, sleep impossible after a bone-crunching march that day. "What's in it for him?"

"What would you think? Why are you and I here? Tell me. Come on, laddie."

"I suppose that, like the chicken that crosses the road," Robert said, "we want to get to the other side."

"Yes, but for what?" Ethan persisted. "What's over there on the other side?"

"Money, and position?"

"Hell yes, laddie. The fabled land of the *conquistadors*. The most beautiful spot in the world. One day soon it'll be our newest state in the Union, where free men can live in peace. That's why we're sitting here gasping away like fish out of water, but not ready to die yet. No, Ethan Drew isn't going to give up in a wilderness like this."

Each day before dawn, Carson rode out far ahead of the army, then rode back into camp before noon. Mounts died under him. Twice he returned on foot, picked up by his rear guard, half-dead on the trail, but still fighting stubbornly to stay conscious.

Robert imagined that Old Walnut, as the soldiers began calling their feared and some-times-hated commander, could compliment himself only on one stroke of wisdom at this time. Thank God, he must have said to himself in his reveries at night, that he'd had the sense to force Kit Carson to accompany the expedition. Otherwise they might all have disappeared into the desert, never to be seen alive again, their carcasses bleached white and strewn along the route.

It must have been the jerky, Robert felt, but it could simply have been the bad air of the region that brought Ethan to his bed one night, nauseated and vomiting. The army's doctor looked in on him but could prescribe nothing. The illness persisted as burning fever the next morning, after the vomiting subsided. Finally Ethan grew cold as ice and immobile.

Robert was beside himself, wondering what he could do to save his friend's life. He called on Carson, who had returned from another exploratory mission.

"Indian fever," Carson said, which meant nothing to Robert. He went away, returning in a few minutes with a packet of leaves. "Make some tea," he advised Robert. "Force it down him. It will break the chill and he'll be all right after a good night's sleep."

The prescription worked. By the following evening Ethan was lustily cursing Kearny and the world, and Robert breathed a sigh of relief.

Under Carson's expert guidance, Kearny's army finally reached the mountains, only to be marooned there by torrential rains driving up from the south, and by cold, thick fogs.

Pushing wearily on when the rains let up, Kearny's tattered, worn-out forces managed to reach San Pasqual by the first week in December. They bivouacked there to rest and gain strength, but they were not yet through their ordeal. They were set upon by fierce Mexican insurgents who refused to accept American control of California. In the continuing wet weather, the Americans had allowed their powder to dampen. Thus, they had no fire-power to raise against the Mexicans, who charged them medieval-style with lances. Of the dragoons, eighteen were killed in the first assault wave, and again as many wounded. Surrounded and besieged in unfamiliar hilly terrain, the army begged Kearny to surrender, but the General wouldn't hear of it.

Carson suggested a ploy that had worked in other situations. "Let me take a small band of men, sir, and we'll slip through the lines and go for help." The harassed commander granted Carson's request. The alternative was surrender.

That same cold and drizzly night, Kit Carson came to Ethan's tent to bid farewell to his friend and Robert.

"I'd take you both along," Carson told them, "but the smaller the party the less chance we have of being caught by the Mexicans. I'm taking Lt. Beale because I think he's the best-trained for the job."

"We'll miss you," said Ethan.

Carson patted Ethan's massive shoulder.

"And I'll miss you, old friend," Carson said. "If something should happen to me, I have a commission for you. Will you accept it?"

"You know I will."

"Write a letter to my wife in Taos. Here—" Carson handed Ethan a slip of paper. "She's a strong woman who understands the risks I take. She'll appreciate your getting in touch."

"Nothing's going to happen to you," Ethan said. "You've got years ahead of you yet."

"Stay calm, keep your hopes up, and wait."

"We can't go anywhere without you, Kit. We're stuck right here." Ethan brought out the last of his wagon supplies, a mess of jerky, and gave it to Carson.

"Here's all we have to offer you. I know how short your general rations'll be. We can survive on empty stomachs for a while. You can't."

"We'll get help through to you. Don't worry."

"When you're out there I don't worry," said Ethan. "*Vaya con Dios.*"

Robert wondered how Ethan could remain so unemotional as Carson, Beale and the small band disappeared from camp in the vaporous night. Without Carson, even Kearny would have an uneasy night. They were as isolated from the world as they would be on the highest mountain of the world in a blizzard. They had barely a half a chance to survive.

"You keep the faith in us and we'll get through," Carson had assured them.

Robert didn't think that they could make it. All through that long night and the next cold day and following night, Robert brooded about his life, about his selfishness in running away, just at the time when old Henry Calder needed him. He tried to think that survival would mean the opening of a new life in the West. This was, he told himself, all he should consider.

As he lay in the wagon next to Ethan, Robert resolved that if he ever got out of this siege alive he'd settle down in California, find himself a woman worthy of Sarah's memory, marry her and start a family.

"If we get out of this place, what'll you do with your future, Ethan?" he asked in the damp darkness.

"I was thinking about going into business in California," Ethan told him. "It's bound to grow. Everybody's coming out here for the rich new land. Wait and see when we settle down there. It'll get so crowded in ten years you'll want to go from the plains to the mountains."

"What business did you have in mind?"

"Oh, something general."

"A store perhaps?"

"Maybe. Whatever we can find that takes the least capital and brings the greatest returns in a hurry. I'm not the most patient man in the world, as you know, nor the longest-tempered."

"You said 'we'—"

"Sure as hell did, laddie. You don't think I'm going into business by myself, do you? I have no heirs; I need a business partner."

Robert thought about this for a moment. Ethan was a strange, moody man, at times volatile, blowing the top off his considerable temper in seconds. Then immediately afterwards he would become as calm and docile as a well-fed infant. Ethan had tenderness, an affectionate concern for folks he liked; but at the same time he could be a raging volcano of a brute. His physical strength was prodigious; he could lift hundred-pound flour sacks as if they were toys, and his endurance allowed him to keep on working like a locomotive when most men had taken to their bunks in exhaustion.

"Well," said Ethan, "what are your plans? You coming in with me?"

It was rare to find a friend like Ethan, Robert

reflected, a trustworthy man, even though they were eons apart in background and attitudes. Robert could ill-afford to put aside such a valuable friendship lightly. A stranger in an alien land, he needed all the support he could get.

"I'll go in with you," Robert promised.

"Good lad," Ethan grunted, and turned over, asleep in moments and snoring loudly.

In the morning there was another dawn attack on the beleaguered camp by Mexican forces. Two more of Kearny's men were killed. When hope was lowest, four days after the siege began, help arrived for the expedition at dawn.

In a savage encounter, the main body of Mexican insurgents were massacred; the survivors were routed in twenty minutes by intense volleys of fire.

That same morning, Kearny broke camp to begin the long march to Los Angeles. The army arrived in Los Angeles without any more military incidents. But, once in the pueblo, there was more fighting as Kearny engaged the stubborn insurgents in several street battles. He won all of them decisively.

Los Angeles surrendered officially to the American forces on January 10th, 1847. The northern portion of the state was also subdued, and the conquest of California was considered complete.

PARTNERS

THE FINAL PEACE treaty between Mexico and Washington, D. C. was ratified by the Senate March 10, 1848. Fifteen days later the Mexican Congress ratified the same treaty. It became fully effective on May 30, 1848.

The territory acquired by the Mexican War settlement included what is now called California, Arizona, New Mexico, Utah, Nevada, and even portions of Colorado, Wyoming and Kansas. The agreement between the United States and Mexico awarded the Mexicans some fifteen million dollars in compensation—an unusual reversal of custom, in that usually it was the vanquished who paid the victor. But there were shameful aspects to the outcome of the war: America's aggression was extreme, its demands excessive. The struggle to make slavery legal in the new territory was a rough and angry one that finally left the new territory a freeman's land.

Although it would be some time before the details of the Mexican settlement could be worked out to everyone's satisfaction, the official agreement was cause for celebration by Ethan and Robert in Los Angeles.

The two men had initiated the first stages of their partnership after they separated from Kearny's forces. They found a wagon yard begging for proper management and started up a fine smithy, a harness and supply counter, and a small stable. Their specialty was servicing wagon trains that moved in and out of the area. But both saw the much larger commercial possibilities of Los Angeles.

It was Ethan who scouted out the building they eventually took over in late 1847. With the cash that Henry Calder had given to Robert, along with Ethan's grubstake of Spanish gold coins, the two bought the building and set about remodeling it to their needs, soon organizing and opening their business.

Located near the old Plaza and the jail, the store specialized in two main departments. Primarily it was engaged in outfitting the Americans who were beginning to funnel into California by the southern route with romantic dreams of easy homesteading, having heard fantastic, outsize tales of the boundless opulence and beauty of California, the "new Eden." The store also catered to the domestic town trade, carrying an extensive range of cloth yardage brought from the East around Cape Horn, and a variety of household utensils and gadgets such as the Knoxville store had carried.

It was soon evident to both men that they could make a great deal of money in a very short time. But they had no desire to take more than a just profit from the business for themselves, and they ploughed much of this back immediately into widening their range of stock. They intended eventually to open branch stores as far south as San Diego and possibly at Monterey Bay.

Since Sarah Calder's death, Robert had not found himself much interested in women. He was quite willing to fill his days with long hours and hard work, so that by the end of his working day he fell into bed exhausted. Next morning he was up at dawn, ready to go again.

This kind of life suited Ethan perfectly. Ethan was neither a drinker nor a womanizer nor a pursuer of men. And yet his possessiveness of Robert might have been called a psychological distortion. He scarcely let Robert out of his sight to do the banking or to go down to the port of San Pedro to purchase goods from the sailing schooners. Ethan discouraged the several young female customers who paid unusual attention to Robert by marked rudeness, to the point where he and Robert had mild words about the matter.

"You don't need to intimidate the patronage," Robert told Ethan. "We're not in business to *lose* custom."

"No, and we're not in business to encourage loose women," Ethan retorted somewhat hotly.

Robert carried the matter no further than to say that they'd both better be as civil to customers as they could be, for other stores were opening and the competition might snatch away their clients—sensible words that registered with Ethan for a time.

All went well in the drygoods store for some months. Then two events took place in January of 1848 that changed the face of California forever and dramatically altered Robert's life.

On January 24th, John Sutter's millwright James Marshall discovered gold flecks in Sutter's sawmill tailrace on the American River. When he shouted, "Boys, by God, I think I've found a gold mine!" it was a cry heard round the world.

That same month, due to growing patronage, Robert persuaded Ethan to agree to hire a responsible clerk instead of putting up with the inexperienced errand boys they had made do with since opening.

Robert let Ethan do the hiring; he felt that this would make it easier for his partner to get along with a third person in the store handling cash and taking orders. Ethan hired a fair blond youth of twenty, fresh off a ship from New York, a city lad with a veneer of sophistication that did not wear too well. Gianni Colli was a first generation American of northern Italian stock. His parents were born in the city of Turin. Handsome, charming, Gianni was bright beyond his education. At first he worked well with both Ethan and Robert and the customers liked him and his sunny disposition.

Colli was not around long, however, before he started drinking. Rumors came to Ethan and Robert that Colli was gambling—rumors verified when Colli asked his bosses for a raise, and in lieu of receiving that, a loan.

"We're not a bank," Ethan told Colli, and

would have fired him then and there, except for Robert's plea to give the young man another chance.

One night, when Ethan had gone out for the evening to see a supplier about some items, Robert invited Colli to have dinner with him at a restaurant near the store.

Into wine, young Colli asked Robert bluntly for the details of his relationship with Ethan. "I know about these things," Colli said over his wine glass, scaling his voice down to an intimate murmur. "I come from New York where you see everything."

Robert suppressed his irritation. "You've had too much wine, Gianni. Let me give you some advice. There's no better man in the world than Ethan Drew. You have to know him to understand what's beneath his moods."

"The color thing, eh?"

"That's part of it. More than that, he's an orphan, he had no childhood, no love, no one to care whether he lived or died. I don't know why I'm telling you all this. I really don't have to."

"Maybe you're thinking of getting out, eh? Going into business for yourself?"

Robert stared at Colli. How could this mere snip of a youth read him so accurately? Yes, he did want to go into business for himself, and not in Los Angeles. He'd been dreaming of going north, perhaps to Sacramento, maybe San Francisco eventually. But there was no easy way to dissociate himself from Ethan, and in his heart he simply couldn't put Ethan through such an ordeal—not without a powerful reason, and he had none.

"Yes, I've thought of it, but it isn't possible."

"Gold's a magnet. Now that it's been discovered in the north that's the place to go."

"I'm not so sure. Anyway, I have no interest in getting rich quick."

"Well, I do," said Colli. "Then I can blow the dust of this stupid town from my shoulders forever, go back to New York, open a business of some sort, and enjoy life."

"You're talking about going north, I gather."

"I'd like to, but I don't have a grubstake."

"You'll need it."

"I know. Why don't you come north, Robert?" Colli asked. "We could go in together, make ourselves a million. It's a lot more exciting than standing behind a counter until your legs give out."

"Maybe," said Robert, amused but certainly not convinced. "Don't let Ethan hear you say all this."

"You mean about us going north together?"

"You haven't seen his temper; it's impressive."

"I don't care," said Colli, "I'm not afraid." He raised his wine glass. "Here's to El Dorado. Think it over."

Robert did exactly that. There was a certain romance to exploring the Sierra Nevada that he found almost irresistible. Always attracted to mountains, these western slopes held the excitement of the unknown. He had no intention, however, of going anywhere with Gianni Colli whose callowness put him off.

The following night the three men took inventory at the store after closing hours. Gianni missed counts on several items. Finally Ethan lost his temper.

"Goddamit, boy, you put your mind to what you're doing or you won't have a job!"

This was more than the excitable Colli could take. He blurted out, "I'm fed up with you, Ethan. I'm not going to stay around here. I'm off to the gold fields, and Robert's coming with me."

A thick, dour silence settled on Ethan's features; for a moment he was so rigid Robert thought he looked made of stone. Then Ethan threw down his clipboard and stalked out of the store, slamming the front door behind him.

"You're a fool," Robert said angrily to Colli. "I don't know if Ethan will fire you, but I will. You're finished as of this moment."

Colli smiled, shrugged indifferently. "So much for that, eh?"

"I mean it, Gianni, you're through here."

"Well, in that case"—Colli held out his hand —"how about my pay? You owe me for five day's work."

Robert took several dollars from the cash drawer and gave them to Colli. "Here! Now get out before Ethan comes back."

Colli smiled, narrowing his eyes. "You like him a lot, don't you?"

"I said get out!" Robert shouted at him.

Colli donned his jacket, went to the front door, touched his fingers to his temple, smiling crookedly. "*Addio, Roberto* . . . See you sometime."

From the store, Colli went immediately to a saloon a block away and got himself drunk. Ethan knew where he was and waited for him. After Colli's money was gone he wandered toward the rooming house where he lived, not far from the saloon. He took a shortcut through a silent alley, which was his mistake. Ethan Drew was waiting for him, boiling with rage that Colli dared to take Robert away. Colli never felt the blow that broke his neck. He was dead before he hit the manure-packed earth.

Robert was still at the store when Ethan appeared, morosely silent. "I sent Colli away," Robert said. "I let him go."

Ethan nodded, sat down heavily in a chair near the potbelly stove, rubbing his hands together slowly.

Robert continued, "I was afraid you might do something."

Ethan nodded again. "I did," he muttered. "The kid's in an alley down the street. I hit him. Just once. I'm sorry . . ." He buried his face in his hands. "I couldn't stand the idea that you'd go away with him."

Robert said, "I wouldn't go away with anybody, Ethan. We're in business. You ought to give me more credit than that. I hope you didn't hurt him, just taught him a lesson . . ."

Ethan shook his head. "He's dead. I killed him."

Robert was stunned. "Oh God," he moaned, leaning against a counter. "What do we do now?"

"I know what I'll do," said Ethan. "I'm leaving on a wagon train heading East in the morning."

A lot of people were being murdered these days, Robert realized, and while justice was often swift for the known miscreants, it seldom served the casual, violent deaths that occurred frequently in frontier Los Angeles.

"No one saw you, I hope?"

"I don't think so," Ethan said.

"What will I do?" Robert asked in anguish.

"Stay here. Take care of the store. Sell it, if you want. How much have we got put away?"

"About six hundred dollars."

"Give me what's there. Everything else is yours—the store, everything."

"Ethan, you're crazy! That's not right."

"It's the way I want it. I'll write a note to that effect, giving my half to you."

"Ethan, you can't."

"Yes, I can. I'm not going to the police. It's best if I go."

The two men sat in the store all night, drinking hot tea, talking in low tones about their lives, about the turn taken with Gianni Colli's death. In another hour or so, at first light, someone would find the body.

Toward five o'clock Ethan packed some belongings in the back bunkroom of the store, embraced Robert and went out the rear entrance, heading toward the area where the wagon trains formed.

Robert watched Ethan's broad back disappear into the early morning mists. He went back inside the store and sat down by the pot-belly stove and wept. He realized then, as never before, how lonely a man can be. He knew that he couldn't bear to stay in Los Angeles, anymore than he could have remained in Knoxville. He wondered what kind of ironic destiny it was that fate had handed him. Maybe Gianni Colli had been right. North was the only place.

He would find a buyer, sell the business and the building, maybe realize enough to keep him going for a while. He didn't believe that he could make it rich as a prospector. In fact, the idea didn't appeal to him all that much; it was the scene that piqued his curiosity. What he intended was to set his mind on the search for a good new life, and this time he would find it. He would not be like brother John and follow the Zionists into the wilderness. He would follow his own religious belief, which was merely the Golden Rule. He couldn't go wrong with that as his credo.

Six weeks later Robert found a cash buyer for the store building and the business. The man thought he was crazy for selling his interests at such a low price. Robert could have waited longer and realized a lot more, but he was impatient to leave Los Angeles, which held only disquieting memories for him.

With part of the sale money Robert bought a fine wagon, horses and supplies and was on his way to northern California in March of 1848. If Ethan had gone north instead of East, Robert still had no idea where to find him; Ethan hadn't bothered to send him a letter. Only chance would bring them together—the store was sold, Robert had no permanent address. This was regrettable, for he now had no way to give his ex-partner his rightful split of the money gained from the sale of the business.

Gold fever was rampant in California, but especially in the Mother Lode Country. The fabulous riches thought by sixteenth-century Spanish explorers to exist in South American were luring men from around the world to the new El Dorado, California. Robert joined the throngs of excited hopefuls, men and women of all persuasions, one among many thousands hurrying North to make their fantasies of wealth a glittering reality.

Only a handful of the seekers found fulfillment. Robert was one of these, but not in any way that he could have imagined.

GOLD FEVER

"THE WHOLE COUNTRY is now moving on the mines," Robert wrote his mother Caroline in Washington, D. C. It was the first time that Robert had written her since he reached Los Angeles. "I expect that you hear more of this news than we do, being at the capital. Monterey, San Francisco, Sonoma, San Jose and Santa Cruz are devoid of male population. Every able-bodied man who isn't in jail has taken off for the gold fields. Blacksmiths, carpenters, even lawyers and doctors, are leaving the comfort of the coast for the wilds of the Sierra Nevada foothills. Ships are abandoned at their moorings in San Francisco Bay. Soldiers are deserting their posts, family men are disappearing. You perhaps would wonder why I am here. Well, dear mother, I am uncertain that coming here was the wisest thing to do. My partner dissolved our relationship, I had some money, and it seemed like a good idea at the moment of decision. However, I am not cut from the cloth to make me kneel stoically in icy water half the day in hopes of obtaining a few dollars in gold dust, immediately spent to obtain the expensive creature comforts hereabouts. Eggs are a dollar a piece, and if there were any hotels about, a decent dinner and a good night's sleep between linen sheets would be fifty dollars.

"I first came up to Sutter's Fort but found it much too crowded. There must be some two thousand people working the streams in and around the Fort. So I drove twenty-five miles into hill country, beautiful and serene it is, and soon found people digging . . ."

From all he'd heard in the past weeks, Robert believed that he might find gold on several branches of the Sacramento and San Joaquin Rivers, which were less crowded areas. Here, of course, where the prospecting population was not as dense as around Sutter's Fort, the choice of river banks was broader, also the chances of robbery, or even murder, were much less.

Along with the decent people who came to what later would be called the Mother Lode Country, there were cutthroats, adventurers, highwaymen and thieving prostitutes. Robert carried arms, a pistol and a rifle, the latter prominently displayed whenever he approached a new area and its inhabitants. Men sought gold within ten to twenty yards of the streams, so as to be convenient to water for sifting out the precious metal. From time to time, as Robert moved about, he saw families. Generally these were a man and wife, both young, with one or two small children, a team obviously trying to make its fortune and get out fast, for the hill country was no place for raising a family.

At one creek branch, Robert ran across a large tent camp occupied by several Americans: a couple of sailors, a clerk, a pair of carpenters and three laborers. One of the carpenters had been on General Kearny's wagon train to California, had moved on to San Francisco and thence to the gold fields. This was the first time that Robert had seen Tom Torrence since they parted company in Los Angeles.

Robert stopped his wagon above a creek, scouting for a spot to camp for the night. Robert's intent was to find a quiet spot for himself away from other prospectors and settle in for a few days. He'd been traveling every day since leaving Los Angeles and needed a rest. The weather had turned warm and sunny, the mountains were drying out after heavy rains, a perfect time to relax.

A shout from Tom brought the two men together. Robert was relieved to find someone he knew, for he missed Ethan more than he cared to admit.

Tom Torrence was about Robert's age, a big bear of a man with a booming voice, much given to whiskey and cigars, basically a good fellow with a friendly nature.

"By God, it's good to see you, Bob," Tom Torrence told him, nearly paralyzing his hand in a hearty welcome shake. "Where's your partner, Ethan?"

"We sold the business we started," Robert

explained, "and Ethan went East for a while."

"I guess you miss him?"

"Very much." He would say no more.

"Why hell, since you're alone, camp with us. It's safer, you'll have companionship. My partners will welcome you."

Robert was grateful for Tom's kind offer of hospitality. "You sure I won't be in the way?" he asked. "Some of the prospectors are pretty touchy about having strangers around."

"It's a free country out here," said Tom. "You got as much right to stay as we do."

"Since you put it that way, all right," Robert agreed. "I'll stay a while. By the way, what's that?" He pointed to a wooden contraption that straddled one finger of the rocky river course.

"It's called a canoe," Tom explained. "It channels water-propelled earth through the trough where we sift it for gold. Mighty effective piece of equipment. We could sell it for a pretty piece if we wanted. Have to stand guard by it nights. There's another one downstream a ways. They each took one hundred board feet of lumber."

"It looks like a baby's cradle," Robert observed.

"It sure does. Ten feet long and a real money maker."

"Then the prospecting's good here?"

"Yessir," Tom lowered his voice to a discreet whisper, "we been makin' about fifty dollars a day, each one of us. We stick together for safety. Where you headed?"

"Just looking around," Robert said, "trying to get the feel of this world. What are your plans?"

"Us, we're makin' it while we can and get-

tin' out fast. The big push is just startin'. Soon
there'll be thousands of folks here, crazy ones,
all jostlin', shovin' and maybe killin' each other.
It won't be no place for a delicate, sensitive
creature like me," Tom declared, and sent his
booming laugh clear down to the river.

"Sounds like you'll each make a tidy pile
before you're through," Robert observed.

"That's it. And you can't find a better place
to be than right here with us. We got a cooperative deal working. We take turns doin' the
chores, cookin', washin' up, guard duty. You
got to find your own spot on the stream, but I'll
speak for the gang that you're welcome to hang
around for a spell, so long as you'll contribute
and do chores."

"I'll be glad to join up."

"All right, fine. Now let's get you unpacked,
set you up and put you to work. Got to get
movin' if you want to make your fortune," Tom
said, and slapped Robert on the back. "Boy, I
sure wish old Ethan was here. Never was a
wagon master to match him. I'm surprised he
didn't decide to come up north. He was born
for a challenge like this one."

"Maybe he'll show up yet," Robert said, but
he doubted it very much. Next best was being
asked to join Tom's group for a time. It would
keep him from being lonely, from thinking
about the strange direction his life had taken
since Sarah's death. He would have to live instead of reflect.

Robert liked being an associate of the mining
cooperative. He wasn't asked to join the working canoe shifts—this was a closed operation.

But he shared the food and clean-up duties, and he contributed cash toward the purchase of staples. Tom helped him set up his own works. Soon he began to operate his miniature mining kingdom just south of the two canoes and started to do the actual placer panning.

Robert would dig up a foot or so of the upper soil near the water with his sturdy shovel. He would then fill one of the tin mining pans he'd brought along with a shovel full of loose dirt and stones. Placing the basin a couple of inches under the clear, flowing water of the stream, he would stir up the dirt with one hand, agitating it enough to allow the current to carry away the light earth. Then he would pick out the stones and cast them into the stream. After continuing this painstaking operation for sometimes as long as twenty minutes, he would end up with a few spoonfuls of fine black sand. Next he would dry this on a piece of cloth in the warm sunshine, then blow away the sand gently. What remained was gold dust, valued at about two dollars. One day he made twenty dollars, according to Tom's evaluation, and another day he made nearly thirty-five dollars.

By the end of the week, Robert had come to the depressing conclusion that a prospector's life, and fortune, weren't for him. Unless he could join a concerted group effort such as Tom and his friends had established, then panning for gold was simply too damned hard, not worth the backbreaking effort it demanded. Besides, the good weather probably wouldn't hold, everyone assured him of that. And when the spring torrents of rain came there would be many cold, damp days ahead when he'd be miserable and lonely, having to lie bundled up in the bed of his wagon with not even a stick of dry wood for a fire. It wasn't that he was too soft for the work, or a tenderfoot, Robert reflected, he just wasn't cut out for the mental monotony, the uncertainty of prospecting.

Tom said something to him Saturday night, a time when the canoe gang would open up a half-gallon jug of whiskey and pass it around ritually, drinking until it was empty. What Tom said stuck in his head after retiring: "Too bad you can't finance a store up in these parts— you'd make a pile."

"You could be right," Robert agreed, realizing that he had enough cash to organize his needs in Sacramento, or even San Francisco. But the incentive to open another store wasn't there; he needed someone to double his strengths, to minimize weaknesses, make the days and off-hours worthwhile. Although not exceptionally gregarious, Robert knew that he couldn't and wouldn't go it alone indefinitely.

On Monday morning Robert packed his belongings, loaded his wagon, hitched up his horses and said good-bye to Tom and his partners. He would head back toward civilization, lower into the foothills.

Two days later he camped on an embankment of the American River, about fifty miles upstream from Sutter's Fort. As he made camp he observed that another tent was pitched across the stream and down some sixty yards from him, partially screened by trees. It was usual to run across one or two persons in the course of a couple of hours and to expect these to camp close by, so Robert gave the tent no more than cursory notice.

At dusk while he was making a soup of lentils and pork bits, Robert heard the shot. The concussion was followed immediately by a high, piercing scream, then silence. The direction of the shot was unmistakable—across the river in the vicinity of the neighboring tent.

Robert's credo in traveling alone was: Mind your own business; keep your gun loaded at all times and never interfere in a fight—you might get your head blown off. He didn't know if this was a fight, of course, but the scream was a woman's, frightened and anguished. He felt a sudden obligation to investigate.

Picking up his rifle he walked downstream to a shallow ford where some flat grey boulders enabled him to cross the stream without wading the icy water. He'd reached the opposite bank when he heard the woman's voice again utter a cry, then a terrified protest: "No, no, you can't!"

Someone obviously was in deep trouble. Then he saw the saddled horse, and immediately beside it the man in sombrero and leatherns, his back toward Robert.

Thirty yards separated Robert from the man. Fortunately, the sound of Robert's advance was covered by the babbling stream. He heard no further female cry, wondering if he'd imagined it. But as he crouched and began to creep forward behind a line of low shrubs, he saw the woman.

She stood fully revealed by the flickering fire at her feet, the gloom gathering like a dark nimbus around her head and shoulders. She was young and strongly beautiful, with a clear, fresh complexion and rich brown hair brushed back and secured to reveal the exquisite oval of her face. Her large eyes were dark with fear, though probably blue, he judged. Her slim, well-proportioned figure was clad in a simple grey ankle-length dress with long sleeves and a modest edging of white lace at the high neckline.

She kept staring down to her right from time to time. Robert followed her frantic darting glances and saw the body, its back toward him. He couldn't tell if it were a man or a woman. But he needed no more information to realize that the blast he'd heard minutes earlier had felled whoever lay there, and that the girl was in great physical danger.

Robert's distaste for violence was strong enough to prevent him from killing a chicken for dinner or drowning a litter of unwanted kittens. He had recently shot rabbits for food, but only the urgency of his situation with fresh supplies had forced him into it. At this point, however, he knew he would have to use his rifle in some way, and had no idea just how.

The man, probably a bandit, moved closer to the girl, pointing his gun at her, using it as an indicator.

"Gimme the gold dust," he demanded roughly, almost shouting his order.

"There isn't any," said the girl. "Believe me, there's nothing here you want. Go away. Leave me alone."

The man's harsh laugh rang out. "Get the gold dust, woman. You're coming with me."

It seemed impossible to Robert that the bandit hadn't seen his tent and campfire. But then, he'd built his fire on the far side of his tent, screened by the trees, so perhaps the man was unaware of someone close by.

"Go ahead, kill me," the girl said, pressing both hands against her bosom. "God sees everything, He'll know what you've done. You won't ever be able to escape Him and His judgment."

"Shut your goddam mouth!" the bandit warned her sharply, and moved in closer.

The girl stepped back involuntarily with a small gasp, nearly tripping over the inert form at her feet. Apparently thinking that she was about to run away, the bandit threw down his weapon and lunged for her, pinioning her arms, grabbing her around the waist. He dragged her toward his horse. Robert saw the rope that was coiled around the saddlehorn.

Robert stood up, aimed his rifle and called out in a loud voice, "Stop where you are or I'll shoot!"

Stunned, the bandit let go of his frightened captive. The girl stumbled away from him, picked up the discarded gun.

"Get out, you filthy cur!" she cried, aiming the gun at his stomach.

"Bitch!" the bandit cursed between clenched teeth, but didn't move an inch, acutely aware of Robert behind him.

"Get on that horse and go!" the girl ordered. "I'll shoot at the count of ten! One . . . two . . . three . . ."

The intruder jumped onto his horse. Robert got a flashing impression of swarthy features, a handlebar moustache—probably some halfbreed gambler down on his luck, desperate. The man shot one last hateful glance into the gloom where Robert stood, then galloped off down the river bank, melting quickly into the early darkness.

Robert stepped forward, his gun held down so that the girl wouldn't shoot him. He took only enough paces to let her see him fully.

"Who are you?" the woman demanded.

"Robert Sanderson," he said, dropping his rifle. "I'm all alone across the river. I heard the shot and your scream, so I came over. Please, drop that gun before it goes off. I'm not going to hurt you."

"The shot," the girl said in a daze. "Oh God, no!"

Dropping the gun she turned and hurried to the still figure by the fire. She knelt and cradled it in her arms as Robert approached slowly, so as not to alarm her.

She embraced an elderly man. Robert saw that he had been shot high in the chest; he was pale as wax.

"I should have killed that miserable vermin," the girl said bitterly.

"Who's he?" Robert asked, nodding at the man whose eyes flickered open momentarily at the sound of his voice, then closed again.

"My father. He's hurt, what'll we do? Needs a doctor." She was almost weeping.

"Let me see him, please." Robert crouched down by the wounded man. The single shot had penetrated high into the chest cavity; he saw the bloody hole in the man's shirt. The nearest medical aid was at Sutter's Fort, at least two days away and no journey to begin at night. Robert could put him into the bed of his wagon, but he'd be thrown about, suffer terrible pain probably, and he might not survive the trip.

"We'll make him comfortable by the fire," Robert said. "In the morning we'll see what we can do about moving him into my wagon. I see you don't have one."

"No, we had to sell it," the girl told him. "We came up here on horseback." Among the trees, Robert saw two tethered horses and a pack mule.

"I'll stay with you tonight, just in case."

"What about that thief?"

"He won't come back, not now. He doesn't know how many of us there are."

"Thank God for you," the girl sighed. "I'm Jane Parker. This is my father, Jacob."

They made Jacob Parker as comfortable as possible. Robert went back across the stream and brought his knapsack over, and then his horses, settling himself close to the Parker girl and the old man.

"I'll make something to eat," the girl said.

The girl busied herself in silence, making biscuits which they shared with Robert's pot of soup. Later she seemed to relax, Robert observed, and told him something of the events that had brought her to this spot.

"My father and I came out West with a wagon train," she explained, filtering in through Los Angeles to make the long valley drive north. In Sacramento the old man had fallen ill with fever and nearly died. A retired grocer from Ohio, he wanted to go back home. "It's probably my fault that he was shot," she said. " I wouldn't let him go. Eventually we had to sell our wagon to get enough money to come prospecting."

She shook her head mournfully. "He might

even die," she declared, "and I'm responsible. I had no business forcing him to come up to this terrible wilderness where we don't have a single friend."

"You have me," Robert said sincerely.

Jane looked at him, her eyes bright, as if seeing him for the first time. "Yes," she murmured, with a trace of a smile, "I guess I have, and I thank God for it." Then she shivered, pulled her shawl tighter about her shoulders and leaned toward the fire. "When I think what could have happened. That foul creature was going to—" She broke off, shaking her head, unable to finish.

"It's late," Robert said, "and you're exhausted. I'll keep watch, I'm not tired. You go ahead and get some sleep; you'll need it for tomorrow. I can look after your father. If there's any change I'll call you. And if you wake up before dawn, you can spell me on sentinel duty for an hour or so."

"You're a kind man," Jane said softly. She went into the tent and pulled the flap closed. Robert tried not to think how she would look under her long, plain dress. As he reflected on this, Jane stuck her head through the tent flap. "By the way, I was telling the truth," she declared. "We don't have any gold dust, nothing at all of any value."

Robert thought he could cite one item—her fresh appeal. "None of my business if you did," he replied.

"Oh yes it is," she insisted. "You entered our lives and saved them. You have the right to know. Good night, Mr. Sanderson, and thank you for everything."

Robert settled back against an outcropping of

grey rock, his rifle across his knees. Tomorrow would be a difficult day, particularly if the old man died on the journey, God forbid. But he mustn't think ahead; his duty was to stay awake, just in case that bandit might return, which was highly unlikely. They were cowards unless in a gang, and this one was probably operating alone.

Jane . . . He rolled her name around on his tongue, savoring it. A plain name for such a remarkably beautiful and spirited woman. He realized with a warm, sensuous satisfaction that he was responding wholly to a woman for the first time since Sarah's death. He knew nothing about this girl-woman, not even her age, but he was immediately caught up in her charm. The father was fairly old, maybe in his sixties, but Jane was young, not yet twenty, he was sure. It would be interesting to see if he and this girl could become friends. Beyond that he dared not let his mind speculate. He yawned, settled himself upright and stared moodily off into the chilly darkness, the fire roaring at his feet, prepared to stay awake until morning.

Jacob Parker died toward dawn. Robert must have dozed off for a few moments, for he opened his eyes to a soft moaning sound. He threw off his blanket and got up to check on the old man. Parker lay on his back, his mouth agape. Robert didn't need to take his pulse to know that he was dead. He'd seen enough fresh corpses with Kearny to be able to recognize one instantly. He covered the old man with his blanket, wondering where they'd bury him, and what Jane's reaction would be. He sat down by the fire, hugged himself for warmth and drifted off to sleep, thinking that dawn would be soon enough to confront Jane with her father's unfortunate death.

He awakened at sunrise, called to Jane, put coffee on to boil.

Jane emerged from the tent tousled, sleepy-eyed.

"You didn't waken me," Jane said.

"There was no need to," Robert answered quietly.

"Why?" Then Jane saw the covered body of her father. She cried out, fell to the ground and threw herself across the corpse. She began to sob brokenly.

Robert took her by the shoulders, made her sit by the fire. As she wept he put a blanket around her. She stayed sobbing for a long while, her face buried in her hands.

Finally she stopped weeping, dried her eyes and stood up, saying calmly, "We'll bury him over there beyond the trees. He'd like that. The last thing he said to me before that bandit entered our lives was how much he liked it here by the river, it was so peaceful. Nice enough for a house. He'll rest well here."

Together they dug a shallow grave on a small rise that overlooked the wooded bend in the river. They wrapped Jacob Parker in a piece of canvas, placed him in the ground and covered him over. They carried smooth grey stones from the river to make a cairn over his grave. After that, there was no point in lingering, so Robert first packed his equipment, then loaded Jane's. In his wagon, with Jane's horses and mule trailing after them, they made their somber way down the valley toward Sacramento.

Jane was understandably silent that first day out, distracted and moody. She spoke to Robert when he addressed her, but she was distant, mourning the death of her father. They pitched camp that night away from the river, near a family with two small children.

Robert insisted that Jane sleep in the wagon bed. He pitched his tent close by. Several times during the night he was awakened by Jane's weeping, but in the morning she was up, clear-eyed, long before he was, making him breakfast from dried oatmeal, with bacon and coffee.

Jane greeted him with a cheery smile, apparently having resolved her melancholy during the night. Robert soon learned that Jane's ability to shed a dark mood lightning-quick was one of her most positive character points.

"I've been thinking," she told him over coffee, "and I've come to an important conclusion. *I* think it is, anyway."

"Such as?"

"I'm alone in California, as you know. I'm only nineteen. And from the way things can be here, I can't wander around by myself. I have some education, and I have to support myself. I suppose I could be a governess, get a position in Sacramento, perhaps settle down for a time, decide what I shall do with my life. But that's not too appealing."

"You could get married," Robert said.

She smiled at him, amused. "Well, I expect I shall sometime. I don't see the urgency now."

"It won't be easy on your own," Robert said.

"This is still a primitive society in the midst of turbulent growth. California isn't truly a part of the Union, although it'll go through the formalities of statehood before long, I imagine. Then the growth will be phenomenal, people will rush here by the tens of thousands."

Jane thought about this for a moment. "I suppose there's a place somewhere for me when I'm ready. I think I'll try for a job of some kind. What do you intend to do? All I know is, you had a store in Los Angeles and now you're a prospector."

"Observing the prospectors," he corrected her. "I honestly think I'd like to become a merchant again in Sacramento."

"And give up looking for gold?"

"I'm not very good at it. And besides, merchandising can be as lucrative as prospecting any day."

"Do you really think so?"

"I'm absolutely positive."

"Sounds interesting. Forgive me for asking, but how will you finance this business?"

Robert had no intention of telling Jane he was solvent. "I have credit," he replied. "I'll manage."

"Well then, your future's all settled. My father had nothing, nor have I. The idea of becoming a governess doesn't really appeal much," she confessed, "and I certainly don't relish the idea of marrying until I'm truly ready."

"So what will you do?"

There was something bizarre about this young woman, Robert thought, so easily able to slip off the mantle of grief. But then, maybe this was just her superficial visage, making it easier for her to deal with sadness.

"That's still to be decided," she said. "I'll probably get married though, eventually."

"You keep coming back to that. Anyone in mind?" His pulse accelerated. He found it refreshing that she could be so open. Most women talked around the subject while diligently scouting for a likely candidate or submitting placidly to some family arrangement.

"No one, but from the few single women I've seen, it shouldn't be difficult," Jane declared, neither modestly nor arrogantly. "I think I can find an eligible bachelor in Sacramento, and if not, I'll move on. According to you, every young man in California's looking for gold. Sooner or later a rich one will pass through Sacramento."

"That's the dream," he said. "At one time there were ten women for every male in California. In the colonial days, that is. It's just the opposite now."

"Then I shouldn't have any trouble in picking and choosing."

Robert smiled. "Putting yourself on the block, you mean?"

Jane flushed. "On the contrary, it's the bachelors who'll be on the block, not me."

"Got it all figured out, eh?"

"Certainly. I'm the one who'll make the choice."

"Good luck," Robert said. He was deeply attracted to Jane but determined not to reveal this until he knew much more about her. He held out his tin cup. "How about some more of your good coffee?" As she filled the cup he glanced at the grey clouds racing toward the Sierra Nevada. "We'd better pack up soon, it looks like rain . . ."

The rain came in torrents and made their progress extremely slow. They reached Sacramento late the following day. Robert located a compound where they could leave his wagon, his and Jane's horses, and the mule.

A family took Jane in, allowing her to exchange domestic duties for her room and board, a temporary arrangement that suited her. Robert bunked in a shack half-open to wind and rain along with several other prospectors, dirty and noisome; but he was glad for a place to rest, especially since it was adjacent to the compound where his equipment was stored.

Within two weeks Robert had his immediate future set up. He made a trip to San Francisco to negotiate for supplies, ignoring the lustier aspects of the town. There he met Sam Brannan, probably the first Gold Rush publicity agent. Brannan was already stocking his San Francisco and Coloma stores with mining gear and related supplies. Later he would run through the streets of San Francisco, waving his hat and a bottle of gold dust and shouting, "Gold, gold! From the American River! Come and get it!"

"You simply can't lose, son," Brannan told Robert. "I'm proud of you, a young man, having the foresight to become a merchant. By summer there'll be fifty thousand people prospecting the Sierras. You'll be able to ask any price you want for any item in stock. Your only problem will be supplies. I suggest you open a lumber yard next to a general store and watch the stampede."

Brannan gave Robert invaluable assistance, since he felt certain that there would be room for both and many others in business to the north and south of the San Francisco Bay Region. "Sacramento will be a way-station, seething with people and prosperity by late summer," Brannan said. "Then the whores and thieves will come. Talk about carnivals, wait and see!"

Robert returned to a Jane eager for the details of his trip. He said, "I'll have to buy or build a store and set up a yard next to it."

Jubilant, Jane wanted to be part of the venture. "While you were gone," she said, "I lined up a store site for you, and there's a good piece of yard land right next door."

With Jane, Robert inspected the location and found it admirable. Jane was shrewd, he was discovering. He bought the land, close to the busy, crowded riverfront, and when his first order of lumber arrived from the north, he started building.

Jane spent as much time as she could helping him oversee the carpenters, who grumbled about a young woman bossing them; but these were unusual times and the pay was fantastic. Jane's sharp eye for details saved Robert time and money. It was her suggestion to include two separate living units within the portion of the structure.

"The larger one will be your office and sleeping quarters," Jane explained. "Isn't that logical?"

"And the other—?"

"Mine, of course," she replied, "containing a kitchen and sleeping alcove."

Robert grinned. He wanted to ask if there would be an adjoining door; instead he asked, "What will people say?"

Jane shrugged. "Let them say what they will. I don't care, if you don't. We've nothing to be ashamed of. We're friends only."

"This won't help your quest of that eligible bachelor," Robert pointed out.

"Nor will it hinder me," Jane retorted. "And of course I'll be working days in the store with you, so the proximity of our quarters is logical."

"You'll be working with me?" Robert said, both surprised and pleased. Jane had the kind of pragmatic sensibility Sarah had possessed, which was one of the reasons she attracted him.

"Yes, certainly. I don't want to be a domestic another day after the store's completed. With a kitchen I'll be able to cook. You'll take your meals with me."

"I will?"

She glanced sharply at him. "What's the matter? I thought you'd be pleased to have an assistant who's trustworthy and willing to look after your interests."

"Oh I am," Robert assured her. "But remember, we'll be living very close together. You may grow tired of the arrangement for a number of reasons."

Jane smiled. "I'm experienced. I'm not soft and yielding, I can take care of myself. I never told you, but when my mother died I went to live for some time with my maiden aunt who raised me. She taught me to take a dim view of fleshly sin. I'm not a churchgoer, but Aunt Emma's religious ideas rubbed off on me a little. I do believe in God and the sanctity of a relationship. Even in marriage, there must be love before anything else. Otherwise it's not a marriage in heaven's eyes."

"You seem to know a lot about marriage," Robert observed.

"No, not much. But I do know about people."

"You think our closeness in business will work?" he said, actually posing the question for himself.

"It *has* to work," Jane declared with finality. "At least for the time being, until I can settle my future."

"How do you propose to do that?"

"Oh," she said mysteriously, "I have ideas," and changed the subject . . .

In 1848 gold seekers began to arrive in California in swarms from Oregon, northern Mexico, from Chile and Peru, Hawaii and Australia. The search for gold took place in widely separated areas on the western slopes of the Sierra Nevada foothills. Ranchers and farmers, soldiers and sailors, merchants, hunters of many different ethnic backgrounds rapidly became miners. At no other period in previous centuries had there been such a polyglot instant population gather in any one place on earth in so short a time.

The incredible rush took off from two focal points: one was from Sacramento, branching out along the tributaries of the Sacramento River; the other from Stockton and the tributaries of the San Joaquin River. The seekers found gold particles and nuggets on the banks of flowing streams in deep winter under freezing conditions, and in the dust of dry stream beds in the blazing hot summer.

A miner's life was a grinding existence. Miners worked at hard physical labor from dawn to sunset, digging, sifting, sloshing through icy water, burnt by the sun, always bending, squatting, repeating monotonously the same boring process day in and day out. By the end of 1848 almost five thousand miners were at work in the foothills.

The forty-eighters were a tough lot. They were basically friendly to one another, and often shared food with the less fortunate. They lived as best they could, a gypsy-like existence in temporary shacks hastily erected and quickly abandoned when they moved to other diggings. They paid a great deal of money for food and drink—eggs were sometimes a dollar apiece—and for the women who went into the fields in search of husbands or simply to sell themselves for gold dust.

Storekeepers like Robert Sanderson supplied the prospectors with food, mining implements, lumber and whatever other merchandise they required. Prices were governed by supply and demand. There were often severe shortages, and transportation of goods was slow and expensive. But the improvident spending habits of the miners made merchandising worthwhile. It was not uncommon for miners to come into the store and give Robert one hundred dollars worth of gold dust for a packful of items, often at prices they could ill afford to pay.

Some struck it rich; however, most came away from the fields with only a modest profit, soon eaten up by the high cost of living. Men who had come to California dreaming of riches they could carry back to their homeland were forced in the end to settle in California and begin life all over again, with no hope of ever getting back home. What made life among the miners worth-

while was the strong camaraderie that bound
them together as pioneers. It was this quality
that Robert admired in many of the men he
met—and often at the expense of high profit. He
seldom charged what other merchants were
charging for identical items. Consequently, his
store was packed all day with buyers, and he
made a good profit, although not a quick fortune.

Once the Sacramento store was open and
doing well, Robert realized how astute Jane had
been to influence him to build living quarters
for both of them at the back of the store. With
the long hours they had to keep, the convenience
of quarters only a few steps from the business
proved a Godsend for them both.

Soon Jane hired a young girl to assist her in
the store, as well as in the preparation of meals.
Robert found a young male assistant who could
oversee the loading of supplies, both in the
lumber yard and in the store, and the transportation of goods from the docks to the store.

One day Tom Torrence appeared at the store,
much to Robert's delight, passing through on
his way to a brief vacation in San Francisco. He
and his prospecting partners had made good
money with their canoe mining venture in the
foothills. But the area became mined thin and
overrun with a new wave of miners, so they had
decided to break up their corporation, each man
going his own way.

Tom had money, of course, but couldn't find
a bunk for the night, so Robert invited him to
stay in his quarters; there was room enough.

After the store closed, Jane served the two
men supper, keeping a keen bead on Tom as she

worked. Robert watched her moving back and forth with various dishes. From the glint in her eyes, which he could read quite accurately by this time, he wondered if she wasn't actually a bit jealous of Tom's unexpected presence. In the past several months Jane had pretty well had Robert to herself. It was apparent tonight that she didn't like sharing him, even with a male friend. And while this pleased Robert in a way he didn't care to analyze right then, it also perplexed him a bit. Jane attracted many male customers; almost to a man they responded to her. She was unfailingly cheerful and pleasant to anyone who showed decent manners, yet her consideration was impartial. She treated those who warranted it as gentlemen, and the remainder as they deserved. But with Tom, her manner changed.

The two men lay in their bunks and talked far into the night next door to Jane's quarters. As Jane listened to the indistinct murmur of their low voices through the wall, she made herself a promise. She had been too lax in her plans; it was time to think about her next move, and it must not fail.

"You got it all worked out," Tom told Robert as the two relaxed in their bunks. "Pretty little woman to do your bidding, nice, prosperous business. Sure wish I had somethin' like it goin' for me. All I got's uncertainty."

"You could do it too," Robert pointed out, "if you wanted to settle down and put your nose to the grindstone."

"Don't think I do. Too lazy. But maybe I would if I had me a prize like you got."

Robert propped his head up on the heel of

one except Tom believed they were living together as man and wife. But even without that, Robert had come to love her deeply. And he had been so insensitive to her feelings, so shy about his own, that he hadn't once asked her how she might feel about him.

He hadn't tried to kiss her, to make love to her, respecting the invisible boundary between them he believed she had set up. Without personal intimacy there was only a professional one. In a few well-chosen exchanges, Tom had said more to Jane than he'd said in all the time he'd known her. Damn his stupid soul! he raged, as he returned from the docks seeing Tom off. He'd better do something about Jane, and soon, before he lost her!

That afternoon Robert took a half hour from work to visit a local merchant. He returned with a bottle of good French Burgundy and a small red plush box.

After Jane's beef stew supper, he asked her to sit down and listen carefully to what he had to say. Fortified by the wine, which he rarely drank, he found the going easier.

"What I have to say may come as a surprise to you," he began stiffly.

Jane smiled. "Nothing you say would surprise me, Bob. I suppose you can read me the same way."

"I've only said this once before in my life, in Knoxville. I meant it then and I mean it now. Will you marry me?"

Jane sat down across the table from him and folded her arms.

"And what, may I ask, prompts this sudden proposal?"

"Tom's visit."

"Tom? I don't understand," she said, wide-eyed.

"I saw the way you responded to him. It made me realize—"

"I responded courteously," Jane said, "that was all. Tom doesn't mean anything to me, he couldn't ever."

"But you—"

"I was only being polite."

"But then—" he started to protest, and Jane interrupted him.

"Bob," she asked patiently, "why is it so difficult for you to say what you think? You've asked me to marry you. What else is there to say?"

"I love you," Robert blurted out. "I don't know if you love me, but I want you to be my wife."

Jane jumped up, came around the table and drew Robert to his feet. She put her arms around his neck, and kissed him on the lips.

"There," she said, "does this answer your question? Yes, I'll be your wife."

Robert shook his head. "But you've never given any indication of interest in me, only in the store and working together."

"You're slow to catch on, Bob. A woman can't spell it out like a man. And besides, there were your memories—I had to compete with them. You had to heal your heartbreak."

"You mean Sarah?"

"Who else? A period of mourning had to be observed."

"Since I first saw you by the river there's never been anyone else."

"I know that," Jane said. "Do you suppose I'd have done what I did if I thought you were chasing wenches like most other men?"

"Then you really do care?"

"Yes, my dear Bob, I do care! Ever since you saved my life and were so good to Jacob."

"Jacob?" For a moment Robert couldn't place the name.

"Of course. Jacob Parker. He was my husband, not my father. I should have told you a long time ago, but the thought never occurred to you so I let it go. I married Jacob when my fiancé died in Ohio two years ago. It was the only way I could leave my aunt who would have tied me to her forever. Jacob was too old for me, but I had no choice. I made him come West; it was a condition of our marriage. And you know what finally happened. Well, now that you know you may not want me to be your wife."

"Your marriage to Jacob couldn't change the way I feel, Jane. Your life before you met me is your own province."

"And so is yours, Bob. Still, I had to tell you." She laughed. "Oh, there are secrets in my life, small ones, but nothing you need to worry over. What matters is what we make of life together."

Robert began to understand many things: why Jane was so determined to join him as an undeclared partner in the store; why she had worked so hard but had left the initiative regarding their future up to him, which he had been so long in taking up; why she had been indifferent to all the men who came into the store, many just to see her; and why, at last, she'd found it expedient to bend to Tom in order to make him jealous and force his hand.

"I'm glad you told me about your marriage to Parker. Now we're both free."

He kissed her, savoring her substance. He held her close; she was trembling, as he was, and on the verge of tears. He sat her down in a chair, afraid to trust his passion, and said softly, "Look, my love, I have something for you, all I could find today. We'll go to San Francisco on our honeymoon and I'll buy you something more appropriate."

He produced the plush ring box and presented it to her. Inside was a plain golden circlet with a pronged setting that held a large garnet. He slipped the ring on her finger and kissed her again.

"It's beautiful," she said breathlessly, "and just right. *Now* we're married."

"But that's only your temporary engagement ring."

"Nonsense! We've already had our engagement, and for much too long. Tonight you'll share my bed!"

They slept together that night for the first time. In the morning they were married quietly, their employees as witnesses. Robert saw a lawyer in the afternoon and made a will that covered his estate in Jane's favor. The following day he ran a door from his quarters into Jane's, making all the rooms into one large apartment.

There was no honeymoon in San Francisco. The lumber yard was beginning to receive huge shipments of cut wood to be sent inland on order, and going away would have been highly impractical, they both agreed. While their young assistants were reliable, they were too inexperienced to handle the store and the yard together in the Sandersons' absence. So instead of a honeymoon, they decided to have a large sign erected over the store which read SANDERSONS' GENERAL STORE. Jane was quite definite about the position of the apostrophe.

"Plural possessive," she said when it was being nailed into position. "I know *that* much about the language."

Six weeks later Jane told Robert that she was pregnant, wonderful news for them both.

They spent endless hours planning for the child. There was never any question about their absolute agreement it would be the perfect child, sweet and bright. Of course it also had to be a boy to carry on the Sanderson line.

Jane was determined not to let her pregnancy interfere with the running of the business. "We'll just work around my condition," Jane told Robert. "It'll be a nuisance toward the last, but I'm not giving up the store until I have to. I love it as much as you do—but you know that!"

Probably much more than he did, thought Robert. Her energy was even greater than his own, and her enthusiasm for their future boundless.

Esther, Jane's assistant, knew of a young Indian girl who was clean, reliable, and very good with babies. They planned to bring her in at the baby's birth, so that Jane could get back to work soon afterwards. The child would be only a few steps in the back of the store if either Jane or Robert were needed, and Jane could pop in to see the infant when she took a luncheon pause.

A letter arrived from Tom some months after his visit. He told them that he had found a good woman in San Francisco—"Lots of them down here these days, more than men," he wrote—and he had married her. They had gone south to Santa Barbara, one of the largest towns in California. "We plan to raise oranges and other citrus fruits," Tom told them. "We wish you two would get married and join us. I bought me a boat and may become a commercial fisherman."

Jane had a difficult pregnancy. Nauseated a large part of the time, their doctor advised her to stay out of the store, get someone to do her daily housework, take as much rest as she could. When she blithely ignored the doctor's orders, Robert begged her to take better care of herself, but she refused to listen to him.

"I'm perfectly all right," she insisted, "I'm healthier than you are. I never get headaches, you do. It's ridiculous to coddle myself, I haven't the time for such a luxury. I'll go right on working," she vowed, and did, much to Robert's discomfort.

On a ladder in the store one day while shelving some items, Jane suffered an attack of vertigo and fell several feet against a counter piled high with bolts of yard goods. Fortunately her injuries weren't serious. A few bad bruises, a wrenched wrist and a skinned elbow resulted, and she went about the business of the day, glad that Robert was down on the docks supervising the unloading of a lumber shipment, and no customers were present, her assistant at lunch.

That night Jane began to have pains. Toward morning, in the doctor's presence, she miscarried and lost the child. It was a girl.

Both Jane and Robert were grief-stricken.

"It's my fault, my own stupid fault," Jane cried in Robert's arms. "How can I ever forgive myself?"

"We'll try again, darling."

"We have to," Jane said. "I'll be very careful next time. But I'm scared."

"No need to be if you take good care, like the doc said. You just did too much. Next time I forbid you to work. You're going to lie around the house eating bon-bons and coddling yourself. Your expression, I should add."

"I'll go mad," Jane threatened.

"That's enough," Robert replied sharply. "You're not to set a foot in the store. Is that agreed?"

"Yes, Bob," Jane said in a meek voice, "I promise."

Jane was pregnant again in two months. She grew quite submissive, relishing the fuss Robert made over her, adoring his many small attentions, his tenderness, and the way he cherished her in every look and gesture. Although she had always admired him, thought him handsome, serious and gentle, now she began to love him passionately. And under the warmth of her adoration, Robert entered into the happiest, sweetest time of his life.

The second pregnancy occurred in the spring of 1850, when business at Sandersons' was at its highest peak ever. Occasionally Jane fretted a bit about having to spend most of her waking hours in the rear apartment, but she knew better this time than to over-exert herself. She prepared only the easiest of meals; she alternated long afternoon naps with a new pastime, reading. Someone brought her Dickens' *Dombey and Son*. She read Trollope's first novel, *The Macdermots of Ballycloran*, and she took up knitting with a vengeance. She made several baby garments and a blanket, a muffler and some mittens for Robert. On Sundays he would take her out in a carriage for some fresh air and a change, but as always the roads were rough and filled with potholes, so these excursions had to be abandoned finally as too dangerous for Jane's condition.

In her seventh month, Jane had a series of brief attacks that the doctor diagnosed as heart complications. They were unusual in such a young and generally robust woman, the doctor told Robert privately, and cautioned him not to leave Jane alone at any time. So someone always had to be in the apartment with her. Fortunately, her health slowly began to stabilize itself under constant precautionary care.

Eighteen-fifty was the year that California was admitted to the Union as a state. Already Californians were establishing the foundation for an Americanized society, a far cry from the semi-feudal, easy-going life of the haciendas and vast land grants that had existed under Spanish and Mexican rule.

There were plenty of reasons why Jane and Robert looked forward with great hope to having a son this time. A boy child, if that's what the infant turned out to be, would have an open field to achieve almost any kind of career that appealed. Nothing, Robert felt, including the

governorship of California, would be too good
for a Sanderson male. If, on the other hand, the
child turned out to be another girl, then they
would raise her in a sheltered manner, turn her
into a lady, and see that she married well—for
love.

Jane's labor began in the middle of a stormy
night in late December 1850. Her travail was
agonizing, due to the position of the child, and
although the doctor was skillful and experienced, he could only do so much to ease and
shorten the painful birth. Finally the child came,
a nine-pound boy. Twenty minutes later, after
seeing the child and talking weakly with Robert, Jane was dead from a massive coronary
attack.

It was days before Robert could bear seeing
the infant, fed by an Indian wet nurse that the
doctor brought in. The child was nearly two
weeks old before Robert could begin to think
about a name for him. He and Jane had composed a long list of possible male and female
names. Jane settled on several boys' names for
favorites. One in particular caught her fancy:
Rebstock, which could be shortened to Reb.
Rebstock was a family surname of Jane's, unusual and easy to remember. While Jane was
alive, Robert might have argued for Lemuel,
his father's Christian name, but with Jane gone,
Rebstock would be a fine way of perpetuating
her memory. Robert settled on Reb, and went
about the melancholy business of living without
his precious Jane.

It was a long time before Robert could think
of the child as theirs, or his, a being in itself,

and much longer before he saw flashes of Jane in the boy's dark blue eyes, his infectious smile, his hearty laugh. It was even longer before he could accept the fact that the boy was not responsible for his mother's death. The most tragic thing was Reb would grow up without knowing her.

SAN FRANCISCO VENTURES

ROBERT HAD ALWAYS kept long and arduous working hours at the Sacramento store, but after Jane's death he plunged into a frenzy of buying and selling. He expanded his lumber yard, built an addition onto the store to house new products, and hired more personnel. What he lacked in devotion to young Reb, he more than compensated for in his slavish allegiance to the business.

As more sophisticated commercial methods of mining were introduced into the Mother Lode Country, Robert made Sandersons' General Store a key focal point of supplies, and he began to make more money than he had ever dreamed possible. There was only superficial satisfaction in this; it would have meant something only if Jane were alive to share his success with him.

As things stood, Robert felt isolated and

alone. He had never made close friends easily,
and now he didn't even try. He was very well-
liked, personable, neat and attractive, but he
sidestepped politely the whirligig of Sacramento's social life. He could have married at any
time; instead he didn't even seek the company
of free women for pleasure. He tended strictly
to business while regarding his tenure in the
river town as temporary. San Francisco had always been his dream goal, and where he intended to locate eventually. But he needed
more than a vague dream to move him in that
direction. He needed the motivation of a friend.

Reb grew into a healthy, happy infant, well-
attended by a girl assistant Robert hired after
the boy's weaning. Robert made some effort to
feel comfortable with the child but found it difficult, which reaction would drive him back to
work with renewed zeal, as if to prove his love
in the only way left open to him—his business,
which Reb would inherit.

In the autumn of 1853, as Reb was approaching his third birthday, Ethan Drew appeared at
the store, well-dressed, heavier, hardly the ebullient wagon master of former years.

Robert hadn't thought of Ethan Drew in a
long time. Overjoyed to see his old partner,
Robert took him back to the apartment to meet
little Reb, who stared in wonder at the huge
stranger who shook his hand, patted his head,
and told him he was a fine child.

"Where are you staying?" Robert asked
Ethan.

"I was thinking about a hotel."

"You'll stay with me. There's plenty of room."

Ethan accepted; the two men dined at Robert's, and over a bottle of whiskey later discussed their lives since they had last seen each other.

"I went to Oregon for a while," Ethan explained.

"You could have let me know."

"I thought it best not to, after what happened in Los Angeles. I didn't want to involve you, just in case."

So, thought Robert, Gianni Colli's accidental death was still on Ethan's mind. "What did you do then?"

"Went to San Francisco. Been there ever since. Never going to leave."

"What brought you to Sacramento?"

"You."

"Me? How's that?"

"I found out you were here in 1850."

"Why didn't you get in touch sooner?"

"Had to think about it for a spell," said Ethan. "You were married, you had a decent life, from what I heard."

"I've been a widower for the last three years. My wife died in childbirth."

"Yes, I just found that out. I'm sorry, Bob."

"You needn't be, I've learned to live with it," Robert said, and changed the subject. "How do you like the store and the yard?"

"I'm impressed," Ethan said. "You got a going concern, all right, and you're on your way to a comfortable fortune."

"It's damned hard work."

"You don't have to convince me."

"Part of all this belongs to you," Robert said. "You left Los Angeles before the business was sold and never collected your share."

Ethan shrugged. "I didn't come for that, Bob. It's not important. I'm doing fine these days."

"Good! I'm glad for your sake, not for mine. I was about to offer you a job."

"And I had something similar in mind for you, laddie," Ethan grinned.

"For me? All right, I'll listen. But only if you'll take your share of the Los Angeles sale. I've kept a separate account for you ever since. It's all down in black and white."

"Good old honest Bob," Ethan said, "I might have known you wouldn't change. You're the same reliable man."

"You've changed a lot," Robert declared.

Ethan had aged strikingly. His black hair was streaked with grey, and in place of his fiery enthusiasms of earlier years he had acquired a certain sophistication, which probably meant that he had at last learned to control his explosive temper, his most vulnerable point. Where Ethan used to be sloppy, unshaven, careless of his dress, he was now stylish and immaculate, even to wearing a brocaded vest with an opulent gold watch chain hanging across his stomach. His shoes were handmade and expensive, and on his fingers flashed two diamond rings.

"Well," said Ethan, "there's a good reason for the change. I'm getting older. Also, I'm married."

"Married? You?" Robert was surprised and pleased. "My congratulations."

"Accepted. I never thought it would happen. But then, she's a mighty unusual woman, Flora is. You'll meet her one day soon."

"I hope so," Robert said. "What do you think of Sacramento?"

"It's growing; that's about all I can say for it."
Ethan shook his head. "But by God, laddie,
you're wasting your life here. The activity's in
San Francisco, not Sacramento."

"I know, Ethan, I know. I'm in a terrible rut.
Ever since Jane died, I've buried myself in
work and more work. Little Reb's not getting
the best of my attention, not by a long shot.
One of these days I'll have to face the fact that
he has no family life, that he'll need a good
education, friends, a proper society in which to
grow up. All signs point to my going away, but
I haven't wanted to face the reality. In fact, I
haven't even voiced these ideas to anyone but
you."

"I'm glad you have, old boy. There's nothing
more here for you on the river."

"It's a tie for me. Memories. It's my home."

"Now, now. You just said you have no life
outside your work. All business and no pleasure.
That's not a life," Ethan pointed out, "that's a
prison sentence. We're going to change all that
for you."

"What have you got in mind?"

"Have you a potential buyer for your business?"

Robert stared at Ethan. "A buyer?"

"You must have. A store like this one is
worth a lot."

Offhand, Robert could think of two people
who would jump at the chance to buy the business, one a cattleman up from Texas, the other
a riverboat owner who was developing his fleet
of passenger and freight vessels to ply the river
between Sacramento and San Francisco.

"I think so," said Robert, "but what would I

do for work? I can't stay idle, you know how I am."

"You won't have to. Now, here's what you do. Line up your buyer, prime him, so to speak, and then come down and visit us for a few days, Flora and me. You'll see how easy it is to enjoy yourself and still make a lot of money. Times are in our favor. With Pierce in the White House the slavery question doesn't look too good, but one day that'll change."

Naturally, thought Robert, slavery was an issue Ethan with his mixed blood would follow closely.

"Then there's another indicator you can't afford to ignore," Ethan went on. "California's changing by the day. It's the age of speculation."

Robert had heard about the get-rich-quick schemes infecting almost every phase of state life, in mining, agriculture, transportation. These were already bringing wealth to some and disappointment to many others. The hustle was on in politics; it was a time for personality, lax morals, unrestrained profits. Grease a palm and all avenues were open.

Ethan said, "San Francisco's a melting pot, a hot center for men and money, and women too."

"I'm not interested there," Robert said, and Ethan didn't pursue the subject. "By the way, you haven't said what your business is."

"A hotel. Posh, high-priced, exclusive."

"I can't imagine you in the hotel business."

"It's a starting point," said Ethan. "We have some of the choicest people in California come to us. But I'm not the one who gives it class, Bob. That's Flora's department; she has the touch. Wait till you meet her. You'll see how lucky I am. When can you come down for a visit?"

"I could manage at the end of the month. I just hired a new bookkeeper who's totally responsible. He'll take charge for a few days, no worry there."

"Good," said Ethan, "let's drink on it. Now I won't let you off the hook. You're not going to throw away the best years of your young life here, not if I can help it."

While Ethan snored away the night in the bunk across from him, Robert's mind raced ahead to the possibilities of a new life. Even if he didn't find business interests in the Bay region immediately, he had to consider a grammar school for Reb. San Francisco was the logical place. What he'd been doing, cloistering himself, having no existence at all, wasn't what Jane would have wanted, he knew. She hadn't died, he told himself, so that he could negate Reb's life and his own. It was good that Ethan had come back into his days. This meant change, and none too soon.

Robert left Reb with his hired girl and went down to San Francisco for three days at the month's end. He'd barely glanced at San Francisco on his first visit. Now, its colorful atmosphere stimulated him the moment he stepped onto the waterfront dock and into another world. The weather was sparkling clear, the sea air brisk and tangy, fog-cooled, a welcome relief after the blazing heat that still hung like a pall over the scorched flatlands of Sacramento in late October.

The city, as San Francisco was already called by its citizens, had grown to almost forty-five thousand persons by 1853. Robert was impressed immediately on landing by the glutted wharves piled high with goods of every description. Robert knew that Eastern shippers had sent merchandise around the Horn indiscriminately since the gold fever started, but he was unprepared for the enormous physical bulk of these shipments, now rotting on the docks. It pained him to see such waste, although his discomfort was only momentary, and his attention soon occupied with other sights of a more colorful nature—the town rising haphazardly on steep hills, the motley crowds of people moving about, a heady mixture of races and costumes. Ethan, however, was not there to meet him.

A horse-drawn van for hire took him up a dirt street with board sidewalks to the Hotel Splendide, a gaudy white and maroon-trimmed gingerbread-fronted building of three stories. In a parlor of red plush sofas, handsome frosted lamps and red damask walls, Robert was greeted effusively by Ethan, who hadn't expected his boat in for another hour. Ethan took Robert's valise and led him into the rear portion of the hotel to a small private parlor. There at a Chippendale desk sat a young woman with hennaed hair and a soft ivory complexion.

As Flora Drew rose to greet Robert with a flashing smile and warm green eyes, Robert understood instantly why Ethan had married her: she was a marvelously subtle blend of black and white, an impressive woman. Not exactly beautiful, she combined the presence of a lady of quality with a gamine air of spicy innocence. Her small, well-defined features needed no artificial color to enhance them. Just a suggestion of mascara around her eyes, however, served to set off their emerald beauty. Robert was favorably impressed.

"I've been looking forward to this meeting for a long time," Flora told him with the faint trace of a southern accent.

"So have I," Robert assured her, and was immediately seated and served champagne from a bottle chilling in a silver bucket.

"Welcome to San Francisco," Flora said. "I think it's going to enjoy you and vice versa."

Both men raised their glasses to join Flora in her toast.

Half an hour later Robert was settled in a comfortable and airy chamber at the rear of the hotel, on its top floor. Between buildings he caught a view of the sapphire Bay and the filigreed mastheads of ships.

Ethan opened a window and said, "You'll love it. This is the quietest room in the house." Later Robert would understand why he was being tucked away in such a location.

In the afternoon Ethan took Robert on a tour of the town. They walked up its irregular streets to the highest point of the new construction. Surveying the vast Bay panorama, Robert listened to Ethan's rambling talk about "the California potential," as he called it.

"All of it starts right here, not up the river in Sacramento," Ethan explained. "Take the fruit industry, for example. One day there'll be orchards in this state that'll stretch from the north to the south. Soon there'll be vegetable-preserving factories, facilities for making jams and jellies."

"You're thinking on a very grand scale," Robert pointed out.

"Laddie, when you think at all in California, think *big*. That's been your only problem. You've scaled yourself down to small dimensions, instead of letting your commercial soul expand. I guarantee you," Ethan said, "before the decade's out we'll be shipping canned fruit all over the United States, for by that time we ought to have a railroad through from the East."

"Aren't you being a little premature?"

"Perhaps, perhaps. But the California potential is endless. It depends on men like us to realize it."

Robert had to agree as they walked back to the hotel that Ethan's excitement was contagious. He decided that he couldn't afford to bypass San Francisco's future.

It was Flora's responsibility, Robert decided later, to introduce him to the true *raison d'etre* of the Hotel Splendide and allow him to discover naturally how and why it functioned.

After an hour's nap, freshened with a bath and a change of clothes, Robert descended from his room to the hotel lounge to join Flora and Ethan.

It was dusk and people began to arrive at the Splendide. Ethan presided at the small lounge bar, while Flora greeted each new arrival as they entered.

First to arrive were several young women. They were all extremely attractive, even beautiful, although they wore startling costumes and their faces were carefully painted. They were each in turn introduced to Robert by Flora, and while their conversation was limited, they were courteous and subdued. After a few moments of superficial chit-chat they passed through the parlor to the central staircase and disappeared to the floors above, leaving a soft trail of perfume behind them.

Flora acted for all the world like a society lady introducing young matrons arriving for a charity bee, and Ethan did nothing to dispell this atmosphere so cleverly created.

A maid entered to prime the rosy-frosted lounge lamps. As if by signal, about ten minutes after the lamps were lighted, the men began to arrive. All were distinguished, either by Flora's warm reception of them, or by their exceptional bearing and rich attire. The men took drinks at the downstairs bar, making polite conversation with Flora and Ethan, or among one another, then they too disappeared upstairs to their assignations.

The scene confirmed what Robert had already suspected was going on. The Splendide was no ordinary hotel. Flora and Ethan were operating a whorehouse, albeit one with class. The "girls" were well-mannereed, attractive young women, their clients the essence of respectability: merchants, tycoons, lawyers and doctors, and various other wealthy entrepreneurs-about-town.

The prices at the Hotel Splendide fixed rooms at an hourly rate, not a daily or weekly one, and other services at whatever custom would allow. Short-ordered food was served in the rooms out of the downstairs kitchen, wine and liquor too; and nothing was cheap, of course. Flora had

convinced Ethan that she could run an un-
paralleled establishment in San Francisco that
would draw the very finest clientele in the city
—and this had happened. But the bonus or
fringe benefits were the real substance of the
business, Ethan explained to Robert.

"I get tips on merchandise coming in at
wholesale prices, or even free when the stuff
will just sit on the docks without any takers,"
Ethan explained. "I have an ear on most every
investment opportunity that crops up here.
You'd be surprised how often I'm able to turn
a fast dollar."

Robert was confused. "I thought you were
talking about a reliable business for me when
I said I might come down. I can't see myself
as a middleman or hotelier."

"Hell no, you can't!" Ethan clapped him on
the back. "Laddie, I know you don't want to
be in a gaudy business like this. And we wouldn't
want the competition if you did. I've something
else in mind, something big for us. It's an investment that'll pay immediate profits. But quite
legitimate, don't worry. I think you'll approve."

"What is it?" Robert asked eagerly.

Ethan grinned, looking mysterious. "Oh, we'll
talk about it tomorrow."

Late that night, Flora's maid served the three
of them a delicious cold supper in the Drews'
private dining alcove adjoining their rear parlor.

During supper Flora did her best to put Robert at ease. "I was worried about meeting you,"
she confessed as Ethan inundated them with
champagne. "I wanted to measure up to the role
of wife and hostess."

Robert smiled, heard himself say, "We do

what we have to do, Flora. How could I fault you on the best-run hotel I've ever seen in California?"

Flora laughed. "Your manners are impeccable. Ethan could use some of your tact."

Ethan guffawed, and Robert said, "Not tact, he has that. The obvious truth is you're the best thing that's ever happened to Ethan."

"Now that I've met you," Flora replied, "I think *you* are."

Ethan talked over supper about the rapid growth of commerce in California, and San Francisco as the center of the West's future development.

"What you saw today at the docks is only the muddled beginning. Everybody's crowding in on us, everybody wants a wedge of the riches. Some'll get hurt, some'll make it big. When we get larger carriers, cargo ships will be coming around the Horn by the scores. San Francisco will become one of the busiest ports of entry on earth. It's damned exciting to be a part of it all. Love for sale may seem like a very gaudy business to you, Bob, but it's a lever and makes it possible for us to lay aside enough to invest where it counts. Which is why you're here, too."

Ethan led the conversation on to agriculture. "Next to commerce, this is where the growth will come. California's a natural garden of Eden. There's no end to the potential. All those picks and shovels and millraces up in the Sierra foothills will soon be rusting in the fields, mark my word. The whole state will turn from gold mining to agriculture and manufacturing, which will make more sense to you tomorrow."

It was midnight when they finished eating

and talking. Robert said goodnight to his hosts
and climbed the stairs wearily to his room, wondering what sort of love idylls had gone on behind those gilt-trimmed hotel doors earlier in
the evening. Trying, actually, not to think about
it, for the thought inflamed him, set his groin
to tingling. His sexual self had lain dormant so
long. He was reminded of how fragile his re-
solve was to remain faithful to Jane's memory
when he measured it against what he had seen
today—beautiful, yielding women, artists skilled
at love; distinguished gentlemen from the high
life, masterful lords. Even if it was all happening in a whorehouse, this was San Francisco.
No, the Hotel Splendide hadn't shocked him, it
had titillated.

He was happy he'd come to San Francisco.
An awakening was what he needed. Maybe he
was moving forward to a point in his life where
he could actually enjoy himself again. Ethan
was right; he'd lived under a glass bell up in
Sacramento for much too long, his head buried
in the sands of business, blind to the world.

He undressed slowly, climbed into the fra-
grant bed, sank deep into the soft mattress and
settled himself against downy pillows, thinking
that whatever happened between him and
Ethan, it was about time. Apparently fate had
decided to team them up once again. He would
change, he *had* to change. It was grossly unfair
to Reb to circumscribe the boy's life as he had
done his own.

Robert was just drifting off to sleep when he
heard a gentle, persistent knocking at his door.
Thinking that it was Ethan with some special
titbit he might not feel free to reveal in Flora's

presence, he grabbed a large bathtowel, wrapped it around his hips and went to open the door.

A stunning black-haired beauty with grey eyes stood in the doorway. She was dressed in a white satin negligée trimmed in lace. Robert could see that she wore nothing beneath it. She smiled provocatively and leaned against the door frame.

"Mr. Sanderson?" she enquired in a breathy, intoxicating voice. "Robert Sanderson?" Her eyes danced.

"Yes," he said, adding unnecessarily, "what can I do for you?"

"Madam Flora thought you might be lonely, or troubled with insomnia. She sent me up to help if I can."

Robert experienced a rush of need so explicit that it made him slightly dizzy. Smiling, he reached forward, took the young woman's proffered hand and drew her into the room, then closed and locked the door.

"I'm Emily," she murmured, loosening the belt of her negligee, reaching down and ripping away Robert's towel, floating into his arms, flesh against flesh.

"Thank God," he breathed, tasting her mouth.

Emily stayed with him until dawn. When he awakened at mid-morning with the sun streaming in his window, there were only the faintest traces of her musky scent to remind him that she'd stayed the night.

At coffee with Ethan in the rear parlor later he said, "Thanks for the gift. I'd like to see Emily again."

"Perhaps," said Ethan.

"But she's—"

"Laddie," Ethan said, "we have other more vital subjects to occupy our minds this morning than the ladies. If there's one thing in over-abundance in this town, it's beautiful and available women. Emily's a rare prize, I grant you, and our gift to welcome you properly to San Francisco. But don't get anxious, she won't run away. You'll see her tonight, if you wish. Now, let's get on with the business at hand and the real purpose of your visit."

As the two men breakfasted on herb omelets and French rolls, Ethan recapped some history for Robert, explaining that the quickest route to the gold fields was by water carrier. "Either through San Pablo Bay, Carquinez Strait and Suisun Bay, thence up the San Joaquin River to the port of Stockton, or up the Sacramento River to your port."

The Bay's first steamer was a thirty-seven-foot sidewheeler, the *Sitka*, but the trip to inland ports took six days then. Soon necessity dictated that vessels specifically designed for river runs be imported and pressed immediately into service. By 1835, local craft such as William Richardson's two thirty-ton schooners with their Indian crews were operating around the Bay. These ships lightered produce from the missions and ranches of San Jose and San Francisco to large trading vessels anchored in the Bay.

In 1850 Captain Thomas Gray's propeller steamer, the *Kangaroo*, began its first scheduled twice-weekly run between San Francisco and San Antonio Landing across the Bay. In the next two years, Ethan declared, several other

similar vessels had joined the lucrative operation, with such a market for their services that
they were never idle, and could in fact have
operated nights as well as days because of the
great demand.

After Ethan's brief historical resume on water
transport in San Francisco Bay, he took Robert
down to the south docks of the city and into a
small shipyard bustling with activity. Two fifty-
ton steam schooners were in the final stages of
drydock finishing, prior to being launched, out-
fitted and tested for service.

"'Those beauties belong to Will Murphy, a
client at the Splendide," Ethan said. "A lot of
people want them, but they're ours, first choice."

"Aren't there competitive bids?" Robert asked.

Ethan shrugged. "Who's to say that Will can't
bend a little in our direction? If we wish, we
can turn out to be the high bidder. They'll out-
run anything now operating on the Bay. Think
of it. And they'll be ready for service in about
six weeks. Makes your flesh tingle, eh, laddie?"

"How much?"

Ethan mentioned a sum that seemed reasonable enough to Robert, his thinking geared to
what Sandersons' would bring when sold. "Murphy wants cash on the line, but he might take
a promissory note from us," Ethan added.

"How soon will he need money?"

"A substantial down payment will secure the
deal right now, which I can manage for us.
Balance is due on completion, guaranteed outfitting, trial runs, etcetera. Well, laddie, what
do you think? Are we to be shipping magnates?"

"It'll take everything my store can bring plus
most of my savings."

"Join the club. You won't be the only one who's betting his underdrawers. I'm laying the Spendide on the line. I'll be right there beside you, and just as bare-assed. Well, what do you say? Want to gamble on what I feel is a sure thing?"

"Let me mull it over."

"Can't be for long. I took a three-day option with Murphy to give us a free field. I get it back if we don't buy, but the three days are up tomorrow morning. So think fast."

"I will," Robert promised, and after a light lunch spent the afternoon closeted in his room, going over his assets. His bank in San Francisco would advance him several thousand dollars on the strength of his letter of credit. He could liquidate the store in a fairly brief time. His down payment, plus the cash that Ethan would produce, could secure the two vessels and leave them a narrow margin of cash to finance operation.

Suddenly a new life was opening up for Robert. His heart jumped at the prospect of coming to San Francisco and setting up in business with Ethan, of giving Reb a fair chance, meeting new people, important men, lovely women. The whole idea was wildly romantic as well as risky, but for the first time in his life Robert was enormously stimulated by the idea of risk. He had a deep responsibility to Reb, of course, committed to the boy for Jane's sake, as well as his own. He and Reb would adapt; they might even become good friends, allies. What a staggering idea to realize that, if he and Ethan played their cards right, they'd both soon be millionaires. Anything was possible now in California.

The available riches from business were a lot easier to come by than gold. Robert felt Lazarus-like, about to rise from the shroud of his self-willed isolation.

He came bounding downstairs to join Ethan and Flora in the back parlor.

"It's all right, we can do it," he told Ethan, who embraced him, while Flora kissed him on the cheek. "You can count me in."

"You're in, laddie," Ethan said, "and you'll never regret it."

That night Emily King came to Robert's room again.

It turned out that Emily wasn't, as Robert had supposed, one of Flora's "girls" at all. She had traveled northwest from Texas with a gambler who was killed in a row over a poker game. She had known Flora in Flora's earlier New Orleans days, when both were supported by wealthy men.

"I was in the back parlor when you arrived," she told Robert. "That's how I first saw you, through the bar mirror. If I hadn't liked what I saw, you wouldn't have had a midnight visitor. When are you leaving for Sacramento?"

"As soon as I can."

"How sad."

"I'll be back soon, to stay. You like me and I like you. Where does that put us?"

Emily was just as blunt. "I have a patron who supports me, an older man, with a family in the East. He's away now, but he'll return in a week or two. I don't love him, Robert, but I don't want to lose him, either."

Robert intended to concentrate on work and

Reb. Marriage or anything permanent with Emily was obviously not practical. At least not for the time being.

"I guess that leaves us where we are," he said.

"I think we'd better let things take care of themselves," said Emily. "We'll meet again . . ."

She departed before dawn, so that she could move unseen through the silent streets by carriage to her apartment.

Robert took the first steamer he could get to Sacramento. Within a week he had settled the sale of the store and the lumber yard. By the end of the month he moved to San Francisco with Reb and their household effects, and was ready to go into business with Ethan, who had found him a small rented house, while Flora found him a reliable girl to look after Reb.

Shipbuilder Will Murphy met his promised deadline for the operation of the schooners. Designed essentially for cargo, Murphy had built a roomy cabin for deck passengers. It was the partners' plan to schedule regular daily runs around the Bay, with each vessel covering half the area, both returning to their home port evenings, a dock south of the shipyard.

With their runs well-advertised by poster and newspaper, the schooners christened the *San Jose* and the *Benecia* were soon being offered a good deal more business than they could possibly handle. When Ethan wanted to raise the shipping rates, Robert agreed but talked him out of raising passenger fares as well, arguing that a bargain was the best possible advertisement. Thus their El Dorado Steamship Company, as they named it, became the lowest-priced travel commodity in the Bay region.

By 1855 San Francisco was the state's largest city and its chief port and commercial center. The city was comprised of some good, substantial homes and business buildings, but the balance was a motley jungle of tents and jerry-built structures, with defined areas for the city hall, for vice dens and ethnic neighborhoods, a large one for Latin Americans, another called Sydney Town that harbored a raw assortment of Australian gangsters lured to the gold fields and now living off the spoils taken from petty theft or worse.

The city was under continuous construction, an expanding commercial prosperity, wild speculation, factional politics, and rampant crime. Flora's modest business was probably the town's most genteel of its kind, due to Ethan's vigilant eye, but just beyond the Splendide's walls, violence and greed were everywhere. Fortunes were made and lost daily.

With Ethan as operating manager of El Dorado Steamship, it soon grew into a wildly profitable enterprise, so much so that the partners decided to expand. They commissioned Will Murphy to design and build them a ferry boat with limited cargo space and extensive passenger facilities, and El Dorado's passenger volume soared when the *Yerba Buena* went into service. San Francisco at that time was teeming with a young, highly mobile population—scarcely a grey head was visible on the streets—so that there was no shortage of passengers wanting to traverse the Bay regularly by the fastest means possible.

* * *

Between 1849 and 1854, a shocking history of violence plagued California. There were 4,200 murders during that time. Ethan and Robert were deeply concerned as conservative businessmen about what was going on in San Francisco among the criminal element—especially Ethan, whose own earlier record of violence still disturbed him, Robert knew.

Gold fever had attracted a horde of enterprising men and women to California. Like Ethan and Robert, many of the men were law-abiding citizens who wanted nothing more than to settle down peaceably and follow the American work ethic to fame and fortune, once the gold rush died away. But criminals and parasites were equally attracted to the advantages of the state. These undisciplined creatures lived by antisocial codes of conduct far beyond the law. Notable among such elements were toughs from New York, Southern firebrands, and Sydney Ducks. As the pressure against these criminals grew in San Francisco, they organized themselves into gangs, stronger and more vicious than ever. Very few souls ventured out at night, none but the hardiest, and those only with firearms. Embittered at failing to make their fortunes in gold, the gangs took out their rancor on the innocent. Knives and guns were their common weapons.

One night on the way home from his shift as dockman for the El Dorado Steamship Company, Gus Stern was brutally murdered in an alley by several toughs. Next morning Ethan came storming into the downtown office Robert had set up in his house to handle El Dorado's shipping, mayhem in his eyes.

"Damn those nasty sons of bitches," Ethan raged, "the whole bleeding lot aren't worth one of old Gus's short hairs!"

As angry as Ethan over the loss of the *Benecia*'s dockman, a good man, Robert readily agreed with Ethan.

"What's to be done about it?"

"We take the law into our own hands, that's what," said Ethan. "I stopped in to talk to Bill Coleman on the way over." Coleman was a prominent merchant who ran a store similar to Robert's Sacramento venture. "The law's got the toughs who did it, but you know how slow they are. Bill says we ought to revive the Vigilante Committee and deal with the scum in our own way. And I agree. What do you say?"

"It's illegal," Robert protested. "You can't right one wrong with another."

"Oh for christssake, what makes you so righteous?" Ethan demanded. "Gus is dead—who cares what's legal? I'm out for guilty blood. I know what you're thinking: Los Angeles. That I'll act without thinking. This is different."

"You needn't have said that, Ethan," Robert said mildly. "I'm in complete agreement about justice for Gus. But I don't like the idea of vigilantes. They get out of hand."

"Are you with us or against us?" Ethan asked.

Robert sighed. "With you, of course."

The powerful desire for vengeance in Gus Stern's death spread like gold fever among the city's solid citizenry. Pros and cons were hotly debated. Some men wanted due process of law, others a quick solution to their fury. A considerable group began to line up with the vigilante idea, and it wasn't long until a twenty-five-hundred-member committee was recruited, Ethan and Robert among them. By majority agreement, the Committee decided to form a military organization with fortified headquarters called Fort Gunnysacks.

That same night the most militant of the Vigilantes broke into the city jail. They seized the two toughs who were responsible for several other recent murders besides Gus Stern's and summarily hanged them in an eerie torch-light ritual from a building in Sacramento street. The blood-thirsty crowd, rowdy and mean, jeered as the men died, raising fists and bottles to the night sky. The public lynching was a savage, undisciplined act, reviled in the morning press as just another form of unlicensed murder, since it did not have the sanction of the state.

Opinions on the executions ran for and against. Many women from all classes openly condemned the kangaroo court trial and executions, Emily and Flora among them. That night after the hangings, Flora locked Ethan out of their bedroom, deaf to his pleas about citizens' justice. Emily refused to meet Robert for their regular rendezvous. "I'm ashamed that you, of all people, would involve yourself in that disgraceful scene," Emily told Robert later.

The city was sharply divided on the behavior of the Committee, but this wasn't the end of the Vigilante action. The Committee leaders intercepted a San Francisco-bound ship in the Bay carrying U.S. arms destined for the state militia and confiscated its weapons shipment, a Federal offense. Continuing to make their own laws, the Committee then jailed one David Terry who had stabbed a Vigilante policeman in a fracas over the arms piracy.

Pitched skirmishes broke out all over the city. In a series of engagements, the Committee resisted pressure by the mayor, the sheriff, and a force of militia under William Sherman.

By the time the Committee was officially disbanded three months after it was formed, in July, it had been responsible for the hanging of three men, and a fourth hung himself in his cell before the Vigilantes could reach him. It was also active in rounding up and deporting thirty hardened criminals. These actions put the fear of God into even the pettiest of criminals, who began to reduce their visibility around the city, day and night.

After the first two hangings, Robert withdrew from the Committee's operations. Ethan did not; he was active to the end, defending his participation by declaring, "Somebody has to do the dirty work and get rid of the scum."

Robert and Ethan argued frequently about the Committee and its takeover of legal process.

"It was permissible before 1850," Robert allowed, "because there wasn't proper legal machinery. Now we have courts of law, and some order. We should use them; it's the only way to strengthen them, not make our own rules."

"Waiting for the courts to handle matters wasn't stopping the terrible crime wave," Ethan declared, and he had a point. "Anyway, we're not gangsters. There are lots of decent men in the Vigilantes."

"Granted, but that doesn't make it legal," said Robert. "And besides the good men, there's a bunch of raving dissolute drunks and drifters among them who scream for blood—anybody's."

"You were hot enough to join up at the start," Ethan reminded him.

"I was thinking of poor old Gus and his wife and kids."

"What do you think I was doing?"

"It's no way to go and I'm glad it's over," said Robert. "I hope it doesn't break out again soon."

"If it ever does, I'll join up again," Ethan vowed, and Robert let the matter rest there. He refrained from pointing out that while the Vigilantes had made it safe to walk the streets for a while, they hadn't set a shining example, nor won accelerated punishment and reformed the courts.

After the Vigilante rumpus died down, the city returned to its normal preoccupation of getting rich quick. Robert felt slightly depressed that Ethan's volatile nature had never really been tamed, but at least his partner deliberated now before he meted out justice. One of the few things they'd agreed upon since the Vigilante explosion was a cash settlement awarded by El Dorado Steamship to Gus Stern's widow and family. The sum enabled them to travel East to the shelter of a sister's arms, and remain there.

The bickering about the Vigilantes did not disrupt Robert's friendship with Ethan. However both men skirted inflammatory subjects after that, and increasingly began to go their separate ways. Fortunately for both, their major business continued to prosper, each making more money than they knew what to do with.

As the city grew up around Robert's rented

house, he decided to build a more suitable one for himself and Reb. The boy was now of school age and needed a private room.

Robert bought land on the Bay slope of Sacramento street, drew up a rough design and submitted it to a young shipyard carpenter, Gulley Walsh, a skilled craftsman anxious to become a building contractor.

In Robert's design he included an office suite, so that he could conduct new enterprises on his own, independent of El Dorado obligations. Robert was pleased with the completed Walsh-built structure. Even before he moved in he was deluged with offers to buy the building for cash. This suggested to him that he should capitalize with Walsh on future enterprises, then act as agent for the new buildings, bringing profit to both of them.

Ethan was decidedly annoyed when he learned of Robert's association with Gulley Walsh.

"What has he got to offer you? You're my business partner, not that pipsqueak's."

"He's very young and very ambitious, and he's starting to get a group of men together so that he can form a company," Robert explained.

"You going in with him, besides just financing houses and selling them?"

"I don't think so. By the way, why don't you draw up some plans for a house? Flora's been talking about one for sometime now. You don't have to continue living at the hotel."

"That's an idea," Ethan said, suddenly mollified. "I'll build it and surprise her."

"Good. Talk to Gulley. He's a bright boy."

Ethan did just that. Before long he was bragging to Robert that Gulley was the smartest lad he'd met in the trades, somebody to watch.

"A real winner," Ethan said, and when Flora was taken to her new house on Sutter street, her joy sent Ethan into ecstasies, with high praise for Gulley. It wasn't too long before Ethan was treating young Walsh with the same avuncular warmth that he'd bestowed upon Robert.

A year after Robert and Gulley were associated as builders, El Dorado Steamship Company needed offices of its own, their shed at the docks having burned in a fire. Gulley erected an extensive building and warehouse sheds alongside a new pier to house El Dorado's operations. There was even enough floor space left over to house several small associated firms serving El Dorado's ancillary needs.

Construction became the rage in San Francisco after the first frenetic years that gold prospecting peaked, then settled into the development of large commercial mining interests. New lumber mills kept opening to supply the city with new structures which it badly needed, since most of the city managed, like the El Dorado offices, to burn down two or three times a year.

There were new stagecoach and wagon factories, a flour mill, breweries. Boot and shoe factories sprang up, and plants for the grading and manufacture of wool. Metal was scarce, so machine shops were built. Iron moulders were kept busy from the early 1850s on, hammering iron wagonwheel rims and harness chains into building tools.

Both Ethan and Robert dabbled independently in small business ventures; it was the only way to put their cash to work. Whatever they turned a hand to was eminently successful; they seemed unable to fail. Inflation gave them less than ever for their money, but since they were never without resources, they didn't worry about spending money as it rolled in.

Being constantly occupied, Robert rarely felt the isolated position of his life on the San Francisco peninsula. San Franciscans, however, were often embroiled in state politics. The national issue of slavery was vigorously argued by transplanted Southerners who wanted to have slaves brought in to work their fields, and by the antislavery forces that fought against the bondage involved.

In the Bay area there were many small towns springing up that appeared to be more or less permanent. With his constant involvement in building projects, Robert did give some thought to land outside of the city, but beyond owning so many acres at such-and-such a place, he gave the idea little consideration. Land was something you simply bought and wrote off, he felt. Maybe later on something could be done with it.

His attitude changed, naturally, in the course of time, and meanwhile, Ethan had grandiose dreams of a rich, vast business empire dominating all of northern California, perhaps even stretching south to Baja California.

"Wait until the railroad comes through, laddie," he was fond of telling Robert over a glass of whiskey. "Then see our smoke. We'll be millionaires overnight for sure then."

A fire that burnt half of the new El Dorado offices down made Robert reevaluate his investments, thinking that he mustn't spread himself too thin in city businesses that could be swept away in minutes by fire and earthquake.

Once again he began to think of land in the undeveloped peninsula countryside a few miles south of the city. Owning land, he recalled, was his brother John's great dream, and Robert wrote to John urging him to leave the Mormon cause in Utah and come to the West Coast to join him.

"I'll set you up in a home, dear brother, and see that you get started in some enterprise. There's no lack of work here for the industrious, sober man, which you are. I know we'll work well together, and it will be the joy of my life to have you out here with me. Who knows, we might even persuade Mother to join us . . ."

While Robert was hardly a prolific correspondent, he wrote to John as often as his brother wrote to him, which was twice a year. John's letters were filled with homilies about God and slight details about the exotic religion that had lured him away from Virginia. In John's letters Robert could read undertones of dissatisfaction that seemed to deepen each year. Still, John refused to make a break with his Utah sect, to accept Robert's generous invitation to come and live in San Francisco, bringing his young wife, Mary Dale, with him. In a community where fertility was next to Godliness, John and Mary had produced no children, so John's warm letter to Robert in the summer of 1855 conveyed joyful news. Mary was finally pregnant; they expected a child in the spring.

"If it's a boy, we shall name it after you, dear brother," John wrote, and Robert sent back an immediate message begging John to leave Utah and come West as soon as the baby was old enough to travel.

John's letter announcing the future arrival of the child was his last to Robert. While out in the wilderness with a group of church members surveying land near Great Salt Lake, John was bitten by a rattlesnake and died later from gangrene. Caroline Sanderson, the boys' mother, received the news earlier than Robert. Both were stricken by the shock of John's death. Caroline, grieving, died a few months later, inconsolable over the wasted life of her youngest son.

Mary Dale, John's wife, left Utah immediately after John was buried, traveling pregnant from Utah to her home in Indiana. She wrote to Robert to give him a forwarding address, but in a fire that burned out Robert's office, the address was lost. Robert had no way of getting in touch with Mary Dale, and the young widow did not contact him again.

The loss of John turned Robert toward Reb. He knew he must bring a deeper friendship to bear on their relationship. The boy was bright and eager to please; it was up to him to capture Reb's total confidence, something he hadn't done yet.

From his sixth to eighth year, young Reb was privately tutored by a clerk from El Dorado Steamship. Despite all of the rough-and-tumble atmosphere of San Francisco in the mid-1800s, the argonauts, or gold pioneers, were almost as interested in education and the arts as they were in license and quick money. The earliest saloons sported handsome oil paintings on their walls; some of them even featured decorous musicales for the patrons.

Schoolmaster Tom Douglas opened the first California public school in San Francisco in 1848. In 1851 an ordinance was passed to establish the free common school system. A man named John Pelton came around the Horn with his wife about that time, with only a dollar-fifty in his pockets, but accompanied by books, globes, maps and a school bell. As soon as Mrs. Pelton could open a boarding house, Pelton started a free school in the basement of San Francisco's Baptist church. Reb attended this school for a time.

In 1860 Abe Lincoln won the presidency over Stephen Douglas by a narrow margin, and Reb Sanderson turned ten. It was nearly seven years since Robert began his affair with Emily King. For the first two years of that period, Emily was still attached to her affluent patron. But when business and family matters took him East permanently, a commitment of sorts was defined between Emily and Robert.

"I don't want marriage," Emily said, clearing the air immediately for Robert, who had foreseen a lengthy, involved exchange of pros and cons.

"I'm not prepared for it, either," he said, thinking of Reb. "But I want you to be comfortable. I'm arranging my situation so that you'll be provided for in case something happens to me. I'm young, strong, in good health, but one never knows."

While Emily was pleased with Robert's thoughtfulness, she was neither greedy nor lazy.

"Commendable gesture, darling," she told him. "I'm flattered you care that much about my welfare. But I can't think that far into the future, I don't even want to. Why not deal with the practical moment and help me set up in business?"

"Business?" This was the first Robert had heard about any enterprise, wondering if she meant something like Hotel Splendide. He frowned. "What kind of business?"

Emily laughed, reading his expression. "Not that kind, silly. You know how much I adore clothes?"

"Yes, a little more and it would be an obsession." She not only liked them, he thought, she had fine taste and criticized mercilessly the dowdy fashions that women brought with them to California from various parts of the world, or the ones that were created here. "It's a good thing you're so clever with your needle or we'd both be penniless," Robert teased. "Especially me."

"Yes, well, I'd like to apply those 'expensive' ideas of mine to making money. I know I can do it."

"You want to become a modiste?"

"I already am, I think. And a little bit more. I want to open the finest, most exclusive dress and hat shop in California," Emily declared, "and I can do it."

"Hats too, eh?" he said. "I guess they go together."

THE GOLDEN STATERS

"OF COURSE. I see no reason why women should go to someone else to buy their hats for my dresses. I think that combining the two businesses is a sound business idea."

"Smart girl. So do I," Robert approved. "Where will you get your materials?"

"First I'll need a building with overhead living quarters, so I can be close to the shop. Meanwhile I'll scout around for the most reliable supply sources. Eventually this will mean importing silks and cottons from China, the more expensive fabrics from Europe, and fashions from Paris, London, and New York. And I'll design for California, not copy world fashions—most of them aren't even practical for us here. Ultimately I'll do something nobody else can do—create originals."

In the several years that Robert had known Emily, he was always discovering hidden depths. At one time he was amazed at her comprehensive knowledge of history. While having no more than the barest of educations, she had an avid thirst for knowledge that was seemingly unquenchable. She could do a good many things that men could, including swing a hammer, wallpaper a room, race a horse, drive a mule team, shoot a gun and pitch horseshoes, the last one of her passions. She was a fantastic cook, interested in European haute cuisine, but just as capable of turning out a Hangtown Fry as any chef. Emily had a fine head for mathematics; she could read a balance sheet and set up business ledgers. She loved books and devoured everything she could find. In fact, she had even borrowed some schoolbooks from young Reb. "To refresh my cavernous ignorance," she quipped to Robert. But even Robert was unprepared for Emily's desire to go into commerce for herself.

"Well," he said, "if anyone can make a success of that kind of business, you can."

"And I shall," Emily vowed. "Now, about the building." She brought out some surprisingly clear, graphic renderings she had made of floor plans for her building, and a sketch of its glass-windowed façade. Robert studied these for a minute.

"You're not going to be able to get simulated brick façade sheet out here," he told her.

Emily smiled. "Who said anything about 'simulated'? The outer shell will be brick, with iron rod reinforcements."

"Hold on, that's expensive and impractical. We'll have to bring in the bricks from San Jose."

"That's easy. You know Ethan's been talking about the two of you setting up a brickyard of your own just south of Mt. San Bruno. Do it, and I'll be your first customer. I'm not going to have a business of mine going up in flames just because it's wooden. The second floor may have to be made from timber, but the ground floor will be brick, and covered with carpeting."

Robert wanted to argue with her that she was too visionary, that she'd have to settle for the same type of structure everybody else did, but from the look in Emily's eyes he knew she'd abandon the project entirely, and freeze him out for a while—she'd done it before—unless he did her bidding.

"All right,`my dear," he capitulated, "brick it'll be." And brick it was.

When Reb heard about Emily's business venture he said to his father, wrinkling his nose, "Women's clothes. Nobody'll buy them, father."

"Don't tell Emily that."

Reb and Emily had always been friendly, Reb accepting her as a friend, later as his father's mistress. Reb was as fascinated with learning as Emily was, and it was a common meeting ground for them through the years, each learning from the other. In some ways, Robert often thought, Emily made up for Jane's absence, often feeling that under the circumstances Emily was the best thing that could have happened to him.

Ambitious schoolmasters like John Pelton took special pride in cramming masses of unusable data into the heads of their pupils. Pelton bore down especially hard on boys like Reb, whose memory was photographic—very much like his grandfather's, Robert noted.

Reb came home from school one day at nine, dazed and frustrated. Robert's door was open and Reb leaned against the doorframe. A handsome boy, Robert observed critically, really as good-looking a youngster as any in San Francisco. He had Jane's beautiful complexion; his soft, mellow voice would one day be baritone; he had a physique that would develop to solid, even heroic, proportions.

"Father," Reb said, "do you have an atlas?"

"I did a few years ago, but it was burned. Why?"

"Well, Mr. Pelton gave us an assignment for tomorrow—to name all the rivers on earth, all the bays, gulfs, oceans and lakes."

"Good heavens, that's a lifetime memory feat. He's loading it onto you."

"That's what I thought. But I don't know how to get out of it."

"I think Emily has an atlas, an old one."

"I'll go see her."

"Wait till the shop closes. You know how busy she is."

"All right. We're also to name all the major cities of the world, Mr. Pelton says. Does San Francisco qualify along with Paris, London and Rome?"

Robert smiled at Reb's question. "It certainly does for us, son. It's the center of the earth. By the way, what if you don't go to school tomorrow?"

Reb's eyes sparkled. "I could be sick, but I'd need a note from you."

"Good, you'll get it. Come in and sit down. I've a question for you."

Reb pulled up a chair, sat down astride it with his arms across its back, chin on his wrists.

"I hope the question's an easy one," he said.

"In a way," Robert said. "I've been mulling this over for quite a while now, ever since I discovered that you're too bright for your britches."

"I wish so," Reb said modestly, pleased.

"Your grandfather was a brilliant man, Reb. My father, that is—I never knew your mother's father. Lem Sanderson should have been a politician, but I've always thought he was too sage for that. At any rate, it looks as if you've inherited your grandfather's intellect."

"I'd like to have your sense of business, father."

"Maybe you've both, we'll have to see. Anyhow, at the pace you're developing you'll soon be ready for more education than we can find for you in California right now. So, where will you get it? I'm not satisfied that the answers are here. Nothing's quite the proper thing. Do you have any ideas?"

It was Robert's policy to be extremely open with the boy. Unlike some of the fathers he knew, who used a fearful respect to keep their children in line, Robert had not found it necessary to discipline Reb since he was quite small. He employed candor, gentleness and honesty in their association, and so far it had worked perfectly.

Reb said, "I have one idea. I'd like to go into business with you, father."

"I thought perhaps you'd like to go East to school next year. New England, or Washington, D. C. You could stay with my Aunt Cissie. She still lives in that big old house; it must have a dozen rooms. You'd have privacy."

"Stay with an old lady?" Reb pursed his lips. "I wouldn't know what to say to her, father."

"Oh, I imagine you'd find things. She's been a teacher all her life, you know. And eventually you could attend Georgetown University."

Reb jumped up from the chair and shook his head vigorously.

"No," he exclaimed firmly, "I don't want to go away. I'm a Californian, father, I was born here and it's my home. I'm a native son and proud of it!"

Robert was unprepared for the boy's vehemence but admired his honesty. He hadn't really wanted Reb to leave anyway, even though it did seem the best thing for him. Already young women turned to look at him in the streets, and he would unabashedly return their glances with a broad smile. It wouldn't be long before he'd seek out easy girls, and at the rate he was growing he'd be a man by fourteen. What troubled Robert most about California was the continuing violence that even Vigilantism hadn't entirely controlled.

"Well, son," Robert said, "we'll talk about this another time. If you want to go into business you've got to make judicious choices. I've not always done that, but then I've been extraordinarily lucky. You like surprises, so tomorrow I shall give you an object lesson, necessary if you intend to be partners with me."

"I intend to, father," Reb said with fervor, and meant it.

That afternoon Robert's male clerk Albert told him that a woman who would not divulge her name was waiting in the outer office to see him. "She says she's a friend of Mr. Drew's, sir," Albert explained.

"Did she state her business?" Robert rarely received a female visitor except Emily during business hours. Emily would occasionally drop over from her nearby dress salon simply to get away from the crush of business.

"No, sir," Albert advised, "she wouldn't say."

"Very well, show her in, please."

The black-clad woman who entered the office with somber dispatch was tall, her figure superbly slim with its narrow waist. She had a dusky, patrician beauty. Her coat and hat were of fine material, elegantly cut. Her features were delicately chiseled, the mouth wide, well-defined. Under the broad brow, her eyes were exotically unmatched, one blue, the other brown, but of blending intensity.

Robert had rarely seen such commanding presence in a woman. He was certain that she could have demanded the moon from the heavens and received it. Regal and reserved, she concentrated on Robert to the point where his flesh began to crawl, either from anxiety or lust, he couldn't decide. He rose to offer her a chair, knowing that she could be only one person, the legendary, the formidable and seldom visible Mary Ellen Pleasant, known more familiarly to some San Franciscans as Mammy Pleasant, the mulatto companion of trickster-entrepreneur Thomas Bell of the New Almaden Mine.

Robert had also heard from Ethan about the house of pleasure that Mammy Pleasant operated. "It's not for you," Ethan had warned him. The ritual for admission to the parlor was bizarre. Mammy Pleasant would sit concealed behind the curtains of a bay window with a view of the front steps of her establishment. When a customer would ring, a half-door would open onto the street and a pale blond Negro butler would appear. The customer would place a ten dollar gold piece on a silver card tray and the butler would then shut the door in the man's face. If the applicant were acceptable to Mammy, then he was allowed to place another ten dollar gold piece on the card tray and enter the house.

Sometimes the door didn't open a second time. To be rejected thus by Mammy when applying at a whorehouse must be the final ignominy, Robert decided, rising to greet his visitor, intensely curious about her mission.

"Mr. Sanderson"—the Pleasant voice was rich and soft, yet as penetrating as a carillon—"I will not bandy words. I am here on an errand of mercy."

"Please sit down, ma'am," he replied, wondering what the truly proper mode of address was for such a figure, variously rumored a voodoo queen, the owner of several laundries, an ex-slave, now keeper of a brothel that was the most influential in San Francisco, if not as cozy as Flora's Spendide.

"You may call me Mary Ellen if you wish, and

I shall call you *Mister* Sanderson, since I've come to you," Mammy Pleasant said, seating herself and placing her telescope bag on her knees. "As I said, my errand is merciful. You are a compassionate man, so I am told from reliable sources. You've befriended Flora and Ethan Drew, you've helped others establish themselves in business, namely, Emily King. You are growing rich in San Francisco without robbing people, in this capital of the free world for people of color."

Robert was about to speak, but Mammy Pleasant shook her head almost imperceptibly. "There's no need for you to act modestly, Mr. Sanderson. We all know your affinity. I know, for instance, that you come from Southern parents who refused to own slaves."

"That's true, ma'am."

"And that you came to California with Kearny's troops and went into business with Ethan Drew in Los Angeles, when others might have hesitated, Ethan being the definite person he is. Also that you went to the gold fields where you met your deceased wife, settled in Sacramento, and that your son is the apple of your eye."

"These are all facts," Robert acknowledged, wondering where she was going.

Mammy Pleasant gave him an approving smile, showing perfect teeth. He speculated as to what her age might be. Thirty? Forty perhaps? Impossible to tell.

"From facts we shall go to figures," Mammy Pleasant continued. "As you know, there is a man aligned with our cause called John Brown, whom we have already helped."

Could it be, Robert reflected, that Mammy Pleasant had been involved financially in the raid at Harper's Ferry, Virginia, which had brought down government wrath on John Brown's head, put him on trial where he was sentenced to death by hanging?

"I've heard of John Brown," Robert said.

"But you haven't heard his latest words," Mammy Pleasant told him, "which have just come to us. He has said that he's too young to understand that God is no respecter of persons. Brown interfered as he did, as he's always admitted, on behalf of his despised and oppressed Negro friends. He has never admitted to being wrong. He has always espoused his belief in the right. Now they will murder him. But dead or alive, he needs our support, our prayers and our money for the cause. I am asking you, Mr. Sanderson, to make a contribution to the plight of the Negro slave in America. By giving, you will help to swing the ax at the root of the tree. And one day soon, I promise you, that tree will be felled."

Robert experienced a prickly sensation at the back of his neck. He was indeed highly sympathetic to the miserable plight of slaves. There were ex-slaves working for the El Dorado Steamship Company as deckhands—or maybe they weren't freemen at all, but escaped slaves. Ethan would know, and anyway, Robert didn't care; he was glad that they were able to shed the terrible yoke of slavery and could maintain their dignity in a free place. He would not knowingly do business with any man who held that slavery was justifiable, and he would try to pass this credo on to Reb. He was glad to make a contribution; Mammy Pleasant was just the charismatic sort of force needed in the fight against slavery. Whatever she may have done in the past—some said she had poisoned her husband many years ago—she was now pleading a righteous cause.

"Do I detect a certain reluctance in your manner, Mr. Sanderson?" his visitor asked.

"I am listening," said Robert.

"That is good. I see no weakness of principle in your thinking," Mammy Pleasant went on, as if divining this from a secret fount of knowledge. "Yours is a debate over what you should contribute. Let me put your mind at ease. One hundred dollars will bring a slave through the line to freedom in the north. A thousand dollars will bring ten human beings to liberty and salvation."

Whether this was true or not, Robert knew that he would probably end up giving the larger amount.

"I won't charm you with the sweet promise of even greater success in your business enterprises, sir, but the omens are impressive."

"What else do you see, then?"

"You will not marry again until memory can be replaced in kind. You have savored the best. At present you don't believe there is anything better."

He wanted to ask about Reb but felt unable to do so. He said, "Is there anything more?"

"In later years there is a dark period," Mammy Pleasant declared. "You will lose something very precious, but it will be replaced with an equal treasure. You will leave this life fulfilled, seeing continuity ahead. Having cast your bread generously upon the waters of life, it will come back to you manifold."

Abruptly Mammy Pleasant stood up, clutching her telescope bag in both hands. Robert imagined that the shiny bag might be filled right now with ten dollar gold pieces from the way in which she clamped it under her right arm.

"I will make a donation, ma'am," Robert said, also rising. "I'll need a little time to organize it."

"Take all the time you need." She drew a calling card from the waist pocket of her black linen coat. "Your assistant may deliver the cash parcel to this address. You have my solemn oath that it will be used to help the downtrodden in the cause of freedom." She exhaled sharply, lowering her voice to a whisper. "I do not admire most white folk, Mr. Sanderson. I have suffered too grievously at the hands of most. But you are a decent man. I have respect for men of integrity."

Nodding curtly, she turned and left Robert's office as briskly as she had entered. Moments after her departure Robert rang the bell for his clerk. He was signing a check when Albert entered. He said, "Please take this to the bank at once. Ask for it in gold and deliver the money promptly to this address." He handed Albert the calling card.

Albert glanced briefly at the card and tried to mask his shock of awareness at the visitor's identity.

"Very good, sir," Albert replied, hurrying from the room as Robert sat back in his armchair, speculating on the significance of Mammy Pleasant's prediction. Something precious lost, something precious gained. An indication that the Sandersons would survive. Well, whatever the strange woman had meant, he wouldn't dwell on it. He had a good relationship with Emily, with Reb; he was successful, prosperous, and, at 36, in the prime of his life.

That night he went to the Hotel Splendide to visit Ethan and Flora. He told them of his unusual meeting with Mammy Pleasant.

"So you contributed," said Ethan. A statement of fact, not a question.

"Something, yes."

"Probably a lot," said Flora.

"Enough to salve my pure white conscience," said Robert, knowing the irony would be appreciated.

"It won't stem the tide," said Ethan. "There'll be a bitter war in three or four years."

"I'm glad you two are in California," said Robert. "I wouldn't be as lucky without you."

"You'd be luckier married," Flora spoke up.

Ethan laughed. "Spoken like a true woman. She means Emily."

"When the time is right, I'll know," Robert told them both, and left the matter there . . .

Robert had very little leisure time with Reb away from their shared daily routines. Next morning he awoke long before dawn, excited that they were going to have a fine, uninterrupted day together.

The two started out from San Francisco shortly after daybreak in Robert's shiny new carriage. They took with them a large wicker food hamper containing a bountiful picnic luncheon, following El Camino Real's well-traveled stagecoach route south toward San Jose. This was the route the padres had established during early California mission days and still the main link between San Francisco and the south.

Their carriage had gone some nine miles when Robert turned off at a crumbling wayside inn onto a mere cowpath of a road that wandered aimlessly beneath giant oaks for a mile or so, gradually ascending into low foothills. Robert halted the horses on a rise of ground that afforded a breathtaking vista of the Bay's sprawling tidelands to the east, and the Bay's sapphire waters beyond.

This far from San Francisco, the land was virtually untouched yet by farming. It was grazed by cattle in the spring, but otherwise as virgin as it had been under the early Indians who lived within the balance of nature instead of destroying it. On the crest of the hill stood a small wooden shedlike shelter, weathered silver and flimsy with age, the only sign around that human beings had ever even thought of settling here.

Robert got out the hamper and Reb walked the horses into the shade of a great oak tree; the sun was quite hot for December, although the air was cool.

"Well, son," Robert said, putting down the hamper, "here it is."

"Here is what?"

"Our very first business venture."

Reb looked all around him. "But there's nothing here, father, except that old shack."

"Don't you see anything else? Look closely."

"You mean the scenery? Well, it's pretty enough."

"A bit more perhaps?"

"The land around us?"

"Smart lad. The land, of course."

"Who owns it?"

"It's a fragment of an old Mexican land grant, son, and owned by the Mendez family."

"Do you know them?"

"Let's say I've a formal speaking acquaintance with the matriarch, Doña Maria Mendez. Quite a formidable old lady . . . And the little girl, Pilar, her granddaughter. Doña Maria wants to sell the piece we're standing on."

"How big is it?" Reb asked with the tone of a mature man considering a bid.

"Two thousand acres."

"And the asking price?"

Robert mentioned a fairly large sum.

"Whew! That's a lot of money, father."

"I know. I should explain that this is a negotiated price. The old lady won't go any lower. But it's still a bargain, which you'll realize when you consider how close we are to town. One day when you're grown up, the San Francisco community will start building homes and businesses down this way. It's inevitable. But even now, the property's valuable, in direct ratio to what we intend to do with it, of course. What do you see as a possibility?"

Reb spread a picnic blanket on the fresh young winter grass, thinking of his father's question, as Robert began to unpack the luncheon.

At length he said, "Speak up, son, I'd like to hear your ideas."

Reb pulled a stalk of grass from the earth and twirled it in his fingers. "Well," he said, "there are lots of ways to take. I think a dairy farm and a chicken ranch combined would be the best thing. We could sell eggs in the city anytime. We could make cheese from the milk, and in the winter sell the milk itself. We could even raise alfalfa and irrigate it with windmills. I'll bet there's always a breeze on these hills. Then we could raise seasonal vegetables and ship them to city markets. There must be a lot of other uses for the land, but I'd have to think about them. And, of course, there's the building that would have to be done, fences run out—"

Robert held up his hands in mock surrender. "You win, Reb. You've convinced me. I'll buy the property, it's ours."

Reb clapped his hands together, ecstatic. "Honestly? You mean we're in business?"

"Absolutely, son. Just the two of us. Your name will go on the property deed as co-owner. All responsibility will be on a fifty-fifty basis. Do you realize what this means?"

"I sure do, father. It means I'm probably the youngest *ranchero* in California."

"It won't be all joy," Robert pointed out.

"It will be for me. Father, I'm excited!" Reb scrambled across the blanket, nearly sinking his knee in the potato salad. He flung his arms around his father's neck in sheer exuberance.

"I'll come out every weekend," he said when he'd calmed down. "I'll spend all my vacations here. I'll oversee everything that goes on. First off, we'll build us a corral for the cows and horses, then a fence for the chicken run. We'll tear down this shack and build a large, sturdy cabin, put in a windmill, outhouses. Golly, there's a million things to do!"

And so there would be, Robert reflected, as they began to eat the fried chicken, marinated vegetables and potato salad from the hamper. To have this kind of rapport with a boy only ten years old was one of the most joyous and rewarding moments of his life.

"The Sanderson Ranch," Reb said dreamily a few moments later, gazing out at the land with deep affection. "Nobody ever had a better birthday present. This one's good for a lifetime. Thanks, father."

Bright and eager, Reb would turn out to be quite a man one day, Robert thought proudly. The boy was right, an eastern university wasn't his milieu. He'd be as out of place as an Eskimo in the Sahara. Reb had an almost mystical love of the land. Yes, no doubt about it, Robert knew he'd made a wise move that would bring endless dividends to them both. Reb's was a youthful vision of his times, of his place. He was indeed a true Golden Stater; California belonged to him.

THE BONANZA YEARS

LAND WAS A PRIME focal point for the new California settlers once the territory became a state. Many incoming Americans sought land for ranches. Some communities needed public lands for townships, planning to subdivide eventually or merely to hold for long-term investment. There was a good deal of rank speculation; and endless, complex legal battles went on over the rights of squatters versus Mexican land grant claims. Time-consuming, often bitter controversies were common between private citizens and the government.

Over a five-year period preceding 1860, the land commission processed some nine-hundred claims. Practically all of these went on for appeal, some as far as the U.S. Supreme Court. The Catholic church managed to acquire title to Indian pueblo lands and mission church sites, while the Indians themselves, naive in American ways, failed to lay any claim to what had been rightfully theirs under the Spanish. Thus they lost their lands.

The wooden shed on the Sanderson ranch had been built by squatters long before Robert bought the property from the Mendez family. Elderly Doña Maria was one of the few long-established California citizens who had received fairly quick free title to the family's fifty-thousand acres south of San Francisco. If the land hadn't been free and clear, Robert would not have been interested in buying the parcel for himself and Reb.

All went peacefully along on the Sanderson ranch at the height of the title disputes. But only twenty miles south near San Jose, the wrangle over the Berryessa grant took a tragic toll. Three people were lynched in disputes, several went insane, many were victimized by fraud, litigation and violence.

Eventually public lands were explicitly designated by Congress, enacting in the 1860s four landmark decisions of vital importance to the development of California. The Pacific Railroad Act of 1862 gave to the Central Pacific and Union Pacific Railways rights-of-way and lands in public domain as incentives to contruct a badly needed transcontinental railroad route. A second significant measure was the College Land Grant of 1862, giving public lands to institutions of higher learning. The 1862 Homestead Act gave 160-acre parcels of land to settlers, with clear titles after five years' residence and proper improvement.

By 1870 the shape of the new California had

definitely emerged. A handful of men controlled vast segments of California; some owned more than seventy thousand acres apiece. One of these speculators was William Chapman, who eventually through dummy corporations and bribery acquired over a million acres. Chapman was, however, a man of vision. He fostered crop experimentation, he built irrigation canals in desert areas, he settled immigrants in agrarian communities when they would otherwise have had nothing. There were some landowners who used their lands purely for speculation, while others developed them by rotation farming, mining, lumbering.

In 1860 Robert began to develop the Sanderson ranch as a supplier of farm products. They were unable, however, to find a reliable city outlet for their poultry, eggs, milk, cheese and butter. It was Reb's suggestion that they open their own small specialty market in the city. This outlet was strategically located and was an instant success with housewives. They couldn't keep it fully stocked between the regular ranch runs, so popular were their quality products. At first occasional ranch-matured beef was offered, but this item was eventually eliminated, due to the unpredictability of the weather and the competition that was developing in the San Joaquin Valley. They concentrated on poultry, eggs and cheese, staples that could be produced easily in poor seasons or good ones, and that met a constant market demand.

At fourteen, Reb announced to Robert that he thought he'd had enough of formal education.

"I want to leave school, father."

"But you still have to attend university," Robert pointed out, wondering if it mattered. Reb was already far better informed than he himself was, than even many San Francisco professional men were. His keen thirst for knowledge and his photographic memory made him exceptional.

"I've already got the equivalent of the first two years of university from independent reading," Reb explained. "I can study on my own if I need special knowledge. Anyway, books teach me more than the instructors."

"But you're still very young. What will you do?"

"I may be young, sir, but I'm already a man."

Indeed he was, Robert observed. Almost six feet tall, well muscled out, handsome, with wide blue eyes and curly brown hair, these attributes and his strong, mature face belied his age. He could pass easily for nineteen or twenty and had already bedded young women, although he hadn't yet had the temerity to show up at the Hotel Splendide or Mammy Pleasant's parlor to buy favors. That wouldn't be long in coming, Robert decided, feeling that if he didn't favor Reb about his schooling, Reb might one day decide to take off for parts unknown—he was that independent.

"Very well, Reb. You may leave school at term's end. You'll return, however, if things don't work out."

"Thank you, sir!"

"Now wait, there's another condition—"

"What's that?"

"You will live down on the ranch for the time being and supervise the development of it. You'll come into town on Saturday night and stay Sundays with me, or whenever business demands."

Reb brightened. He had an even keener eye than Robert for ranch details and would assist the present supervisor, Jim Hull, a former employee of El Dorado Steamship, who, like Reb, preferred to live out of the city. Hull was planning to go into the poultry business for himself at San Jose, and would be leaving the ranch soon. Reb's full-time residence there would guarantee production, spark his talents, or at least absorb his bountiful energy, leaving him very little idle time for the many attractions of the city.

"Goddam, that's wonderful!" Reb said enthusiastically.

"Watch your language, son."

"Yes, sir. I'll move my things down tomorrow. Jim will be glad to have me around."

Reb remained on the ranch all through the Civil War. He had no strong feeling for the preservation of the Union, or against slavery, as Robert and Ethan had. He felt that the issue belonged to the East, North and South, not to his California, the detached and most western frontier.

In any case, Reb became totally caught up in the care and development of the ranch after Jim Hull left. First of all, he had a decent residence built so that Robert could come down overnight whenever he wished, and an adequate bunkhouse erected for the mixed group of laborers who lived on the property: Chinese, Indians, a few cowboys of both black and white ethnic backgrounds. Reb was an excellent overseer and

boss, Robert was pleased to discover. He picked
his men with an eye toward their congeniality
and ability, and he was seldom wrong about
his hired hands.

Reb kept to the agreement with his father
about visiting town only on weekends, but still
he managed to drop in on the gaming tables
and court women. With his father's example of
continuing singleness, Reb himself was in no
hurry to wed. No need to buy a cow when milk
was cheap. The fact was, despite his affable
promiscuity in the city, he had not yet fallen in
love; his taste for women was catholic. Already
he had sampled the charms of black women,
Indian girls, a Mexican girl, and several older
women from saloons and theatres.

On his eighteenth birthday he got drunk and
tried the door of the Hotel Splendide. Flora and
Ethan offered him champagne but denied him
the company of any of the girls. Later that same
night he went to Mammy Pleasant's parlor and
was refused entrance by the blond butler.

Upset by these rejections, he ended up at the
Bella Union, a famous variety house, or melo-
deon, where a spirit of festive openness prevailed as perhaps nowhere else in the city, or
probably in the country, at that time.

The Black Crook, a melodrama, was playing
at the Bella Union. There were plenty of girls
about, all available, one of whom took an instant
shine to him. She was a saucy blonde with a
halo of ringlets and heavy make-up. Ample of
bosom, with a splendid pair of hips, she minced
no words with Reb about how attractive he was.

They sat at a table and Reb ordered more
champagne as the minstrels played popular

melodies. The burlesque melodrama began, but by this time Reb was quite drunk and getting noisy, so much so that a young man at the next table told him to button his mouth.

Reb jumped up in anger, and a fight started between the pair. It culminated in the street outside the Bella Union, finally broken up by the police. Reb spent the night in jail, receiving a stern lecture next morning from Robert while nursing the worst hangover of his life.

"I'm not going to bandy words with you, son," Robert said over a breakfast Reb couldn't eat. "I'm disappointed."

"I know, father, I asked for it." Reb managed a grin despite his bruised and swollen jaw. "I owe the good name of Sanderson better treatment than that."

"Well, at least you have some sense of contrition," Robert observed. "You're eighteen and a man now. I think the problem is that you don't have enough to do at the ranch. You seem to want to let off excess steam whenever you come to town. Maybe you'd better remain on the ranch for a spell, eh?"

"Possibly, sir," Reb agreed. "We could use more land to work. Then I could keep busy."

Coincidentally, Robert had just that week received a communication from the aging Doña Maria Mendez. She was offering him another section of land contiguous to the acreage that he and Reb already owned. Reb had never met the old lady; it seemed time he should, Robert decided.

"You've never been down to the Mendez house."

"No, just heard about your visit when I was a boy."

"Now's your opportunity. You'll carry a letter from me to Doña Maria. She's ready to sell some more land."

"My Spanish is pretty bad, sir."

"I'm more concerned with your good manners. Doña Maria always has someone about to interpret for her, in her favor, of course. Do you want to be our representative?"

"I'd like that."

"When can you go, do you think?"

"Anytime, sir."

"Good. What do you propose to do with the new land?"

Robert now left all ranch decisions up to Reb; he had proven time and time again that he knew exactly what he was doing. When fences were required, Robert merely paid the bills Reb sent him, knowing that the expenditures were legitimate and needn't be checked out.

"I'm thinking of sheep, sir," Reb said. "We can sell mutton and wool on the local market. I wish to God we had fifty thousand acres, father. We could start our own mills. Wool textiles are always in demand in the city."

"Fifty thousand acres would be a *hacienda*," Robert said. "It's a nice dream, but impossible."

"It could be a reality if we wanted to go into the San Joaquin Valley," Reb suggested. "One day sheep-raising will outdo cattle-ranching. I'm sure of it."

"You may be right . . . Well, go ahead, have some breakfast while I write a letter you'll carry to Doña Maria. Oh yes, one more word of advice. The Mendez family are aristocrats, Reb. I caution you to be the young gentleman at all times."

"You don't have to rub my nose in it, sir, but I guess I deserve it for last night."

"About last evening . . . since *you* brought it up this time. I beg you, for my sake if not for your own, stay away from the whorehouses and saloons. I'd like to have you alive, not dead."

"I promise, father."

"Very well. See that you hold to it on your next visit."

"I will."

It was a long time before Reb was involved in another argument in town. As he departed for the ranch with Robert's letter to Doña Maria, Robert was left with the uneasy feeling that he may have made a mistake in allowing Reb to leave school at such an early age. If he hadn't, the lad would now be in his middle years at Georgetown, a polished and worldly young gentleman. But maybe not, and besides, he reminded himself that this was only what he wanted for Reb, not his son's wish, and dismissed it from his mind, being of a practical turn. Reb was doing fine, considering the rough nature of the times.

A series of responsibilities concerning supplies and construction kept Reb closely confined to the Sanderson ranch for the next two weeks. He was unable to make the proposed visit to the Mendez rancho until nearly three weeks after his birthday.

Reb intended to ride horseback down to the

Mendez case. That way he could cut across country and save almost an hour. But he knew he had to dress up for the occasion in his best clothes, which was incompatible with riding a mount through unmarked terrain. So on the day of the journey he rose early, decided on the buggy, bathed and dressed carefully in his best suit, put on his newest wide brim, hitched up his sleekest, most reliable horse, and drove off to the *rancho* with his father's letter in his pocket, having several days earlier sent a message to the widow, Doña Maria, notifying her of his arrival.

It was a beautiful warm day in late January, the kind of benign weather that often appears briefly in the midst of the cold, wet northern California winters, as calm and sunny as the eye of a hurricane passing over.

Reb drove along the stagecoach route for a couple of hours, then turned off into the foot-hills. He arrived at the impressive Mendez estate toward noon, to be met on the road a few hundred yards from the *hacienda* by a young boy on horseback, or so Reb thought as he reined his buggy to a halt.

The figure on horseback was clad in buck-skin, wore a wide sombrero and was probably one of the very young farmhands, Red decided.

"*Buenas dias, señor*," Reb called politely from the buggy.

"I speak English," the young *caballero* called back, and Reb suddenly realized that he was talking to a young girl, not a boy.

"I'm Reb Sanderson."

"I know who you are. You're here with a letter for my grandmother, Doña Maria. I'm

Pilar Mendez. Welcome to Los Arboles, our home."

"Thank you," Reb said, unable to see much of Pilar Mendez' features beneath the sombrero. What he did see, he liked; she was looking less boyish every second.

"Follow me," said Pilar. "I'll escort you to the corral; Antonio will take your horse."

Reb drove after Pilar past the main house of Los Arboles, a rambling, two-storied hacienda, built of adobe brick, whitewashed, with red-tiled roofs.

Antonio unhitched Reb's horse and led it to water in the corral. Pilar dismounted, hitched her horse to a corral post and joined Reb, pulling off her sombrero and allowing a cascade of black, glistening hair to tumble free over her slim shoulders. Now she bore no resemblance to a boy, but she was rather more an elf than a girl, he decided. Up close, she was quite lovely, her features delicate, her skin light and creamy. Reb couldn't figure her age, but he found her very attractive.

"My grandmother is waiting for you," Pilar said as she led him toward the front gate to the inner house. "She thinks your father is a remarkable man. So do I."

"That makes three of us," Reb said. She was trying to put him at ease, which he appreciated.

"I understand you live on the Sanderson ranch."

"Permanently, with occasional trips into town. You've never been there."

Pilar smiled. "I'm not allowed off the estate without a *dueña*—you know our Spanish customs?—and my chaperone doesn't ride horseback at fifty years of age, only in stagecoaches."

"Have you lived here all your life?" Reb asked.

"Only occasionally until the past year, since my grandmother became ill. My father's dead, in case you're interested. And my mother, well, she went back to Spain where she was born. I refused to go with her. There, that's my biography. It should satisfy your curiosity."

It didn't, of course. Reb said, "Where did you learn your English?"

"In San Francisco, at a convent near the Mission Dolores. Is it all right?"

"Superior. Like a native Californian."

Pilar glanced at him sharply, her black eyes searching his face. "You aren't making fun of me? I *am* a native Californian. Are you?"

"Yes, born in Sacramento." He wanted to say *twenty* years ago, not wishing to be merely eighteen in Pilar's eyes.

"So we are a pair of natives," Pilar said, without warmth, and led him through a heavy oaken door into the casa's inner patio. They walked across cool, polished tiles to the bright, sunny inner garden with a splashing central fountain, set in beds of bright geraniums; the walls of the large patio were ablaze with bougainvillea.

In the central living room the tiled floors were spread with hand-woven Indian throw rugs, the walls hung with dim Spanish tapestries that looked antique to Reb.

In funereal black near the blazing fireplace Doña Maria sat waiting for them, dwarfed by the huge wicker chair that held her frail body. Her figure was almost as slight as Pilar's, while her wrinkled countenance documented her extreme age with a network of tiny lines. She peered at Reb with slitted eyes; her soft white hair was half-hidden by a fine black lace mantilla.

Robert had told Reb, "The widow's above seventy, but very sharp. She'll expect you to present proof of what's already been done on the ranch and what you intend to do with the new property, *if* she decides we can have it. So go easy."

Doña Maria leaned forward, peering up at him as he paused before her. "Welcome to Los Arboles, *señor*," she said in measured English, the last she would speak during his visit, conversing henceforth in Spanish.

Reb bowed deferentially to her with a flourish of his hat. "I'm honored to be here, ma'am," he said, which was immediately translated for Doña Maria by Pilar, apparently their chosen interpreter.

"Is your father well?" Doña Maria enquired.

"He's fine, ma'am. He sends you his most respectful greetings."

Doña Maria waved him into a chair. "Be seated. Will you have some sherry? We make it ourselves. Not Spanish, but we do our best."

Reb allowed politely that he would indeed have a drink. The silver and crystal decanter with the tall silver goblets were brought in on a tray by an elderly female Indian servant. Reb was served first, then the old lady, then Pilar.

Reb sat back, sipped at his sherry, tried to appear casual, feeling himself under scrutiny. He had never tasted sherry before. This *amon-*

tillado was exceptionally light, dry and nutty-flavored; he decided after a few sips that he liked the drink.

"This is really excellent," he observed, hoping he would sound informed.

"I'm glad you like it," Pilar translated for her grandmother. "We sell most of what we make, setting some aside to remind us of our homeland. I was born only a few kilometers from Jerez, where this type of wine originated . . . Well, enough of that. What do you intend to do with the new land, if we reach an agreement?"

Reb produced his father's letter and handed it to Doña Maria, who opened and passed it on to Pilar to translate into Spanish. As Pilar spoke, the old woman studied Reb in silence. After Pilar had read the letter, Doña Maria said, "You're very young to be managing a ranch, *señor*. I imagined that you would be much older."

Reb said with some embarrassment, "I'm eighteen, ma'am. In California that's considered adult." Pilar translated this with ill-concealed relish.

"I suppose," said Doña Maria, "you expect to get rich from the land in a very short time?"

There was a grating tone of irony in Pilar's English translation, Reb noted. He could understand why. Generally *Latinos* had suffered many indignities from the American takeover after the Mexican War. Most of them were but one rung up the ladder from the dispossessed *Indios*. The exploitation of land by the Americans was a touchy subject.

"I hadn't figured on getting rich, ma'am, or ravaging the land. We're not greedy, my father and me. What we make, we put right back into the ranch, hoping one day it will be my real home. For my family, if I ever have one."

"What specifically will you do with more land?" Doña Maria probed.

"I don't know exactly, ma'am. I was thinking of some vineyards, maybe raise some cattle or sheep. My father's left the decision up to me, so I'm moving slowly. I don't want to make mistakes. I did think of fruit orchards. These are practical, they don't ruin the land. When we get irrigation canals put through we might even raise alfalfa. But orchards or vineyards, these are practical. There's always a city market for fruits and wine."

Actually the idea of orchards and vineyards came to him as pure inspiration while he was sipping the sherry. It must have pleased the old woman, for she murmured, "Wisely said," with a smile.

Somewhere a gong sounded.

"Time to refresh yourself before dinner is served, *señor*," Doña Maria said. "Pilar will show you where."

Pilar led Reb down the right wing corridor of the house to a large bedroom dominated by a massive, carved mahogany bed with a brocaded canopy. A chest of drawers and sturdy oak chairs sat against the whitewashed walls. Towels, a pitcherful of water, a basin, were ready for Reb.

"Excuse me, I must change," said Pilar, and she disappeared down the hall.

Fifteen minutes later Reb was seated at one end of an enormous banquet table, Doña Maria at the other. A third place was set between them on Reb's right, for Pilar. She joined them presently, demure in a simple white cotton dress, her hair up and secured at the nape of her slender neck by a heavy silver clasp. The transformation from gamine in buckskins and sombrero to elegant young maiden rendered him speechless. He gawked at her, and Pilar, aware of his attention, stared at him with a superior smile, apparently pleased that she had made the intended impression. Probably she would not have changed for her grandmother.

Doña Maria blessed the table and the meal began. A savory soup was served, then a magnificent *paella* containing pork and lamb, chicken, seafood and vegetables, all combined with pimiento-dotted saffron rice. It was one of the most delicious dishes Reb had ever tasted, and the homemade sauterne served to set off its richness perfectly.

Pilar picked listlessly at her food, as did Doña Maria. Both watched Reb eat. By the time he had accepted a third helping, Doña Maria was smiling happily. She said something quickly to Pilar, who turned to Reb.

"My grandmother says she always trusts a man with a healthy appetite. She says you are such a man."

"That's kind of you, ma'am," Reb said, and proceeded to clean his plate of the last of the *paella*.

Dessert was a caramel flan. Stuffed to the chin, Reb could scarcely rise from the table, to the delight of Doña Maria and the quiet amusement of Pilar.

Bitter black coffee was served in eggshell china demitasses in the living room. The terms of the contract were discussed. Armed with his father's instructions, Reb negotiated points as best he could. Toward three o'clock they reached an agreement satisfactory to Doña Maria. She promised that her lawyer would draw up a contract for Robert's and Reb's signatures. It would be ready within a week; he could come to Los Arboles for it then.

After graciously thanking Doña Maria for her hospitality and the memorable dinner, Reb took his leave. Pilar saw him to the corral.

"You surprise me, Reb Sanderson," she said, as soon as they left the *hacienda*, and Reb asked why. "Well, you are so serious about ranching. The other young men I have met are so silly, out chasing dancehall girls at the melodeons, or losing money at the gaming tables, living for the moment. They don't think about the future. They certainly wouldn't want a *ranchero*'s life as you do."

"I'm not exactly a model of virtue," Reb confessed. "I like a good time like anyone else."

"Are you a fool, then?" she challenged.

"I guess so, if you mean liking women. It's not a crime. Besides, why shouldn't I?"

"Yes, being a man you would think that," she said sarcastically, and he realized that he could not make jokes if he intended to see her again, and he did.

Antonio harnessed his horse to the buggy. Reb got in. "I hope to see you again when I come back."

"You may or may not," she replied. "I might be visiting my aunt in San Jose."

"Well then, another time."

"It would have to be here at Los Arboles."

"Anywhere is all right with me."

"Yes," she said noncommitally. "Good-bye, Reb Sanderson."

She turned away and he drove off. When he had reached the point in the road where Pilar had first greeted him on his arrival, he glanced around and saw her standing motionless under the great oak in front of the *hacienda*.

He took off his hat and waved it at her, but she ran into the house without acknowledging his farewell. Didn't she trust her own responses, he wondered, snapping the horse's reins. Damn the girl's arrogance! Who did she think she was?

It was the first time in Pilar's life that she'd been deeply impressed with a young man; her reaction upset her. True, most young bachelors were frivolous idiots. Here was a man who dazzled her, but she didn't even know why, and it maddened her. All she knew was, she admired his gentle honesty toward her grandmother. Handsome? Yes, he was. But it was his seriousness that had made her heart race.

In the house her grandmother said, "I shall now take my *siesta*, and a good two hours late because of the *Americano*. You seemed strangely silent at dinner, *querida*. Didn't you like the young man?"

Pilar shrugged her shoulders. "Oh," she said, "he's nice enough for an *Americano*."

"You are never easy on young men," Doña Maria observed. "I found him quite charming."

"*If* you like *Americanos*," Pilar replied.

"But we are all *Americanos* now."

"I have chosen not to be."

"It makes no difference. Sooner or later we will all be absorbed into their way of life."

Doña Maria rose stiffly from her chair by the fireside.

"Yes, I liked his sincerity, and his industry. He is very much like his father, one of the few admirable *Americanos*, a true gentleman. I think he will do well in life."

"A *ranchero*'s life," Pilar said contemptuously. "I would never want such a fate."

"You may have no choice, if you are lucky enough to marry into a good family."

"I want to choose what I do with my life," said Pilar. "Like Reb Sanderson."

"Whatever makes you say that?" the old lady demanded. "You're not a man."

"I wouldn't mind being one," she replied, "if I could be like him."

"What are you saying, child? You have no sense of decency. Or was it that second glass of wine I saw you drink that's taken your wits?"

Pilar realized that she had gone too far with her grandmother. Liking Reb, she had refused to go along with Doña Maria's praise of him, which might make her suspect in her grandmother's eyes. The old creature was able to read people clearly. If she guessed how impressed her granddaughter was with Reb, she would be shocked.

"I suppose it was that second glass of wine," Pilar confessed. "I don't feel so well, grandmama. Excuse me . . ."

"Not until you take me to my room." Doña Maria held out her arm, linked it through Pilar's.

"Silly girl, to have such foolish dreams. Well, in any case, the younger Sanderson is a fine boy. He loves the land, he will care for it well . . ."

* * *

Reb dreamed of Pilar that night. His dream was wildly erotic and he awoke in a sweat, too disturbed to get back to sleep immediately. He rose and wrote his father a letter, which one of the hands going into town would deliver to the offices of Sanderson Enterprises.

In it he told his father: "I followed through on all the points you suggested. I admired the old lady, she's remarkable. An aristocrat too, just as you described her. I liked Pilar Mendez— she's very young. The food was excellent. My appetite did it justice. Doña Maria says she will have the contract for us in about a week. I may travel down to Los Arboles at that time to get it then bring it into town for your perusal and signature. As you know, I'm excited about the prospect of the additional acreage and have grandiose plans. If only a fraction of these work out I'll not be disappointed!"

Back in bed before dawn, Reb surrendered to thoughts of Pilar and wished she were lying right beside him. There was only one way to manage that: marriage. Out of the question. For the Spanish were too proud to allow their daughters to marry Anglo-Americans, although Spanish *grandees* had taken American wives. And you just didn't sleep with a Latin girl of good family without marrying her first. Getting married was far into the future where he was concerned. There were too many delights to be sampled still as a single man; he intended to miss nothing.

After second thoughts, stirred up as he was, he decided to go into town and deliver that letter in person, then look into the melodeons,

discreetly of course, and see if he could find a
night's fun, which might be difficult. Now that
he'd met Pilar the whole world looked different.

A note in Spanish from Doña Maria, written
in an ornate and spidery hand, arrived at the
ranch eight days after the luncheon rendezvous
—pretty good time, Reb thought. He gave the
messenger a reply for Doña Maria, informing
her that he'd be down in three days' time, and
that he'd bring his healthy appetite with him,
if that was all right.

This time Reb decided to ride horseback instead of traveling by buggy. He dressed more
informally than he had for his first visit, and
arrived at Los Arboles half an hour before dinner time.

Pilar did not meet him on the road, nor was
she to be seen anywhere as he was ushered into
Doña Maria's presence. Without an interpreter
things moved slowly. The old lady was definitely not as cordial as she'd been on his first visit,
although this did not dim her eagerness to discuss the contract with him. Obviously, she
needed cash.

They took their meal together. This time it
was roast kid, a Mexican specialty. Their basic
language inadequacies had to stand for the
more fluid conversation that Pilar had managed
between them.

No mention was made of Pilar's absence by
Doña Maria. Finally, toward the end of the
meal, Reb did venture a polite query as to the
girl's whereabouts.

Doña Maria stared at him almost irately, as

if he'd committed some unpardonable *faux pas.*

"She is in Los Angeles," the old lady declared. "She belongs there for a time. That is all."

"When will she return?"

"I do not know, she has many relatives down below," the old lady said, so sharply that Reb abandoned the subject.

On the long ride back to the ranch he brooded over what might have happened. Had Pilar been as interested in him as he was in her, and had she made the mistake of confessing this to her grandmother? Well, whatever had happened, Pilar was out of his life, at least for the present, and he could get down to the finer details of developing the new acreage.

In the 1860s railroad construction was on everybody's mind, a vast enterprise that involved the real future of California, a state so large that mass transportation was of vitally urgent importance. Local railroads around San Francisco had not developed rapidly as the more visionary pioneers had hoped they would. By 1860 only one line was working, the Sacramento-Folsom run of twenty-three miles, built by Ted Judah, an old acquaintance of Robert's.

Judah was a brilliant young engineer and a splendid promoter, easily able to infuse skeptics with enthusiasm for his dream of an overland rail route designed to surmount the formidable Sierra Nevada range, negotiating the high pass where the ill-fated Donner party had met its doom in 1846, and link California with the mid-West and East.

Judah lobbied in Congress for support of his plan, and before the state legislature, seeking official support. The Judah plan had plenty of foes, among them diehard get-rich-quickers who didn't want any competition from the influx of settlers that an easy route to California would inevitably precipitate. They foresaw a mass migration that would bring thousands upon thousands to California seeking its wealth and disrupting its established order.

Robert was deeply stirred by the idea of the railroad route, seeing it as something inevitable that California needed badly. If Judah didn't get his scheme in the works, others would dream up a different plan one day. When Ted Judah appealed to Robert and other San Francisco businessmen for financial support, since the government refused to cooperate, only Robert came forth to help. Ethan wanted no part of the plan. "Let the bastards stay on the other side of the mountain," he told Robert. "We got ours the hard way. Why should they walk in and take it away from us?"

"It will develop the state, make us rich."

"How? By bringing more settlers?"

"It'll mean more business."

"We have all we can handle now," Ethan said gruffly. "I wouldn't give a penny to help Judah."

Other businessmen felt as Ethan did. Judah was considered an impractical visionary, his scheme foolish and ill-advised. Financing it would be like throwing good money down a drain, for many men believed sincerely that the railroad could never be built.

Robert was disappointed; he wanted very much to be part of something he steadfastly believed in. He suggested that Ted Judah go to

Sacramento for his financial support, and mentioned the name of Leland Stanford, whom he knew.

"Stanford has friends with money," Robert explained, "and good sense along with vision. I feel that he'll be able to help you. At least he's worth a try."

"I'd like you to be in on it, Robert," Judah told him. "You'll be part of history. Whatever the diehards say, I'm convinced that the railroad will go through and make some people very rich one day."

Robert thought so, too, but at the moment Ethan was pursuing a project related to another aspect of El Dorado's transportation system, the main reason for his refusal to go along with Robert's interests. Later on he would curse himself for his short-sightedness.

Ted Judah journeyed to Sacramento and found a ready disciple in Leland Stanford. He convinced Stanford without much persuasion that he had a magnificent plan that couldn't possibly fail. In turn, Stanford talked up the railroad to several friends of his—Collis Huntington, Charles Crocker, and Mark Hopkins. All these men, later known as the Big Four, combined resources to form the incorporated Central Pacific Railroad Company. Together they built the transcontinental railroad that first linked the East to the West Coast and changed the tranquil face of California forever.

Ted Judah poured his life's energies into his beloved project. The hard work paid off; the railroad was a world-shaking success. But Judah died early in the project's history, worn out by his efforts to get the colossus going, and unfortunately did not see his dream come to reality.

The Big Four continued the monumental task of constructing the railroad. By group agreement, they formed a dummy corporation to construct the line and through it connived and manipulated funds that brought them all prodigious wealth, making each man an instant millionaire and laying the groundwork for their individual empires, the largest that California had thus far seen.

Building a railroad through the rugged barrier of the Sierra Nevadas was truly a labor fit for Hercules. It was achieved by utilizing cheap Chinese laborers to augment white ones. The Chinese were imported by the boatload from famine-ridden mainland China, some of them near-starving and happy to get on a ship and come to work under the grueling conditions of the railroad gangs for the sake of pitifully meager wages. Far better the railroad than starvation back home. Needless to say, under breakneck conditions, life along the rail line was considered cheap. Coolies died all along the route as the punishing work progressed.

Of the Big Four, it was the huge, red-bearded Charles Crocker who was the most influential of the group in the actual construction of the line. "Uncle" Mark Hopkins was the scrimper and the saver, collecting discarded paper in the offices for second use, touring the tracks around the work sites to pick up rusty bolts and spikes, or any other scrap of metal that might be reused.

At one point the white laborers deserted the corporation to chase after elusive fortunes in silver at the Nevada mines. It was then that

Crocker replaced the "traitors" with the sixteen thousand coolies used in the laying of the line. Crocker figured that if the "heathen Chinee" could build the Great Wall of China, they could sure as hell put together a puny old railroad. He was right.

After Robert had set up his own small corporation to deal with supplying several of the railroad's construction requirements—food staples, railroad ties, tools—Crocker asked him to come to the work site out of San Francisco.

"You have to see how the work's going and where your supplies are needed," Crocker said. "It'll give you some ideas on items we may have overlooked."

Robert rode with Crocker as far as the big man's luxurious private railroad car could travel beyond the rearguard supply camps. Once he spent several days with Crocker just watching railroad bed operations. At nights he dined with Crocker on roast beef and pheasant served by a Chinese waiter on damask linen, drank good red wine out of crystal goblets, ate off the finest china. After dinner he and Crocker would study charts and figures, and discuss the need for more supplies.

Then in the morning, after a night of too much drink and a lot of talk, Crocker and Robert would ride out to the work site on horseback, Crocker with saddlebags of silver and gold coins slung across his mount, from which he would pay the workers personally.

One morning Crocker and Robert watched from a distance as a gang of coolies under two white foremen planted charges of dynamite on a sheer granite outcropping. When the preparation was done, the coolies stood nonchalantly to one side with their foremen as the charges were detonated. Usually this was a safe enough practice, but not this time. The explosion caused the mountainside above to shudder and break loose. Before their horrified eyes, the entire cliff above the discharge rumbled down on top of the road gang, killing twenty-five coolies and the two white foremen, burying them under tons of earth and rock.

Robert stayed with Crocker as gangs arrived to dig out the victims. The rubble was removed but there were no survivors. In a few hours the work continued, even while the dead bodies were being carted away.

Another time, Robert came up as the work neared the granite crest of the Sierra range. Under these conditions the progress was slow, since workers had to drill through solid rock, sometimes making no more headway than a few inches a day. The Chinese worked twelve-hour shifts on a twenty-four-hour basis, pausing only to sleep and eat.

Crocker was as profit-motivated as his partners; he never stopped thinking about the railroad, pushing everyone as hard as he drove himself. His searing ambition was to beat the impossible and push the line right through to the eastern Sierra foothills into the Nevada desert long before schedule. This was done, but it placed the workers there at the wrong season, in temperatures that soared to 120°F. Even so, the track was laid in that inferno at the fantastic rate of a mile a day.

Fascinated as much by Crocker's almost inhuman energy as the railroad itself, Robert made many trips to work sites along the Central Pacific route to see Crocker in action.

On the East Coast during all this frenzy of activity, Collis P. Huntington was doing his share to effect completion of the railroad by expediting equipment. On his fleet of ships, locomotives were being freighted from the East Coast to San Francisco, then placed on flatbeds and sent along the line into Nevada.

To Stanford, the most dignified of the Big Four, fell the job of playing diplomat. He traveled ahead of the line as it was built, soothing the tempers of local dignitaries, speaking eloquently to various assemblies, making grandiose promises about the wealth and civilization that the railroad would bring in its wake.

Six years after ground was first broken to lay the Central Pacific roadbed, on May 10, 1869, the Central Pacific met the Union Pacific at Promontory, Utah. Despite the frightful loss of life that occurred during construction, and despite the Big Four's deadly profit-rape, the achievement was the most staggering one to date in American history.

Without the peculiar alchemy of genius and energy that the Big Four brought to the vast project, the work would never have been completed in that time.

For the dedication ceremonies, five hundred people gathered that May day at Promontory to witness the tying-together of the two rail lines. Two steaming locomotives sat facing one another on the track, only a few feet apart. A golden spike would be driven into a simulated final section of track, which was actually a laurelwood tie, and unite the two railroads.

A telegraph wire was rigged to the silver hammer that Leland Stanford would wield to drive the spike. When the spike was driven, a click would be heard transcontinentally, and pandemonium would break loose. It almost didn't, Robert observed from the top of a Central Pacific railroad car behind one of the locomotives. In grandstanding, Stanford missed the spike with the hammer and no click registered. But a quick-thinking telegraph operator saved the day; he depressed his key and the sound signaling the completed railroad was heard across America, if not in Promontory.

That night Robert attended a sumptuous dinner given in a string of private railroad cars by the Big Four and their guests. Robert was pleased to be among those so honored, although he didn't feel he deserved any special consideration for his contribution.

The man to be honored was the deceased Ted Judah, whose dream gave birth to the idea. It was to his memory that Robert raised his glass in silent toast, and to the Chinese and others who died so that the railroad might be.

As he journeyed back to San Francisco over the scenic Sierra route, he thought of how little money had come to mean to him. He acquired it so easily, he spent it the same way; it was only the joy of achievement that held any meaning. Something was missing from his life. Even Emily, good companion and lover that she was, couldn't fill the void. He'd hoped Reb would somehow bring the ingredient of spice to his life, but it hadn't happened yet.

Whatever he lacked he might never find. He was prepared to accept this, but Robert was saddened that he couldn't order what he wanted. He had time, money, intelligence; he could be far more than he wanted to be. But he didn't *want* to be anything; maybe that was the problem.

Let Stanford make speeches and kiss babies; let Crocker be a financial wizard; let Huntington wallow in his empire, and "Uncle" Mark Hopkins indulge his lust for penury. All Robert wanted was peace of mind; and he hadn't found it.

While the transcontinental roadbed was being laid between Sacramento and Utah, a short line was quickly pushed through from San Francisco to San Jose in 1864.

A year earlier the San Francisco and Oakland Company built a spur rail line from central Oakland to the Bay ferry wharf. This meant competition for El Dorado's western Bay connections. However, because the area's population was growing rapidly, this latest development didn't phase Ethan and Robert at all. In any case, they had always welcomed competition, for it always seemed to invigorate their own business.

The Big Four determined that San Francisco would be the center for a Bay region network of railroads. They linked Sacramento to San Jose; they built another rail branch to Oakland, Alameda and the East Bay waterfront. They took over control of a line between Sacramento and Vallejo, extending this to Benecia. There they opened a ferry service to carry their trains across Suisun Bay, introducing the world's largest ferry boat for this purpose. Eventually they were able to buy the San Francisco–San Jose rail line, completing their conquest of San Francisco and the Bay cities.

Robert and Ethan had foreseen the Bay's ultimate rail encompassment. They were constantly correcting their shipping routes to touch at all rail terminals. By such strategy they not only increased their commerce but did so without having to expand their facilities.

By the time the transcontinental railroad was steaming daily to the shores of San Francisco Bay, Robert had turned forty-six, Ethan was over fifty, and Flora was in her forties. Also by this time Robert had known Emily King for close to fifteen years. Emily was in her mid-thirties.

In the early days of the affair between Robert and Emily, while Reb was still a small boy, they were devoted, passionate lovers, meeting and making love frequently at the Hotel Splendide. There were many times during these years when Robert would have gladly married his mistress. Emily, however, was persistently ring-shy, unlike most women Robert knew who were only too eager to marry. Emily had one simple explanation, which was all he got from her. She said, "I like our situation just the way it is. Let's not change it. We both have our freedom, and that's precious."

"We could have a family if we married," Robert suggested, but Emily rejected this. "I've tried hard *not* to have children," she said, "and I don't give a damn how that sounds, I'm just not the type to be a mother. Anyway, you don't need more children. You have Reb."

Emily was very good with Reb, she always had been; and Robert wouldn't have minded another child or two with Emily. But at forty-six that need was past. He'd put on some weight, though not a lot; his hair was turning an attractive blend of silver-grey. He was no longer prey to the torrid emotions that belonged to younger men. He and Emily got on perfectly the way they were; she was still a handsome woman and a considerate lover. No man could ask for more. But he worried that he couldn't persuade Emily to go to the altar. Not that he thought she ever strayed. Nor did he restrict her comings and goings or pry into her personal relationships with friends, which was probably what kept their affair going.

To ensure privacy for their trysts as Reb began to grow up, Robert built himself a small cottage out in Noe Valley, near the upper western reaches of Market street. Here he and Emily could spend weekends together, relaxed and at ease, away from the pressures of their business lives. Sometime they would invite Ethan and Flora out for noonday dinners, which Emily usually cooked. Or occasionally the women would remain at the cottage while the two men sailed out on the Bay in a small ketch they owned, to talk business and fish under the sunshine in windblown privacy.

From the beginning, Emily's modiste salon had been a grand success with San Francisco society. She loved the challenge of being San Francisco's most versatile couturiere and milliner. She worked to bring a definite chic to the city's loveliest women, or at least to those who could afford her prices. But her success was due to more than mere style; she had brought something peculiarly San Franciscan to her business.

It had all started shortly after she opened the salon. Custom was then only fair-to-middling, and while this kept her busy she wasn't making much money, and she got to speculating on what kind of exposure she needed to attract hordes of women to her establishment.

About this time the melodeons and saloons were all wide open and roaring with customers. From this milieu there came to the salon one day a famous entertainer. She requested a special black satin evening gown with a rhinestone-studded cape to match. The actress was Lola Montez, and she required the costume for a new act she would be introducing a few days hence.

The hurried request posed problems. Lola wanted twenty large sequined tarantulas to go with it, intending to shake them loose on the dance floor as she gyrated. Emily could do the job easily, but it would mean hours of late sewing so as not to interfere with current orders. Emily masked her nervousness as she took the redoubtable Lola's famous measurements, and went to work.

Two days later Lola returned for her first fitting, pleasantly surprised at Emily's superior workmanship and speed. While the fitting was progressing in a partially curtained alcove, a Mrs. Hannah Goodman entered the shop. Forty-ish, stout, plain to the point of homeliness, Mrs. Goodman was the wife of an executive at Ralston's Bank of California. The woman would never be chic, no matter how Emily tried, but the salon did its best for such women. This time Mrs. Goodman's order had been pushed aside to make way for Lola's costume. When Mrs. Goodman asked about her ensemble, Emily told her the truth: "Sorry, but we're behind on it. Since you said a few days one way or another didn't matter, I gave priority to this lady's ensemble."

Emily nodded toward Lola, who stood in the alcove by a work table, pinned into her black satin.

It wasn't difficult for Mrs. Goodman to recognize the client in black satin as the fiery Lola Montez, whose reputation was scandalous. Goodman wrinkled her nose in distaste. She tapped the point of her rolled silk parasol on the shop's brick floor impatiently.

"Lady?" she said loudly. "What lady? I see no *lady* in your shop, Miss King."

This was more than Lola Montez could tolerate. She stepped out of the alcove to confront Hannah Goodman, her hands on her hips, her famous eyes flashing.

"Who are you, may I ask?" she demanded of the matron.

"I am Mrs. Grover Goodman," said Hannah Goodman.

Emily saw her clientele melting away.

"You are a fat, ugly toad," Lola said with curled lip, raking Mrs. Goodman from head to toe, and smiling wickedly. "It would be obvious to a blindman that even a modiste as talented as Miss King would need a miracle to make you look as good as a flour sack. And even if you ordered what's being made for me, you'd look no better than a lump of coal swept out by the scullery maid."

Hannah Goodman gasped and turned beetred. No one in San Francisco society would have dared say such things.

"You, you—harlot!" Hannah Goodman shrieked at Lola, abandoning her hauteur. "How dare you even so much as speak to me!"

Emily saw herself being run out of town on a rail. However, Lola was prepared for Mrs. Goodman. She stepped quickly backwards, picked up from the work table the black silver-tipped whip that she often carried around town to ward off overzealous male admirers, and deftly snapped the tip of it at Mrs. Goodman's parasol. The parasol went flying out of the matron's hand and into the backroom where two young apprentices were working, causing them to burst into peals of delighted laughter.

"Now get out!" Lola snarled at Mrs. Goodman. "Get out before I whip that dress from your back and show you up for the fat grub you really are!"

One of the girls scrambled to retrieve Mrs. Goodman's parasol and presented it to her. Then the enraged matron, her cheeks flushed lobster pink, glared in hateful fury at Emily King, a glance that said Emily's professional days were numbered, and stomped out of the salon.

By late afternoon the incident was all over San Francisco. Somebody brought the news to Robert even before Emily could.

Emily was pleased that the straight-laced Mrs. Goodman had been put soundly in her place. "But what about my salon?" she said to Robert, almost in tears. "I'm ruined."

"Maybe not," Robert speculated, and he was right. The next day Emily had a call from her idol and namesake, the musical comedy star,

Emily Melville, whose subtle and sophisticated French style was replacing the more flamboyant reign of entertainers like Lola Montez.

"I need something fresh and saucy in aquamarine fashion," Melville explained. "I'll sketch it out for you, then you create the style."

"I don't originate styles, Miss Melville, but I'll do my best to make your sketch a reality," said Emily modestly. Melville smiled and patted Emily's hand.

"I'm sure you do excellent work, otherwise Lola Montez would not have defended you with her whip."

So whenever a new customer brought a fresh version of the whip scene to the salon, Emily smiled enigmatically and accepted the interpretation. She had received a thousand gold dollars in free publicity from the incident, and from Montez on, Emily's success was guaranteed. It was soon a common sight to see stuffy society matrons and actresses or even ladies of questionable virtue all rubbing elbows as they waited to order new clothes or have a fitting. The salon became so popular that no faction dared start a feud with another, or they might be denied Emily's skills.

Inadvertently, Emily was responsible for helping to create a more democratic society in San Francisco. She made it possible for any doe-eyed demimondaine to walk in off the street and expect to be treated as a lady, just as long as she behaved like one and could pay the high price of Emily's fashionable creations. Emily, as a matter of fact, was the first modiste in San Francisco to ask for and receive half the final price of a garment before she would so much as put scissors to fabric.

Men were still very much in the majority in San Francisco during the mid-1860s. There were many lawyers, judges, stock brokers, gamblers, merchants. They wore silk hats, Prince Albert coats, ruffled silk hats, fancy waistcoats and trousers fitted below the knee to reveal gleaming polished boots. And business, of course, was still the game to play.

While the transcontinental railroad was being built through the Sierra, the Comstock Lode, that fabulous flow of silver ore from the Nevada mines, was changing the face of California and making San Francisco the financial center of the West. In 1862 the Federal government and the Eastern banks deserted the gold standard for silver. William Ralston managed to convince San Francisco businessmen that they must stay on the gold standard.

"You can ship gold East," financier Ralston argued, "and exchange it for greenbacks." A gold dollar was worth two greenbacks each by the end of the Civil War, so the merchants and investors who followed Ralston's suggestion profited handsomely.

With the importance of silver, a new Gold Rush atmosphere engulfed San Francisco. Forty men joined to create the San Francisco Stock and Exchange Board. Robert Sanderson was one of the founders. The Bank of California opened, eventually developing the Comstock Lode, which investment produced riches for its founder, William Ralston. In fact, Ralston lent Bank of California money to the Big Four to complete the railroad across the Sierras, this on personal notes, assuming personal responsibility for the debts.

When the last spike was driven to complete the transcontinental railroad, a collapse in real estate prices occurred. Robert and Ethan had invested all their spare cash in property. If they had over-extended themselves as much as Ralston and some other businessmen had, they would have been wiped out. Fortunately, they were able to keep their sites leased and hold onto them, while Ralston was left with a lot of property south of Market that no one then wanted to develop.

William Ralston was a man who always took the long shot gamble, partly because he followed his instinct, partly because the odds to a deal excited him. But this time he had gone too far.

Robert and Ethan received a hurried summons from Ralston for a private conference and Robert went immediately. When he had needed financing for the original acreage that comprised the Sanderson ranch, Ralston had lent him the cash without so much as a single piece of paper to prove that the transaction existed. Robert paid back the money from another transaction within a year. But he never forgot Ralston's support and consideration at a needful time, so when he received the call from Ralston he couldn't refuse the summons. Ethan came along grudgingly, knowing that he couldn't fail Robert, even if he didn't approve of Ralston's eccentric business practices.

The two men found Ralston pacing his office,

pale and sweaty with panic, in a desperate situation calling for desperate action. Two other men walked in seconds later, named Harpending and Dore, both trusted Ralston colleagues known to Robert and Ethan.

Ralston sat the select company down, produced a bottle of whiskey, and spoke of his dilemma.

"As all four of you know, the bottom's dropped out of real estate, maybe out of San Francisco as well. We'll have to wait and see. Anyway, it's leaked out today that the Comstock Lode is exhausted. Not news to us, but the man in the street hasn't known this before. You're probably way ahead of me already, but I'd better state for the record that the Bank of California has sunk its everything in the Comstock Lode. We have good reason to believe that when the Comstock news becomes generally known there'll be a run on the bank tomorrow morning that could wipe us all out and cause San Francisco economy to collapse."

"What do you have in mind, Bill?" Harpending asked Ralston.

"The only scheme that will work," Ralston replied. "There are five tons of gold sitting in our bank vaults. Tomorrow there may be none, if there's a run on it."

"How do we protect it?" Robert said.

"I've just come from making arrangements for an exchange of gold with the United States Sub-Treasury for coined silver money."

"For God's sake, Bill," Ethan spoke up, "you can't cart gold through the town in broad daylight."

Ralston frowned at Ethan. "Exactly," he

agreed. "That's why I called the four of you together, all good, strong, reliable lads, to help me effect the exchange *tonight*."

"Under cover of darkness," Robert reflected, "that makes good sense."

"*Midnight* darkness," Ralston amended, "when few will be about. Our world's at stake," he glanced at each of the quartet individually. "What do you say? Are we going to save it?"

The four men solemnly agreed with Ralston that there was only one thing for it, and that was to effect the exchange. They met again at ten o'clock that night. Disguised as Chinese coolies, they pulled gold-heavy sledges through the streets in relays until the five tons of gold were transferred from Ralston's bank vaults to the Sub-Treasury. It was an exhausting and tedious job. By first light the work was done, and a weary, strained group under Ralston's supervision dragged their aching bodies home.

The public run on the Bank of California began with the first panicky crowd storming its portal at opening time that morning, just as Bill Ralston had predicted. But since the tellers were able to display inexhaustible mountains of silver coined money in plain sight for even the most skeptical to see, the panic subsided within an hour. The bank and the imperiled local economy were rescued, for the time being.

By 1870, the Comstock Lode was popularly considered mined out. Unobtrusively, however, some shrewd young miners who'd worked in the mines were quietly buying up stock in several of the properties.

Harpending came to Robert with a plan. He'd

worked in the Comstock and knew what was going on.

"I can help you, Bob, if you'll help me," said Harpending.

"What's the scheme?" Robert asked.

"I need some financing. How about you and Drew coming in on the deal?"

"Ethan won't. He's being conservative these days."

"Well, you, then?"

"What's in it for me?"

"Speculation, pure and simple."

"I don't think so." There were improvements Reb wanted to make in the ranch, and upkeep needed for the rental properties.

"Let me explain it to you. Mackay and Fair are two men who used to work in the mines. You wouldn't know them, but they've just formed an association with Jim Flood and Bill O'Brien who've been dabbling in mine stocks for years."

Robert, of course, knew Flood and O'Brien, saloon-keepers with a shrewd instinct for lucrative, short-term investments.

Harpending explained further what was happening.

"For less than one hundred thousand dollars, Flood and O'Brien have obtained control of the California and Consolidated Virginia mines."

"Do the properties show any promise?" Robert asked at once.

"Well, not so far."

"Then why invest in them?"

"Trust me," said Harpending. "There's a game afoot and we can be in on it."

"I'm not much for games. Sounds risky, unless there's something more substantial you haven't told me."

"Bob, take my word. Get some money together, as much as you can, and stand by. I'll go halvers with you on whatever you can scrape up. Whether we win or lose, I'll pay you twenty per cent on whatever you lend me. Fair enough?"

"Sounds reasonable," Robert said, and he agreed. But more than just reasonable, tricky. Robert got a flutter in his groin over the idea and decided that instead of following logic he'd follow instinct.

Harpending came back to Robert in three months' time. Meanwhile Robert had put together fifty thousand dollars, to be split between the two of them. Harpending signed a note with the details of the interest payment on which they had agreed. The stock purchased was five thousand shares from three mines.

A week later the discovery of a few veins of silver ore in Nevada's Comstock caused an absolute sensation on the San Francisco Stock Exchange, and the market boomed, especially in Consolidated Virginia and two other properties.

Harpending came to Robert with a smile of triumph. "Didn't I tell you?" he said. "Look what we've already made!"

"You knew something I didn't."

Harpending shrugged. "Me? I'm just an innocent babe in the woods, Bob. Want to sell now or hang on? We've already made a fortune."

"Let's hang on."

By the following week, Consolidated had

jumped from $100 a share to nearly $800, a phenomenal rise.

Harpending insisted on selling enough stock to pay Robert for his original loan, plus the twenty per cent interest rate. With the surging of the Comstock mines stock, San Francisco went stock-gambling crazy. No one talked of much else. Emily King spent as much time discussing stocks with her clients as high fashion. The names of such mines as the Kentucky, the Yellow Jacket, Crown Point, the Consolidated and the Ophir became household words. A feeling that inexhaustible riches lay under the Lode swept through the business houses of San Francisco.

Robert had a hard time thinking of himself as a millionaire, which he now was. He'd bought a small chunk of stock for Emily, which she watched rise meteorically and then cashed in for gold. Robert gave Reb a block of stock, but Reb soon exchanged it for farm equipment. Robert gave Flora some stock as a birthday present and its value increased fivefold in as many weeks. Ethan refused to accept any stock gift, angry that he'd stubbornly rejected Robert's initial suggestion to come in with him and Harpending.

The situation was to get even better. One day Montgomery street was shaken by the news that the two mines known everywhere as the Big Bonanza contained the richest vein of silver ore in the entire Comstock Lode. Flood and O'Brien, plus two additional speculators, Fair and Mackay, took the precaution of buying up nearly all the available stock just before the news of the Big Bonanza was made public. The remainder of the stock was cornered by Robert and Harpending through the latter's sources.

A war began between the newly rich Big Four and Bill Ralston's Bank of California, with the objective being the control of the immensely rich Comstock mines. As the battle between the tycoons and Ralston raged, the city went wild with speculation. The financial district's female brokers hawked stocks on street corners. Women in diamonds crowded the exchanges mornings, fresh from the half-world of saloons and melodeons, anxious to be in on the kill.

The dethronement of Ralston happened in 1875 and brought financial San Francisco down with it. The Nevada group was determined to break the Bank of California and open a rival bank. Ralston wanted control of the Ophir mine, valued at an improbable thirty-one million dollars.

Harpending came to Robert with bad news about the Ophir, whose stock they owned.

"We've got to sell it."

Robert had an instinctive fondness and pride concerning the Ophir; this time he wanted a full explanation from Harpending before he would sell.

Harpending told him, "It's worthless, that's why we have to sell. The mine's an empty hole, Bob. Ralston is overloaded as the single largest stockholder. If we don't get out we'll go down with the ship."

"My God, we'd better tell him."

"You do and you're as good as dead," Harpending advised.

"So what do we do?"

"We unload everything, if you want to keep your millionaire status, and I gather you do."

"All right," Robert agreed, and the two men quietly disengaged themselves from their stock; it took a week. Even Ralston's right hand man, William Sharon, was unloading his Ophir shares secretly, spreading them around.

In February a rumor hit San Francisco that the Big Bonanza was worthless. The stock market crashed and the holders of mine stocks were wiped out. It was said that the Bank of California was ready to close its doors, and that Bill Ralston was to blame for it all with his insane speculation. The new Bank of Nevada, backed by the Nevada Four, withdrew its deposits from San Francisco's largest banks so that it could open its own doors for business. These huge withdrawals sent all banks to the brink of ruin. In a panic, Ralston sold his holdings indiscriminately in order to raise money, but he was too late. By August the Bank of California was forced to close its doors.

Robert went to Ralston's house that night to tell him how sorry he was over the bank's failure, and to ease his conscience. He intended to make a confession to the fallen financier about his own pre-knowledge of the Ophir's worthlessness. His collusion with Harpending had been preying on his mind for some time.

The meeting never took place. Ralston sent out word to Robert that he was indisposed, so Robert went to Emily's to talk. Whenever he was low, or had a problem that weighed on his mind, he visited Emily in her apartment. In many ways Emily was the strongest person he had ever known, possessor of a steely will. She was also extremely stubborn.

Emily was getting rich. Not that the salon did that much for her purse, but from time to time Robert would drop small investment parcels in her lap and she always knew how to manage them, to turn them from stones into golden eggs. It would be safe to say, Robert reflected as he knocked on Emily's door, that she was or would soon be one of the wealthiest single women in San Francisco.

Glad to see him as always, Emily welcomed him into the apartment. She had recently redecorated the unit over the salon where she still lived, although she could have afforded to build a house on the Polk street side of Nob Hill had she wanted.

"I went to see Ralston," Robert said, and told her why as she served him a cognac.

"You let your conscience get in the way of your business intuition," she said, and when he asked what that meant she added, "You could be ten times richer than you are."

"I don't see any point in piling up money," he said irritably. "I didn't come to you for a lecture."

"My, my, aren't we edgy tonight?"

"Forgive me. I've been working too hard."

"You can say it another way. *We've* been working too hard. I'm not picking at you, darling, but it's high time we left this town. Its avarice is getting to us both. Reb has the right idea, living out of town."

"Leave here? Where would we go?" It hadn't occurred to Robert in recent years that he could possibly live anywhere else, that he'd even consider it.

"Personally there are lots of places I'd like to see," Emily went on. "The great European capitals, the Orient. I'm no longer young. I've no responsibilities if I want to sell the salon." She studied him for a moment, thinking he was one of the most distinguished men she'd ever seen. "No, not even you. You refuse to let me coddle you, you always have."

"I thought it was the other way around."

Emily laughed. "Anyway, back to changing our style. Ethan can run the steamship company. Your staff can handle things while you're gone. What's to prevent us from taking a trip?"

Really nothing, Robert knew. Reb was doing a superb job of managing the ranch, and he could easily oversee the San Francisco enterprises in Robert's absence. But he wasn't ready for a trip.

"I don't think I'd enjoy the discomforts of travel," he declared.

"My dear Robert, you're thinking of the days when you and Ethan came across the country by wagon during the Mexican War. That was a long time ago. There's a railroad now, just in case you've forgotten, and steamships, and luxury hotels the world over. We could visit exciting places, meet fascinating new people. Just think, we could take a whole year and go all around the world. I don't intend to stay put in this cesspool of commerce and debauchery forever, even if you do."

"Does that mean plans have already been made?" Robert asked uneasily. He didn't relish the idea of her going.

"Yes," she said, "in a way. Do you recall the incident between Lola Montez and Hannah Goodman?"

Robert smiled. "Who could forget it? It made you and your salon famous."

"Well, she came to see me yesterday. I guess her husband salvaged something from the Bank of California because she wants to buy the salon and go to work."

"Your business?" he gasped. "You'd sell it?"

"Possibly. She'll pay cash for the building *and* the good will. I named a steep price and she said yes."

"I'm amazed that you'd sell. My God, Hannah Goodman won't last a month."

"She just may," said Emily. "She's a shrewd old hen. She'll drop the chic and go in for good, sturdy Christian garments, the kind her church ladies can't find professionally made in this high-styled town. At the worst she'll break even."

Robert poured himself another cognac.

"So you're really serious about going away?"

"Yes, Robert. With or without you."

"Stay here. We'll get married."

Emily laughed lightly, fully prepared for his suggestion. "We're as good as married already, Robert, and where has it taken us? Two people, getting older, who see each other occasionally, for moral support and love, but who essentially lead separate lives. I've come to the conclusion that the Sanderson men, you and Reb, aren't the marrying kind."

"I just said I'll marry you."

"Thank you, Robert, but I'll have to think about the offer. And it may take me a while, perhaps as long as a trip around the world, say a year or two. When I come back I'll let you know."

Robert knew Emily well enough to predict that she wouldn't change her mind unless he changed his. They would remain cordial but the deadlock would exist.

"Since you've already made plans, when do you think you'll go?"

"A month from now, I think."

"But that's no time at all." He felt let down, betrayed. "It—it's too soon."

"That's what I thought when Hannah Goodman urged me to sell the salon. The years have rushed by without our enjoying them very much, without their being as important as they should be, so I thought, why not tie up everything neatly and quickly? Get away while the getting's good!"

"Emily, you know I've never had a dull moment in your company, not since the night we met at the Splendide."

"If you have you've never said so. Those were pleasant days. We could have better ones if you'd come along with me. A private compartment on the train to New York, a first-class suite on a ship to England. It's all booked."

"Dear Emily, I can't."

She regarded him with wistful grey eyes. "What you mean is, you can but you won't. I should have expected no more and no less."

"What will I do without you?" Robert mused aloud. Besides Ethan, Emily was his closest friend. He knew a wide range of important people, but they weren't his friends. He realized with a jolting awareness that if it weren't for Emily and Ethan, and Reb, he'd be a very lonely man.

"What you'll do without me," Emily said softly, "is going to be your problem. I can't help you there."

"I love you, Emily," he muttered, mouthing the words he had only told her a few times, long ago, with such direct meaning.

"I love you, too, Robert," Emily replied, "but there are times when that isn't enough—too little, too late. Now, drink up your cognac and come to bed."

"Do you really want to?"

"Of course. You're still attractive, and the very best . . . I trust you aren't bored with that yet, are you?"

"Not yet," Robert conceded.

That night their lovemaking was muted by the sober knowledge that they had made a break in the even continuity of their lives, and that nothing would ever be quite the same again between them. Emily was still a beautiful woman, Robert reflected as she fell asleep with her head on his shoulder. But she had never really been his. First, he had shared her with her rich patron from the East, and then with the salon. And come to think of it, the other women he had loved, Sarah and Jane, were more his in the mirror of memory than they had ever been in life. Emily King would soon join them in the past.

The next afternoon Bill Ralston put on his bathing suit and went down to the Bay near North Beach. It was his custom on summer days, before the fog drifted in through the Golden Gate, to take a swim in the Bay.

Witnesses said later that one minute they saw him enter the water and go splashing away from the shore, but when they looked up again he had disappeared. The sun was hot that day and the water was quite cold. Ralston may have gone out too far deliberately, his mind distraught by the collapse of his financial empire. Or he may simply have misjudged his distance from the shore, and in trying to swim back sustained a fatal heart attack.

In any case, he did not return alive from his swim. His body was found on the beach near Fort Point by fishermen the following morning, washed up by the high tide.

Ralston was the martyr, while the two who profited most heavily from the Ophir mine, Mills and Sharon, eventually reopened the Bank of California, now forced to play second lead to the Bank of Nevada, already the dominant force in the city.

An era was ended, Robert knew, with the death of Bill Ralston and the going of Emily. In a way, the two events were both funerals of similar finality. Robert went to the Ralston services and watched the men who had been made rich by Ralston's vision now patronize his memory. He left feeling melancholy and mortal. He knew he was making a mistake by not going with Emily on the trip—she would leave in less than three weeks and was now living at a hotel while the salon was being transferred to Hannah Goodman and her husband. Yet he couldn't adjust to the weightlessness and mobility that travel entailed. He might be a Golden Stater by adoption, but he was tied forever to the land he knew so well and loved so dearly.

He could accept his inability to rise above habit and good sense—never taking a capricious step, not able to chuck everything for a while and go away with Emily. It was his character, his view of the world, however narrow and restricted that might be.

Going home at midnight from Emily's apartment he breathed deeply of the cool salt breeze, spread his arms out to the night. His life was about to change, and he welcomed his fate, since he did not feel that he could control it.

A week before Emily's departure, Robert arranged a farewell party for her in a suite of offices he had recently taken in the Montgomery Block, the largest commercial building on the Pacific Coast when it was built. James King of William died in one of its rooms after being struck down by assassin James P. Casey in 1856 for venting his wrath on the city's corrupt politicians through his stringent newspaper editorials.

The party was to be intimate: Ethan and Flora, Reb, the two female assistants who had worked in Emily's salon for years, and Emily herself. The affair was supposed to be a surprise, but the news leaked to Emily through one of the assistants. She came to Robert in agitation.

"I don't want a party, Robert," Emily declared. "It's like that damned funeral for Ralston in a way. What makes you think that an expensive party with gifts for everyone, with champagne flowing and more waiters than guests will change anything between us?"

"It wasn't intended to," said Robert. "It was merely meant to be something pleasant to remember."

"I have other memories to carry with me. If you had some important announcement to make a change in plans, then I'd accept the idea of a party. But you haven't."

"No," said Robert, crestfallen, "I haven't. I just wanted to add a graceful note of good luck to your departure."

Emily wasn't to be placated. "My solitary exodus has enough of a burden on its shoulders already," Emily declared. "You can say goodbye to me at the Oakland Station, if you insist on sopping your conscience."

The final week of Emily's time in San Francisco brought Robert and Emily together for a quiet luncheon with Ethan and Flora. Reb came to town on an unexpected visit that changed his life and Robert's considerably, and from which event Emily blithely walked away.

With the new acreage Reb had secured from Doña Maria, the Sanderson ranch became the most productive of its kind on the upper San Francisco Peninsula. Its proximity to San Francisco and the railroad line between the city and San Jose made it a convenient and highly lucrative outlet for its high-quality, fresh-daily products: butter and eggs, milk, cheese and poultry.

Reb had continued to commit himself to the ranch's management, with regular trips into town to see Robert and to let off some steam in the saloons and restaurants that made San Francisco the most sophisticated and notorious city in the West. Reb's passion didn't run to theatre and classical music; he liked the raucous bawdiness of the dens and the flashy melodeons, and because of his exceptional good looks, his impeccable town wardrobe, and his ready cash, he found eager females wherever he went. He chose his beauties at random, sometimes from among the more adventurous daughters of the wealthy merchant class, or from the town's wide assortment of easy-going women to whom virtue was an impediment. Reb was selective in his choices, however. He wanted his women clean, healthy, fun-loving, and as unpossessive as he himself was. They had to be out for a good time and nothing more. He refused to go beyond sexual satisfaction and an evening or two with any of them, and he made this clear to one and all. However, in the process of enjoying himself he managed to break a heart now and then. But he didn't feel that this was his responsibility and accepted no blame.

Nor did Reb make any close male friends during his salad days. Like his father, he saw his position in life clearly. He was on earth to work and eventually to sire an heir who would continue the Sanderson li_e. Reb was intensely his own man and whatever confidences he tendered went exclusively to his father, who was his only true friend.

Reb found good books and the pursuit of general knowledge far more attractive and rewarding than close friends. Books never let you down. He didn't question this aspect of his character; it was simply the way he was. His San Francisco peers spent nearly all their spare time in dissipation that claimed Reb only on the infrequent evenings when he came into town to visit his father and call on certain suppliers. If there were a constant in Reb's life, it was the memory of his single meeting with Pilar Mendez. Although he was unable to define what he felt about her, she hadn't faded from his memory.

There were moments at the ranch when Reb sensed an emptiness in his life that no amount of reading or playing cards with some of the ranch hands seemed to fill, and sometimes he would think of Pilar, wishing he could see her. A few times he even entertained the fantasy that he was in love with her. He toyed vaguely with the idea of finding some way to communicate with her, but he followed it no further than the thought. The pressures of the ranch would always bring him back to his immediate responsibilities.

One day about a year after Pilar Mendez went south to Los Angeles, Ramon Garcia, Reb's Mexican foreman, brought news of her to him.

"The little *señorita*'s getting married," Raoul announced.

"Which one?"

"The Mendez girl, of course."

"Where'd you hear that?" Reb asked, immediately concerned.

"Oh, from one of the hands from the Rancho Los Arboles. I saw him on the road today. They're planning a big wedding down at the Mendez *hacienda* for next month."

"Who is she marrying?" Reb said.

"A man named Manuel Domingo from the south."

"What about him? Is he wealthy, young?"

Ramon shrugged his shoulders. "I didn't ask, *señor*."

"Well, why didn't you?" Reb demanded, realizing the strength of his interest.

Ramon blinked at him in surprise; Reb rarely raised his voice. "I can find out," he said.

"You do that. Today!"

That afternoon Ramon informed Reb that the wedding would take place in three weeks.

"Is my Spanish good enough to warrant me an invitation?" Reb asked. He'd been studying Spanish grammar recently, and while his accent would always be pure American, he was getting reasonably fluent; at least the Latin ranchhands understood him.

Ramon grinned at his boss. "Well, *señor*, your Spanish is probably good enough if you leave out the curses. But you don't have Spanish blood."

"What do you mean?" Reb asked, knowing the answer.

"I would think that Doña Maria will only invite the immediate family, *señor*, and a few close friends. It won't be a big open occasion, like a *fiesta*. Doña Maria is not well enough for that."

"I'm her neighbor. I should be included."

"It's not the same thing, *señor*. You are—"

"I know. A *gringo*."

Ramon spread out his hands to indicate that this was reason enough to be excluded from the guest list.

"Damn! I'm going to find out," Reb declared. What he really wanted was to see Pilar again,

and as soon as possible. "I'll go and see the old
lady."

"As you wish, *señor*. But I don't think you will
get very far. Doña Maria is a lady of high caste,
one of the last still alive here. That doesn't mean
much these days to Americans, but it's her life."

"Nevertheless, I shall pay her a visit," Reb
determined. He sent a rider that afternoon with
a polite note to Doña Maria, asking if he could
have an immediate audience with her about the
possibility of acquiring more land. He made no
mention of Pilar's return to Los Arboles or her
impending marriage, couching the note in such
formal and respectful terms that he thought the
old lady would respond positively. To secure
the visit, he said he was traveling down her way
on other business the next day and would drop
by late in the morning. He instructed the rider
to wait for an answer, and the ranch hand rode
back with one in the evening.

The following day Reb rode down to Los
Arboles. He was received by Doña Maria with
gracious cordiality, quite unlike his reception on
the last visit, and was offered the traditional
sherry. Pilar was not in evidence. During the
course of the conversation, Doña Maria said she
had thought about the land but that she'd decided against a sale.

"We will keep what is left, *señor*. My granddaughter is getting married next month. As you
may have heard."

"I didn't know," Reb said, wondering why he
found it necessary to lie.

Doña Maria nodded, studying his reaction.
"To Don Manuel Domingo, son of Don Felipé

Domingo of Los Angeles. Their illustrious family received one of the first Spanish land grants in California. We are very pleased with the liaison between Mendez and Domingo lines. There is not one drop of Mexican blood in the Domingo family," Doña Maria pointed out. "Not one. The engagement is short because we feel that the marriage will be long and fruitful."

Reb let that one pass with a nod as sagacious as one of the old lady's.

"Is Pilar still in Los Angeles?" he enquired casually, unable to restrain his curiosity any longer.

"She is here. She returned recently with Manuel and his mother."

"I'd very much like to meet the Domingos, *señora,*" Reb said, "and of course pay my respects to your granddaughter and offer her my sincere congratulations."

Doña Maria did not respond at once. She gazed at Reb critically for a moment with bright, hooded eyes. Perhaps she knew the gossip from San Francisco about his womanizing, his reputation for taking pleasure where he wished and never committing himself in marriage. But surely, with Domingo and his mother at the *hacienda,* she still couldn't possibly feel that he was any kind of threat to Pilar's virtue, he thought.

Doña Maria said, "The *señora* and my future son-in-law will be here with Pilar in a few minutes. Meanwhile, tell me about your *rancho.* I hear it is remarkable. If it's progressing as well as your Spanish, *señor,* then you have nothing to fear."

The Domingos and Pilar appeared as Reb was

concluding an account of his poultry-raising methods, to which Doña Maria had listened in attentive silence punctuated by a series of solemn nods. She had no interest in him, he saw, and would probably be relieved when he left after the meal. With her granddaughter betrothed, a great weight must have lifted from her shoulders, Reb imagined.

Señora Domingo was fat, squat and quite ugly, with a mole the size of a black widow spider on her chin. She was typical of the Spanish matrons Reb had seen since he was a child: fussy, fluttery, exploding into rapid-fire expostulations at the slightest provocation, looking through Americans as if they weren't even there.

Manual Domingo was tall, in his thirties, with straight black hair plastered to his skull, hawk-eyed, with a large aquiline nose under which sat a small, twitching moustache. His voice was high-pitched, the tone haughty. Domingo seemed to regard Reb as a necessary inconvenience imposed upon him by his hostess, but of no importance. He barely glanced at Reb as he offered the visitor a cold, limp hand to shake.

Pilar hadn't changed, Reb thought at first. She had a radiance about her that touched him deeply. But on closer inspection, he saw tightness around her eyes, and sensed pain. Her conversation was animated almost to the point of shrillness, as if she were trying to mask an almost overwhelming panic. While *Señora* Domingo made hen talk with *Doña* Maria, Pilar chattered away ceaselessly to Reb about trivia —her residence at the convent in Los Angeles, the long, wet winter of rain and floods just past,

a Santa Anna wind that had nearly suffocated
the southland. Not once did she refer to her
former meeting with Reb, nor did she include
Manuel in her conversation. Occasionally Manuel would interject a question of his own for Reb,
who answered him with polite brevity.

It was apparent to Reb that Pilar was already
desperately unhappy. Her pale, carefully controlled features did nothing to conceal her state
of mind from him. If only he could get her
alone for five minutes! He was determined to
find out what was really going on. But with
Domingo monitoring everything that went on
between them, he saw no chance of this.

All through dinner the same general mood
prevailed. The ceremony ended with brandy
and coffee in the living room.

Domingo offered Reb a Cuban cigar from a
silver case with a patronizing nonchalance. Reb
accepted the cigar and promptly pocketed it,
knowing that protocol required him to smoke
it on the spot, not later. Domingo's moustache
twitched at this, but he lit his own cigar, then
moved to the alcove by himself, where he could
watch Pilar as he puffed away in hostile silence.

Pilar continued her monologue to Reb in
louder tones, as if she were afraid that Manuel
might miss something. Gone was the charming,
spirited gamine he had met a year earlier, and
about whom he had dreamed so often. He felt
trapped and stifled, entirely superfluous in this
heavily Latin atmosphere that was already
charged with the excitement of the coming big
event to which he would not be privy, it
seemed. No one but *Doña* Maria had referred
overly to the approaching nuptials. Had the old

lady briefed the three to avoid any mention of weddings in front of the *gringo*?

At two o'clock Reb rose, thanked *Doña* Maria and Pilar for their hospitality. He bowed low to *Señora* Domingo, shook hands with Manuel Domingo, and left.

Intensely disturbed and frustrated, he walked slowly toward the corral. He was certain that Pilar was deeply unhappy; he read it in her eyes, voice and manner. What perhaps upset him even more was he now knew he loved her. Or else something was affecting him that went a whole lot deeper than the powerful lusts he'd experienced with the women he'd mounted all over San Francisco. Those casual attachments were only the logical culmination of sheer physical exuberance, and nothing to do with the heart. It pained him that Pilar was facing a life sentence. Her basic honesty and sweetness were doubtless still there, but sublimated to social commitment. She must hate the idea of marrying Domingo yet could not resist the magnet of ancient traditions that put concern for family security above the individual's wishes.

The whole idea of arranged marriage was repugnant to Reb. Raised in unorthodox freedom by Robert, who made his own rules but considered the dictums of the heart of prime significance, a credo he had handed down to his son, Reb was certain there must be a way out for Pilar. But what?

Riding away from the gleaming *hacienda*, he forced himself to look back over his shoulder, hoping that Pilar would be standing in the shade of the giant oak tree, her hand raised to bid him good bye. He saw no one.

He rode back to the ranch arguing with himself, thinking foolish, quixotic thoughts about *señoritas* in dire distress, and specifically about arranging Pilar's rescue and running away with her.

Where would he go? His entire life was centered on the land that adjoined the Mendez grant. If he took the initiative with Pilar—and even so, how did he get a personal message to her?—his life might not be worth a red cent, and Pilar would become an outcast. He would have to leave the ranch for good, and the ranch was his whole world. Running away would turn him into a displaced person, a wanderer, and he couldn't let that happen.

At his house on the ranch he got drunk all by himself, up half the night debating what he should do—mind his own business or go back for Pilar? Woozy and depressed, he fell asleep around four o'clock without getting any closer to a solution.

At first light he was awakened by a gentle tapping on the front door. Rubbing the whiskey's blur from his eyes, he went to answer in his night shirt, wondering who would knock on the front door at such an hour. Anyone connected with the ranch would automatically use the back door, which was always open, and tap on his bedroom door, but then, only in an emergency.

He opened the door to find Pilar standing there, her back against the rose-grey dawn sky. In buckskins, she looked much as she had that first time they met.

Wordlessly she stepped across the threshold

and flung herself into Reb's arms and began to sob uncontrollably.

Reb led her into the parlor and sat her down on the black horsehair sofa while he went for a dressing robe. He returned in a moment to find her shivering and hugging herself, a look of agonized fright on her face.

"Here"—he put out his hand—"let's go into the kitchen. I'll make a fire and some coffee. You're chilled from the ride."

She nodded, gave him her hand. He walked her into the big ranch kitchen and sat her down on a wooden chair by the circular oak table.

"What happened?" he said, stoking up the stove.

"Manuel," she murmured, unable to find the strength to speak out.

Reb didn't look at her. "What about him?"

"We had an argument last night. It began right after you left, when we went out for a ride."

She got up from the chair and paced the kitchen floor, hugging herself again. Finally she stopped in the middle of the kitchen and said, "I don't want to talk about it. The subject is unpleasant."

Reb caught her eyes. "You have to," he said firmly. "That's why you're here."

"I guess you're right," she agreed. "Well, we had an argument up in the hills. I rode home ahead of Manuel and locked myself in my room. Grandmama knocked for supper but I wouldn't come out. When I thought they'd all gone to bed I sneaked through the house to get something to eat. Manuel was waiting for me in the dark. He twisted my arm behind my back and forced me into the library. He locked the door and pushed me onto the couch. He accused me of being your lover. He called me filthy names and said he wouldn't marry me unless I could prove that I was still a—"

She broke off; the taboo was so strong she couldn't speak of it.

"That you are a virgin?" Reb finished her sentence.

"Yes," she almost whispered.

"So what did you do?"

"I told him I'd never sleep with him before marriage. I don't love him, I can't." She began to cry. "It was a nightmare dreamed up by his mother and my grandmother. When you came to the house long ago, my grandmother had everything already arranged. Seeing you gave her the reason to send me away to Los Angeles."

"What did Manuel do to you?"

"I don't want to talk about it."

"Tell me." He walked over to her and took her by the wrists. "Pilar, I have to know everything." If he intended to protect her, he had to have the whole story.

"He forced me down on the couch. He put one hand over my mouth and tried to—" She paused. "He tried to enter me. He was like a wild beast, I'd never seen him like that. My fear made me strong and I struggled free. I ran to the glass doors that lead into the patio. I knew they were usually unlocked. He didn't. I got away and ran out into the night, to the corral in the dark. I took my horse without saddling him and came here by the back trail."

She collapsed against his chest, sobbing. As

she had talked, Reb was trying to sort out his thoughts. If Pilar were in real trouble with her family—and he suspected that *Doña* Maria would take the whole business very seriously, believing whatever story Manuel might give her —then he himself was in a much worse mess. Manuel Domingo might come after him to defend the honor of his family name, believing that Reb and Pilar were lovers.

"You haven't said why you came to me."

Pilar wrenched away from him, rubbing the tears from her eyes. She sat down.

"Because I thought you would listen," she said in a melancholy, despairing voice. "I am so alone, so unhappy, Reb. You don't know what it is to be a Spanish woman in our society. A slave to be bartered off to the highest bidder. It has nothing to do with caring or love. Manuel Domingo is my second cousin, thus the lands in the south and our estate here will be joined together. It doesn't matter that our world is falling apart, that people like you begin to own it now. The tradition is strong and my grandmother believes in it. She has a kind heart, except where the family line is concerned. I can't go back, Reb."

She folded her hands, more composed, the tears gone. "The day you first came to the *hacienda* was the first time I had ever really talked with an American man."

"A *gringo?*"

"No," she protested, "an American. You listened, you were kind. We listened to each other. I was content. I wanted to see you again, but my grandmother saw more in my wish than I did, at the time. She means well, she cannot help being steeped in the old ways as most Latins are. She has never known anything else. The family forced her to marry into the Mendez clan and she expects me to marry as she wishes. My father didn't, and I have my mother's blood, good woman that she was." She crossed herself quickly. "My grandmother will not accept change. It isn't her world any longer, it's yours, and mine. Ours . . ."

"I think you know we're both in trouble, Pilar."

"I can go away," she said hurriedly. "I won't cause any trouble. I have a friend from my San Francisco convent days. She's a French girl who lives in Oakland. She might take me in."

"But that's not anything permanent," Reb pointed out.

"It would work for a while. But when her family hears the whole story they'd probably try to send me back to Los Arboles. The sisters at the convent will give me shelter, though not for long. I'd join the order as a novice, if I could, but if they found out about Manuel Domingo, they'd turn me over to him. Oh Reb, I don't know what to do. Tell me!"

"I'm not the wisest man on earth," he said, pouring them both cups of rich, steaming coffee. "Here, drink this. It'll relax you and warm you up."

She accepted the cup gratefully, glad for something to do with her hands.

"I wish I had a solution for you, Pilar. You'll have to make a decision soon, whatever it is."

She said softly, "I want to be with you."

"Do you know what you're saying?"

"I think so," she replied. "Yes, I do. If you feel the same way, then I am yours."

Reb hesitated. The moment was crucial, Pilar's declaration entirely too glib. He took a deep breath, knowing that whatever he said, one way or the other, it would alter his life.

"You've been in my thoughts almost every day since I first met you last year," Reb confessed. "But making a life with you, that's a different matter altogether."

"I know that, Reb. Tell me what I should do."

"If we became lovers we'd have to get married. You know that."

"Why?" she said, almost defiantly. "I'm no child."

"My God, Pilar, use your head. Your family would come after me with bullets otherwise. Even if we got married, that might start a vendetta."

"You are making a debate out of it," said Pilar. "I am going. You don't want me here."

Reb decided that this was probably the strangest conversation he had ever pursued with a woman. He didn't know whether to shout for joy that she had run to him and confessed her feelings, or do what his common sense dictated —tell her to get out of his house, go back to her stupid fiancé, make the best of a dull life; she was really no concern of his. Besides, everybody had to put up with something they detested in life. Why should she be any exception? He'd never even had a mother he could remember.

But the inescapable point was, Pilar had made herself his concern by the simple act of coming to him. This fact was irrevocable. And once he'd slept with her, taken her virginity, married her, in whichever order, she'd be an outcast to the Spanish people in this area, no better than a common whore, his responsibility forever. At this moment his freedom looked like the most precious jewel on earth. He wasn't at all certain he wanted to exchange it for Pilar, who might or might not be as pure as she indicated, playing some game of her own. Manuel may have had her already, she might have even slept with others.

"Honestly, Pilar, this isn't a trick, is it?"

She drew back in genuine shock. "Am I a virgin, do you mean?"

"Well, are you?"

"Reb, I have never been with a man."

"All right," he said briskly, "I'll accept that. We'll go to San Francisco right away. At least, you will. You can't stay here. Domingo may come looking for you with blood in his eye. At least in the city we can hide you until we decide what to do."

"I don't want to go to San Francisco. I want to stay here with you."

"We'll both go," he said, thinking he must be an idiot. He reminded her, "It's still not too late to go back to Los Arboles. You could say you couldn't sleep, you went up into the hills early to think things out."

Pilar shook her head vigorously. "That wouldn't work. Manuel has washed his hands of me. So will grandmama."

"You have the choice of going back."

"There is no choice, Reb, If I hadn't met you last year I could have gone through with marriage to Manuel. My life was already arranged.

then. My grandmother sent me south because of you, so we couldn't become friends." She raised her small, perfect chin and stared up at him with dark, burning eyes.

"I love you, Reb." Her words defined her expression. "I have loved you since I first saw you." She stood up and came to him. "Please don't force me to return to Los Arboles, or go someplace else. My life is over at home or I'd not have come to you."

Even with her statement Reb felt a sudden reluctance to commit himself. He said gently, "I know what you're going through, but you should think about returning home. I like you, Pilar, I admire you. I'm not sure that I—" He simply couldn't utter the words she had found so easy.

"I'll never go back to grandmama's," she vowed. "I'll die first! You don't have to marry me, I'm not begging. You don't even have to touch me. I'll go to the convent, I'll find some way to live. God will take care of me."

Reb did love her. It was beyond all reason and good sense, but there it was. He couldn't reject her.

"Dear Pilar," he said with a sigh, and she accepted his open arms. He kissed her tenderly; she leaned against him, tiny and fragile, so touchingly sweet in her boyish buckskins. Reb was overwhelmed by a fierce desire to protect her from life, to encompass her in a cocoon of love. Yes, he could marry her, he believed, and even find a certain peace and warmth. He thought of the delicate body beneath her clothes as he held her. His groin stirred. Ignoring the insistent signal, he stepped away and took her by the shoulders.

"There now," he said calmly, "I have to get dressed if I'm to take you to San Francisco."

"No, it is I who must get undressed so we can be together," Pilar insisted. "I want your arms around me."

Reb smiled and shook his head. "Not yet. There'll be plenty of time for that later." He left her with a second cup of coffee and went to dress.

Ramon drove them to the station; they caught the early train to San Francisco. Reb gave Ramon strict parting instructions not to discuss Pilar's arrival at the ranch with anyone. None of the hands had seen them depart. Ramon promised he would maintain silence; he was loyal and dependable, and besides, he was glad to see Reb with the girl.

In the city Reb took Pilar in a carriage to Emily King's hotel suite. A rather surprised Emily greeted them in her sitting room, crowded with suitcases and a steamer trunk being packed for her trip.

"This is my neighbor, Pilar Mendez," Reb explained. "From the Los Arboles *rancho;* you know of it. Her grandmother sold us all our land."

Reb had never mentioned Pilar to Emily. She noted Pilar's buckskins, thinking how beautiful the girl looked in her boyish outfit.

"I thought you could find Pilar some garment," Reb said. "Something suitable, and right away, if it won't be too much trouble. She can't go about town in what she has on."

Emily agreed. "We'll find something. But on

you, my dear, that outfit's charming. If I still had my salon I might be tempted to adapt it for younger women. It would be ideal for the perfect figure, which you certainly have."

"It was all I could bring with me," said Pilar, unaware that Emily had paid her a sincere compliment.

"Could I leave Pilar with you?" Reb asked. "I have to arrange a suite for her here and go see my father."

"Of course, darling. Have you eaten?" Emily asked Pilar, and the girl shook her head.

"Good! Then you'll have a bite with me and we'll discuss some proper clothes for you."

Reb was gone a couple of hours. As soon as Emily had ordered a light breakfast for two, she sent off a messenger with a note to her former chief assistant at the salon to bring a street ensemble for Pilar, one that a customer Pilar's size hadn't picked up before she left town. Pilar remained moodily silent as Emily discussed shoes, gloves and undergarments with her. Finally Emily could contain her curiosity no longer. Why hadn't Reb ever talked of this lovely creature? But then, he hadn't brought around any young women for Emily's inspection, nor his father's. Which could mean only one thing, Emily decided—Reb was deadly serious about this exotic Latin flower who seemed intelligent as well as being a young beauty. Either a love affair was already in progress, if she knew Reb, or soon to begin. She was determined to find out more.

"Have you and Reb been friends for long, my dear?" Emily asked, attempting to sound casual.

"About a year," Pilar replied. "We met when Reb came to Los Arboles to talk with my grandmother about buying the new land."

"I don't mean to be curious but I'm an old friend of Reb's, sort of like his aunt, you might say. I've known him since he was a small boy."

"I know. You're Mr. Sanderson's friend."

"Yes. We go back a long time," said Emily, determining not to let the conversation slip away from her.

"But you are leaving San Francisco, Reb said."

"Oh, not forever. I'm taking a trip to Europe, maybe elsewhere. I haven't decided. But I'll be back. This has been my home for many years."

"Then I don't understand why you are leaving your home, if you like it."

This wasn't the way Emily had intended their talk to go. This little beauty might not be sophisticated yet, but she'd have all the answers one day, and soon.

"Tell me," Emily pursued, "what do you intend to do in San Francisco?"

A shadow passed across the young woman's exquisite features, Emily was quick to note.

"That depends on Reb," said Pilar.

"And why is that?" Emily persisted.

"I left Los Arboles early this morning and came to Reb's house. It was my own decision and I cannot go back. I am running away from my fiancé, Manuel Domingo. I will never marry him, he is a hateful man. That means I must also run away from my family, my grandmother. She will no longer recognize me as her grandchild from this day on."

"Incredible," Emily murmured, "to think that kind of thing still exists."

"It's the way we are," Pilar said. "Wishing things were different won't change our way of life. Not in a day anyway."

"I see now why you say your future depends on Reb. Forgive me, my dear, but do you want to marry him?"

"Very much, yes. I love him."

"And how does Reb feel?" Emily considered this a fair question, even if it was a bit snoopy, since she was no more able to read Reb's thoughts than she was to probe with much success behind Robert's handsome, mature and amiable façade. The Sandersons did not wear their emotions on their sleeves.

"Reb *says* he will marry me. If he changes his mind, then I will have to find another way."

"My dear Pilar," Emily said in her most advisory tone, "a word from someone who's had a wealth of experience, for what it's worth. You have three choices. Marriage is the most binding and conventional, certainly not the easiest path to take. Or you could live with Reb as his mistress. San Francisco society has two distinct sides. You can exist as you like: love in freedom beyond custom, or by the law. If you become Reb's mistress, this means you can walk away from the arrangement any time it fails to please you. Now that's a feeling with a lot of power behind it, if you handle it discreetly. But you're also walking on quicksand. Reb could leave you stranded without warning. The third choice is to use what education you have to get yourself a job of some kind, so you'll be eating while you look around and size up the world, see where you really want to go . . . Oh yes, there is a fourth alternative, but it's far too grim for you to consider."

"To be a common prostitute, is that what you mean?"

Emily nodded; the girl was astute, surprising in one so obviously inexperienced. "Passing indiscriminately from one man to another, from youth and beauty to something sordid and depressing, an outcast."

"I would scrub floors first," Pilar said proudly. "I won't be Reb's slave or anyone's. I shan't put myself up for sale in the marketplace. If Reb doesn't want to marry me, I'll go my way. He will never see or hear of me again. There is such a thing as pride. I was raised to respect it, to depend on it. Just because I ran away from Manuel Domingo doesn't mean that I've lost it."

"You have spunk, my dear," Emily declared in admiration. What on earth could she tell Pilar to give her substantial support at such a climactic time in her life? The girl seemed quite able to work things out for herself.

Pilar said, "I write a firm, clear hand, I am as fluent in English as in Spanish. I can act as a translator for business. I'm also good at accounts. Maybe I can find a job . . ." She seemed suddenly to wilt, her eyes misted. "Something must happen," she moaned softly. "I don't know what to do."

"Something will," Emily assured her, thinking it was time she brought her own findings to bear on the situation. "You must listen to what I say, Pilar. I met Robert Sanderson many years ago when I was young and frivolous and desirable. A lot of men liked me, and I mean a *lot*. I was a favorite in San Francisco and could have married well before Robert came along. But I had a particular friend at the time I met Robert, a rich man from the East Coast who supported me. I was his, although we didn't live together. Do you understand me?"

"Yes. You were his mistress."

"I'm telling you something I've never told Reb's father. I deeply loved my friend from the East. So when Robert suggested a permanent union, a marriage, I balked. My friend was married with a family, but I kept hoping against hope that this would change and he'd be free to marry me. It was a foolish dream, really. Robert and I were lovers. He was good for me and to me. I dallied with both men. When my friend went back East, never to return, Robert renewed his plea to get married. But I was enjoying life as it was. I was independent, we had a good casual arrangement, I was content. All I've missed is not having children, a family."

Emily paused reflectively as she poured herself more coffee. It all sounded very complex and rather cheap the way she was telling it, but of course it wasn't. She wished she could get across to Pilar that if you couldn't have precisely what you wanted out of life, you settled for the next best thing, protecting your heart always, just as you protected your physical self.

Pilar read Emily's discomfort. "If it's painful for you, don't tell me anymore," she said.

"That's all right, it's necessary," Emily insisted. "What I'm leading up to is the Sandersons, both of them. They're singular men. Reb is much like his father. Both find it difficult to say what's in their hearts. They're good men, I don't mean to imply otherwise," Emily hastened to emphasize, "but they're much concerned with themselves. Not selfish. Preoccupied is a better definition. Business is their god, women their release. They exact a heavy price, but they're generous."

"Reb is a good man," Pilar interjected. "At least as I know him."

"Don't do as I did, Pilar. I wasted too many years. Marry Reb. For you that's the only way. Marry him while he still feels a sense of responsiblity for you. Once that passes and he takes you for granted, you're on your own."

"I won't force Reb to marry me," said Pilar. "I wouldn't feel right about it."

"Don't be a fool," Emily countered sharply. "That's sheer nonsense. It's a rough world out there, Pilar. Believe me, I know. And you haven't been up against it. I have since I was sixteen, younger than you are. Marriage can sometimes be a ghastly bore, and a headache, but in a world where men still make the rules it's a secure legal refuge."

"You make it sound like a business."

"It's a corporation," said Emily, "with a hard-to-break charter. We Americans look at it differently from you Spanish, especially we women. We set our sights independently of family and it's open season on any eligible man, all are fair game for the hunters. I grant you, your way may be easier for the woman, but ours is more exciting."

"I love Reb," Pilar said firmly. "He's all I need."

"Then you'd better get him while you can," said Emily, "and learn to live with your decision. If it turns out to be something besides

love, at least a friendly husband is the true
binding in a woman's life." Emily laughed. "Oh
yes, I'm the wise one all right. You're listening
to a woman who was foolish enough to bypass
marriage when she should have grabbed at it.
Now, well, that's another story and not very interesting."

"I'll do what Reb wants," Pilar said.

"Then it's up to us to see that Reb wants what
you want. Leave it to me."

A knock on the door announced the arrival
of Emily's former assistant with a liveryman
weighted down with garments and boxes.

Within the hour Pilar was bathed, coiffed and
attired in a beautiful beige moiré-silk suit. There
was a hat to match the floor-length outfit, smart
kid gloves, a handsome purse, button shoes.
Dressed in the latest Paris fashion, Pilar looked
as richly demure as a new bride embarking on
her honeymoon. The subtle make-up Emily skillfully applied to Pilar's face accentuated her
gamine charm.

"This ought to do it," said Emily, a few moments before there was a knock on the door,
announcing the arrival of Reb with Robert in
tow, much to Emily's delighted surprise.

"Well, father," Reb said proudly, his arm
around Pilar's waist, "here she is. What do you
think of her?"

Robert was dazzled; he made no attempt to
conceal his enthusiasm. He'd never seen a more
distinctive Spanish woman, nor one as slender
with such creamy ivory skin, such luminous dark
eyes, such a glistening crown of black hair. Her
perfect nose, generous rosy lips and soft low
voice immediately enchanted him. Robert could

hardly blame Reb for his interest in Pilar, and if Reb hadn't fallen in love with her, he was less of a man than Robert thought he was.

Emily noted Robert's interest with mixed feelings. On the one hand she was pleased at his positive response; on the other she was a bit saddened. Never in all their time together had she received that same look, nor had he showered such fervor on her that he now lavished upon Pilar. She speculated that if Reb weren't in the picture what might Robert's ultimate intentions toward such a fresh young creature be. Robert had reached that time in life when young women began to hold a fatal fascination. But good God, she decided, she was being outrageous.

"Come on, father," Reb urged. "Don't just stand there, say something."

"All I can say is, I admire your taste," Robert said with sober sincerity. "You're to be congratulated."

"I thought you'd say that," Reb said, pleased.

Reb's choice of a bride was his own, so long as he was in love, Robert had already told Reb. He wanted his son to make a salutary choice that he wouldn't ever regret. Reb had a free hand to make his own future. Robert would only interfere if he thought Reb was headed for a major disaster—obviously not the case here.

If Reb cared enough for Pilar to marry her, then Reb's freewheeling career with women had paid off in pure gold. On the pragmatic side, he worried about Doña Maria, and the fact that the girl would now be disinherited. Having broken the rigid family mold, she would be excluded from her grandmother's will.

Actually, this part made no difference to Robert. He was rich enough to buy the Mendez estate, or most of it, for cash on the line. If it ever came up for sale, which was doubtful, he'd buy it at once for Reb and Pilar. The main thing about these two youngsters was that with love there would be fine children. It pleased Robert that good Spanish blood would mix with solid Virginia stock, and that sooner or later he'd have a grandson.

"Will I hear wedding bells before I leave?" Emily asked pointedly.

"Then you approve?" Robert smiled at her.

"Of course I do. But they'd better ring out soon. I'm leaving in three days."

"My God, so you are!" Robert realized.

"I'm ahead of all of you," Reb said, producing a ring box of white satin which he presented solemnly to Pilar. The gesture reminded Robert of another such occasion with Jane, long ago in Sacramento.

Pilar opened the box slowly. Nestled inside on white satin was a blazing three-karat diamond in a simple prong setting. Reb took the ring from the box and placed it on Pilar's ring finger, then kissed her lightly.

"That does it," Robert observed. "A perfect ceremony for a serious event."

"How short is the engagement?" asked Emily.

"The wedding can be at my house tomorrow afternoon," said Robert, turning to Pilar and Reb. "Is that too short notice?"

Emily interrupted by clapping her hands together. "Perfect," she cried. "I'll find the wedding dress."

"Then it's all set up," said Robert.

Emily was content. It certainly hadn't taken Reb as long as she'd expected for him to make up his mind, but she had to bless the propitious circumstances for this. Reb had probably realized that if he didn't make a quick decision Pilar might slip through his fingers.

"I shall be matron of honor in my new canary silk," Emily announced.

Not to be outdone Robert announced, "I'll give the bride away in my new evening suit."

He said this with a sense of fun that Emily hadn't seen in his eyes for years. Why hadn't Robert been able to make up *his* mind at the appropriate time, as Reb had? But that wasn't fair, Emily realized; it was she who put contingency clauses into their relationship. She could at least admit that privately.

"Let's ask Flora and Ethan to be witnesses," Reb said, and that concluded the immediate details.

Emily rang for champagne, and all four joined together in a joyful toast to a joyous betrothal, albeit a short one.

That night Reb had dinner with Pilar, Emily and Robert at a downtown restaurant. Reb stayed with his father, while Pilar slept in a hotel suite down the hall from Emily, totally exhausted from all that had happened to her: the flight from Los Arboles, being plunged into San Francisco and marriage all in the same day. All she had known of San Francisco before this was what her inexperienced school chums had told her at the convent.

The wedding took place at three the following afternoon. Robert's dark Victorian living room was considerably brightened by banks of bright spring flowers.

Emily brought Pilar to the house in a charmingly simple gown of white Spanish lace over white satin. Two of the salon's seamstresses had sat up all night making it.

The ceremony was presided over by an elderly judge, a friend of Robert's. Flora and Emily shed tears. They would have preferred a church wedding, which both Reb and Pilar had elected to circumvent. Reb wasn't at all religious, and Pilar had no taste for a Catholic ceremony, under the circumstances.

The first night of the honeymoon was spent in the Oriental Hotel suite in downtown San Francisco. The pair retired late after a supper given by Emily, at which she proceeded to get quite mellow on wine and almost changed her mind about going away on her trip.

At one point she whispered to Robert, "If I hadn't sold the salon to Hannah Goodman, I might stay on, open another and give the old battle-ax some competition."

"Why didn't you think of that sooner?" Robert said. "Then we could have had a double ceremony."

Emily said, "No, my dear, things are as they are, and God knows why, I don't." She refused an invitation to go to Robert's house that night. Instead she went up to her hotel suite and had a good cry, upbraiding herself for having the perverse balkiness of a mountain mule.

In their luxurious suite at the Oriental Hotel, Reb and Pilar consummated their marriage.

Reb was prepared to be gentle and tender

with Pilar, to go along with her anticipated reluctance, and do no more than hold her all night in his arms, if that was what she wanted.

He lay in bed waiting for her to join him, his heart thumping loudly. This was the first time he had been worried about his performance since he'd lost his virginity. He wanted more than anything else in the world to please Pilar, to make her truly happy. He knew that the success of their marriage might very well depend upon his performance, and he was determined to offer his best.

Pilar was a long time in the bath and dressing room. When she finally emerged she was wearing a provocative semi-transparent nightgown that Emily had given her. She approached the bed modestly, her breasts visible through the sheer fabric of the nightgown.

She dropped the nightgown at the side of the bed and climbed in next to him, her hands cool and trembling. Reb turned and cradled her in his arms. Soon her trembling stopped and she relaxed against him. They remained like that for several minutes. Reb was waiting for some signal to make the first move. When he received none he began to stroke her arms, he ran his fingers over her nipples and breasts, he caressed her soft belly.

Suddenly, as he touched the mound of her sex, her timidity vanished and she came alive. He was unprepared for her passionate aggressiveness; he had usually set the pace in his lovemaking.

Pilar rolled over on top of him, then again on her back with his weight covering her. She reached down, took hold of him and guided him into her, moist and relaxed, pulling his buttocks toward her, emitting a sharp, guttural cry as he penetrated her as gently as he could, but barely able to restrain himself.

Slowly, with gathering rhythm, Pilar's body began to match his stroke for stroke. In too short a time Reb rose to a searing, devastating climax, spending himself in an uncontrollable frenzy of joy. Usually he could prolong his pleasure indefinitely, but Pilar's body had a will of its own; she had set the pace and he was forced to follow.

Exhausted, he remained in Pilar, kissing her softly, while her hands played up and down his back.

After a few minutes he started to withdraw, but she held him in position, whispering, "Was I all right?"

"You were magnificent, darling. You shamed me."

Satisfied, she maneuvered herself from under him and got up to make her ablutions. He noticed then in the dim light from the foyer lamp the thin trickle of blood on her leg and knew for certain she was a virgin. Had she been lying would he have cared? Or was that almost as unimportant as promising eternal sexual fidelity? They loved one another, that was what really mattered. The rest would take care of itself.

They made love again within the hour. This time Reb concentrated on Pilar and raised them simultaneously to a shattering mutual climax. The glorious, arcing rainbow of their orgasms was the most satisfying sexual moment of his life. Afterwards he lay limply against the pillow, Pilar's head on his chest, knowing that he would never be able to duplicate this perfect, luminous moment of love again. He hoped that its essence would remain with him through the thin times they might have to remind him how lovely Pilar was, and how much she meant to him.

Yés, he believed that he really loved her, he had no regrets about the marriage. He could continue to love her deeply and enduringly. This must be what the poets wrote about, an object created by two people, ascending in light and glory to the heavens, eternal.

"Were you satisfied?" Pilar asked softly before he fell asleep. "Are you sorry you married me?"

"Sweetheart, I'm only sorry we didn't run away together the first day I met you. We wasted a whole year apart."

"We need never waste another moment," said Pilar. "I want a son for us, right away. Will you make one?"

Reb laughed. "Give me time, darling, and we'll have a dozen brats."

"I said *one* son. A boy, then a girl. That is all."

"You know what you want, don't you?"

"I don't know *you* yet, Reb. I want to."

"My father says the best thing about a good marriage is the element of mystery between both parties. He thinks there should always be secrets you don't reveal, as well as understanding. You know something, you anticipate nothing. We'll have our secrets, won't we?"

"You may have yours," Pilar teased. "I shall have to think about my own! Goodnight, my darling."

She kissed him, then turned and fitted her trim buttocks against his loins and fell promptly asleep while she was thinking that if the rest of marriage could be as easy and enjoyable as sex it would be heaven on earth. It wouldn't be, of course, but she was glad to experience marriage while she was still young. She was only eighteen.

The following morning Reb lingered over breakfast with Pilar in their suite, reluctant to go to his father's offices where he was due for a business conference at eleven. It was time, Robert had told Reb, to hire a reliable manager for the ranch so that Reb would have more time for his new wife.

"I hate to let you go," said Pilar.

"I promise to be back at one to take you out to lunch," Reb told her. "So make yourself even more beautiful than you already are."

"I'll go talk with Emily. If anybody has beauty secrets, it's Emily."

Reb kissed Pilar good-bye and walked down the long corridor, thinking that this was the finest morning of his life. He stepped out of the hotel lobby into the bright sunshine of a typically breezy San Francisco spring day. The sky was a cloudless blue, the air clear and sparkling. He had every reason on earth to be thankful he was alive, he reflected, and hailed a horse cab.

He was about to step into the cab when he heard someone call out his name. He turned and saw a man he couldn't place at once walking toward him, not ten paces away, The man was dressed in severe black clothes and a wide-brimmed black hat and he was raising his arm in Reb's direction. It wasn't until the man's arm was horizontal that Reb saw the object he was holding. Then the whole picture came into focus. The man was none other than Manuel Domingo, Pilar's jilted fiancé, and the object in his hand was a pistol.

As Reb moved back against the cab he saw an orange flame spurt from the weapon's muzzle. Then he heard the explosion and felt a vicious thump near his right shoulder as the bullet plowed into him, knocking him down, smashing his head against the cobblestones.

Reb regained consciousness on a couch in the hotel manager's office where a pair of employees had brought him. Pilar was bent above him weeping; a white-faced Emily stood protectively beside her. A doctor hovered at Reb's shoulder, staunching the flow of blood.

"What happened?" Reb asked in a faint, dazed voice, unable to make any rational sense of the incident.

"You were shot," said Emily.

"By Manuel Domingo," Pilar added.

"It's all right, darling," Emily said. "They have the bastard in jail. He wanted to get both of you. You first, Pilar next."

Reb glanced at Pilar and managed a weak smile. "Thank God he didn't get to you."

The doctor moved the women back so that he could talk to Reb.

"You're going to be all right, son. The wound's superficial, the bullet didn't break any bones. Went right through the fleshy part between your upper arm and rib cage, missing the shoulder blade. You're lucky. Just a few minutes more and you'll be all right. Got to do some cleansing here, so brace yourself."

Pilar stepped close and took Reb's hand,

squeezed it tight as the doctor worked quickly and skillfully to swab out the wound.

During the process Reb thought he was going to black out, but Pilar's touch kept him from fainting. Then in five minutes it was all over; the doctor had finished bandaging his wound and he could sit up.

"Get him right to bed," the doctor told the women. "Let the wound settle down. I'll be around in the morning to look at him."

A few minutes later Reb was in his marriage bed, more stunned by the incident than injured. Robert arrived not long afterwards, his usually placid features hard with anger.

"At least," he told Reb, "they've got the son of a bitch in jail. A mob wants to string him up. They're shouting outside the jailhouse for his blood right now."

Reb's reaction was disgust at the mob. "They're fools, that won't change anything. I'm not dead."

"Thank God, son. We can all be grateful for that."

"Especially me," Reb said. "I can understand Domingo's feelings. I might have acted the same way, if I'd been in his place."

"But he tried to kill you, son."

"Father, too many people want to take the law into their own hands. You've opposed this many times. Manuel Domingo thought he had a valid reason for getting me."

"You're amazing," said Robert. "I didn't know you had such compassion."

"I do in this case."

"There'll be a trial," Robert said, "and if

Domingo isn't strung up before then, he'll get a stiff sentence." He turned to his daughter-in-law. "Begging your pardon, my dear, *Latinos* aren't wildly popular among *gringos* these days."

"I know," Pilar replied. "It works both ways."

"Why a trial at all?" Reb said. "It won't solve anything. It'll just stir up more hostile feelings between *Latinos* and Americans. And if Domingo gets convicted he'll be more of a martyr than a criminal in the eyes of a lot of people."

"Son, there has to be a trial, with justice done."

"I don't want a trial, father, with the muck and publicity that can dredge up. I'll refuse to testify."

"That won't get you very far," Robert pointed out. "They'll drag you in under guard, if necessary."

"I'll hide out in the hills behind the ranch. They won't find me."

"Reb, I don't understand your reasoning."

"I want them to release Domingo, father. I won't bring charges against him."

"But he meant to kill you."

"I don't care. I want him released. Just so long as he gets out of northern California and doesn't show his face here again, I'll be satisfied. The case is closed for me. Pilar and I have a life to begin leading."

"Dammit, son, you weren't like this a while back," said Robert. "You were always the first one to jump into a barroom brawl."

"That's another time, and long ago. I wasn't married then. I know how Domingo feels. He lost Pilar to me and he couldn't accept it."

"We could both be dead," Pilar said. "Manuel is vindictive. I'm afraid of him."

"Don't worry, darling," Reb said. "He's avenged himself. He'll be grateful now for his life."

"I'll not stop worrying," said Pilar.

"Nor will I," Robert concurred. "But I'll use what influence I have to carry out your wish, Reb."

"Thank you, father."

"On second thoughts, you may have a racial point about Domingo. It's high time *Latinos* and Americans buried the hatchet. I don't think releasing him will please a lot of good folks, but I respect your tolerance, which surprises me. Now, what will you two do about a honeymoon?"

"We thought we would spend it here," said Pilar.

"Nonsense," Robert replied, "I have a much better idea."

Robert talked with Emily later that morning in her cluttered suite.

"Could you postpone your trip to New York for another week, my dear?" he asked her.

"No, Robert. I'm leaving as scheduled."

Robert smiled. "My dear, I'm not talking about *us*. I'm thinking of Reb and Pilar. They need a complete change. Delay your departure another week, until Reb's well enough to travel. Then Pilar and Reb can go to New York with you."

Emily brightened considerably. "That's a wonderful idea! I'll change my reservation to suit their booking."

The honeymoon couple stayed a month in New York. They saw Emily off to Europe, they savored the sights and sounds of the great city, responding to its youthful exuberance. They visited the museums, went to theatres, ate at fine restaurants. Young and much in love, they made the most of their time together.

When Reb and Pilar returned to San Francisco, Manuel Domingo had been released and was in southern California. In their absence Robert had purchased a small, two-storey frame house on Laguna Street opposite Jefferson Square. One of his reasons for doing this was to remove Reb and Pilar from the ranch's proximity to the Mendez estate, since no reconciliation appeared possible between Pilar and Doña Maria. The old lady stoutly refused to answer Robert when he wrote to ask for a visit. His letter came back unopened, with Doña Maria's name crossed out.

The other reason was that Robert had quite pointedly made it unnecessary for Reb to live at the Sanderson ranch any longer. There was a new manager Robert had found while Reb was gone. Reb could now commute down to the ranch a couple of times a week to oversee the production. Pilar was happy with the house and pleased to live away from the ranch. They both adjusted easily to city life.

Not long after they were settled on Laguna Street, Pilar announced that she was pregnant, the best news Robert could have heard. For a fleeting moment the idea of a family so soon made Reb feel trapped. But he adjusted quickly to the idea of a child, a son, and treated Pilar with even greater affection than before.

ENTRANCES AND EXITS

MARIA SANDERSON was born to Pilar and Reb in the winter of 1872. Hers was a difficult birth that left Pilar ill for many months.

From the first Pilar was enchanted with her daughter. Her only regret was that Doña Maria could not see the tiny child who was named for her—or would not see her. Reb sent an announcement of Maria's birth to her grandmother at Los Arboles, but there was no response. And pride prevented Pilar from going there herself with the infant, fearing rejection.

Robert was as happily excited over the new baby as any grandfather could be.

"She'll be my fiftieth birthday gift," Robert announced proudly to Pilar and Reb.

Had the need arisen, he would have taken the child instantly to raise in his own house, forsaking part of his involvement in business in order to have little Maria with him.

From birth, Maria was a happy child, as beautiful as her mother, though fairer-skinned, with hazel eyes and golden hair.

Robert had to admit privately to initial disappointment that Maria was not a boy. This attitude soon evaporated as his attachment to the child grew. It was Reb who acted downright resentful about not having had a son.

"How the hell do we carry on the line with a daughter?" he asked Robert with a sharpness that surprised his father. Robert had thought he wouldn't care if he had a daughter. The next child might be a son.

"Very simple. You try again as soon as you can."

"I thought you didn't like big families."

"Two offspring won't make a dynasty," Robert pointed out. "Anyway, it ought to be a pleasant enough task for you. And while you're working at it, I'd like you to take over more responsibility with our business."

Reb brightened. "I was wondering when you'd suggest that."

"You don't have the full burden of the ranch on your shoulders, so you have the time. Of course I'll remain in the background as senior advisor. You won't have to go it alone, not yet at least."

Reb plunged enthusiastically into the challenges of the various Sanderson enterprises. He suggested new uses for El Dorado Steamship Company which Ethan agreed to. He organized a contracting firm and put Sanderson money into building tract homes. He opened a chain of markets and brought produce up from as far south as the Monterey peninsula. The ranch production was stepped up with endless poultry runs, a new dairy to handle the making of cheeses, and a new distribution company for city milk delivery.

On a more visible scale, Reb's good looks and fluent charm, and his ability to mix easily with men of all classes, made him an extremely popular young man about town. Robert was counting on this plus in Reb's personality to bolster up the Sanderson enterprises, for it was something that didn't come naturally to Robert; he'd had to grub at it and was never as successful as he wished to be.

Reb found enormous satisfaction and excitement in working in San Francisco. These factors wiped out any regrets he still entertained in having to leave the Sanderson ranch and putting the management of it into the hands of the new and highly efficient supervisor. Whenever he went down to visit, which was no oftener than once a week, the place seemed slightly provincial to him, and he wondered how he could have been so content basing himself there for such a long time.

A year after Maria's birth, Pilar became pregnant again. This time her pregnancy was unpleasant; she was ill a good share of the time, finally spending half the day in bed before she felt well enough to dress, go downstairs and think about dinner for Reb. Fortunately, Robert came to her aid with two excellent servants—a Chinese chef and a good practical nurse to take care of little Maria.

The delivery was agonizingly difficult for

Pilar, and the child, a girl, died a few hours after birth.

For a time Pilar was inconsolable. She stayed in bed for two weeks, barely eating, not wanting to see Maria, or Reb, longing for her grandmother to whom she couldn't turn. A permanent sadness settled upon her features that Reb and Robert could not dispell.

Robert took the loss of the child hard, Reb even harder. Up until that crisis, the marriage had worked perfectly for Reb and Pilar. From then on it began to move slowly and inexorably toward separation.

Unfairly, Reb vented his frustration over the sex of the child and its death on Pilar. He could not accept the fact that anyone could lose a child, no matter how careful, and that they could try again later on for a healthy male heir. Reb's disinvolvement with Pilar began when he stopped sleeping in the same bed with her. This was occasioned by the family doctor's stern edict that Pilar must avoid another pregnancy for at least a year, perhaps two. Thus, Reb moved into one of the guest rooms and slept alone. A wordless understanding helped them adjust to this, and both seemed relieved. Reb felt released from the obligations of his marriage bed; Pilar felt liberated from her fear of another pregnancy.

In less than a month Reb was spending most nights away from home. He kept a suite of rooms at the Oriental, with the reasonable excuse that when he worked late it was more convenient to walk a block to lodgings than to worry about riding home in a carriage. But the times that he worked nights became rarer as the months passed; he managed to do whatever was needed during the day.

Handsome as ever, always perfectly groomed, well-mannered and amusing, Reb was very much in demand at the ornate mansions on Nob Hill, and frequently in attendance at the lavish parties given by such nabobs as Leland Stanford, James Flood and others.

One night while he was attending a musicale at the Flood mansion, he was drawn to a young red-haired, green-eyed beauty in white. She was surrounded by several avid male admirers. Studying her, Reb thought there was something very familiar about her. As she gestured and laughed, played coquettishly with her fan and flashed her brilliant smile at her coterie, Reb realized where he'd seen her before. Once, briefly, she had worked as a sales girl for Emily at the salon. It was at least four years back, Reb decided. Then she was a pretty though not spectacular girl, rather quiet and shy, as he recalled. Now here she was, a vivid and seductive creature, beautifully gowned and made up, the center of attention and easily the loveliest woman at the affair.

As he studied the vivid creature, whose name he couldn't recall as yet, she happened to glance in his direction; their eyes met. Whether she recognized him or not from his visits to Emily's salon Reb couldn't say, but she smiled. In that smile was all the promise Reb realized he'd been missing in the last year and more as his marriage had settled into the vise of routine predictability.

His blood raced; he felt himself come tensely alive. Then, abruptly, he recalled her name:

Lida something. Yes, Lida Fulton! She would be about his own age. He speculated on what had taken her from Emily's salon to the Flood mansion and turned her into such a dazzling female. It was a long time since he'd been stirred at gut level by anyone other than Pilar. He knew he had to meet this Lida again, and make love to her. It had nothing to do with Pilar, nothing to do with anything except the passing moment, and it was nobody's business but his.

While he wondered where Lida's escort was, as if by signal she excused herself from the group of doting admirers and walked over to him.

"You're Reb Sanderson, aren't you?" she enquired. "Emily King's nephew? And all grown up, too."

Reb was pleased. "You're Lida Fulton."

"You remembered! I'm Lida Ryan now."

"I'm not Emily's nephew. My father and Emily were old friends; she sort of adopted me. Where did you go when you left the salon?"

"It's a very long tale. I won't burden you now with the details. I went to New York and got married. That'll do for now."

"Where's your husband?"

"In New York. He's directing a show. We sometimes lead separate lives." She flushed slightly as she said this, and Reb changed the subject.

"What are you doing in San Francisco?"

"I just arrived with a company. We're to open at the California Theatre in a musical extravaganza."

"Then you're a singer?"

"I have one of the leads in a new piece."

"I'll come and see you."

"You can see me tonight. I'm one of the artists in tonight's concert. I interpret popular, not classical."

"I look forward to hearing you."

Lida fluttered her fan against her powdered bosom. "I was hoping you would. What are you doing, Reb?"

"In business with my father. Sanderson Enterprises."

"Oh yes, I remember. El Dorado Steamship."

"And other firms," he replied modestly.

"Are you married?" Lida asked.

"With one child."

"But your wife isn't here with you?"

"No. She rarely goes out. She prefers evenings at home with our baby daughter."

"She's taking quite a chance," Lida said, smiling provocatively, warmly—which could mean anything, Reb decided, since she was an actress.

"I'm the one who's taking the chance," he said. "She might bolt the door against me some night."

A lively waltz was struck up in the adjoining ballroom, serving as the overture for the musicale. Guests began filtering into the large hall and finding seats.

"Oh dear, that means I have to go," said Lida. "Will I see you again? Please come to our show, won't you? We open in four days and we're going to be the biggest hit in town."

"I'd like to take you home tonight," Reb said.

"Oh, I'm afraid I already have an escort for this evening." She turned toward a young man with a handlebar moustache who stood apart from the group of male admirers glowering fiercely at them.

"I see what you mean," Reb said.

Lida regarded him for a moment, her green eyes glittering.

"Don't draw any conclusions," she murmured softly, then smiled, tapped him lightly on the chest with the tip of her white lace fan and walked away.

Reb stood at the rear of the ballroom so that he had an unimpaired view across the audience of some one hundred guests.

The first number was a mixed quartet presenting a medley of light opera selections. Lida Ryan's voice was a rich mezzo-soprano, easily outstanding among the other singers, a soprano, tenor and baritone. It was a big, natural voice, with raw vitality. Reb could understand why Lida had said she was a popular singer, not a classical one.

Among the popular melodies interpreted by the quartet were some from a new English light opera recently introduced in New York. It was called *Thespis* and was written by a fresh, unknown team, Gilbert and Sullivan.

After the medley, each member of the quartet took a solo turn. Lida Ryan featured three popular songs of love and longing. She performed them with impeccable clarity and passion, receiving a hearty audience response, especially from the male spectators.

After an orchestral number and another set of songs by the quartet, the concert was over.

Reb lingered in the foyer until the main body of guests had departed, but Lida and her escort did not appear, although the orchestra and the other soloists all departed through the mansion's front portals.

Finally Reb approached the head butler to enquire if all the entertainers had gone. The butler grinned knowingly at him.

"Are you referring to the pretty lady in white, sir?" Reb said that he was. "Well, sir, she left with a gentleman by the side entrance. They had a carriage waiting."

Reb thanked the man and went to his house for a change that evening, in no mood to stay at the hotel or go out on the town, his mind filled with thoughts of Lida.

Four nights later he was seated alone in the orchestra section of the California Theatre, having been greeted at the door by Lawrence Barrett, the actor who had left Tom Maguire's Opera House management to become manager of the newer, finer California.

The piece was *Lonely Hearts*, a melodrama of the 1840s set to new music. Lida Ryan played the heroine's best friend who gets the heroine's rejected suitor. In a dizzy comedic handling of a thin part, Lida was exceptional. With her clarion delivery of lines andsongs, and her innate timing, she was easily the outstanding hit of the show. Applause and bravos brought her back for three solo bows. As she blew final kisses to the audience she spotted Reb and sent him a special smiling kiss. Reb took the gesture on face value and went backstage.

He pressed his way through the backstage crush of grandes dames, gentlemen in tall silk hats, luscious women in furs and jewels. Lida's dressing room, as was to be expected, was filled with male admirers. The handlebar moustache of the Flood mansion party was nowhere in sight, Reb noted, to his relief.

He waited his turn and finally got a minute with Lida.

"Thank you for the gorgeous roses," Lida said, taking his hands in hers, and nodding toward the most sumptuous floral arrangement among many. "You're a darling."

"I'd like to have the chance to prove it," Reb told her. "How about having supper with me tonight? Or am I presuming on your time? I made a reservation just in case you were free."

Lida's generous mouth drooped in a false pout.

"Oh dear, I've got a thousand things to do tomorrow. A pick-up rehearsal, fittings for clothes, luncheon with the cast. Going out's a bore. Isn't there some way we can have a quiet drink together, perhaps a glass of champagne, and simply talk?"

Reb had already anticipated such a possibility.

"My hotel," he said. "I'll be waiting for you at the backstage entrance. Hurry!" He bent and kissed her hand.

At his suite Lida said, "This is perfect, just heavenly." She sipped lightly at her champagne, dressed in a simple grey gown, a far cry from the white vision of the other evening. "I've dreamed of this ever since I left San Francisco."

"This hotel?" Reb said, smiling.

"No, silly, of our success tonight. I'm a local girl, you know."

"I didn't. Where were you born?"

"Sacramento."

"My God, so was I!"

"We fit the mold, don't we?"

"I think we're made for each other," Reb said, sliding over beside her on the velvet sofa.

"I wish Arno could have been here tonight. He'd be so proud of me."

"Won't I do instead? I'm proud of you."

She gazed at him with sparkling eyes; she put down her champagne glass and leaned into his arms.

"I think we'd better find out right now," she said, pushing him back against the sofa. With her body pressed against his, she explored his mouth with her warm tongue until he nearly had to fight for breath. When she finally released him he was giddy with desire.

Lida jumped up. With a few deft gestures she shed her gown. Reb gasped. She was wearing absolutely nothing beneath it. Seeing his reaction, she executed a slow pirouette before him, then walked to the bed, ripped off its silken coverlet, threw back the bedclothes and settled herself with sensuous languor across the linen sheets, looking for all the world like some elegant pseudo-Renoir oil painting that might hang over the bar in a San Francisco saloon.

Reb shed his clothes on the way to Lida.

Moments later they were making love with a savage intensity he'd never known before. It wasn't love as he defined the emotion, but it was gutty and stimulating. Sacrilege to compare it with his intimacies with Pilar, but to be honest, it was infinitely more exciting, more physically satisfying. When he brought Lida at length to a shrieking climax, she dug her nails into his back and raked him raw and bleeding. But in his frenzy he didn't even feel the mark of her talons.

They made love several times, until it was dawn and Lida insisted she must go.

"When will I see you again?" Reb asked as he watched Lida button herself into the grey dress.

"Not tonight," she said. "I have a date with a bank president."

This jolted him a bit. "What about tomorrow?"

"I'm invited aboard a vessel in the Bay for midnight supper with the captain. Sorry, love."

Reb was beginning to feel like a used appendage. "Do I have to make a booking a year in advance?" he asked.

Lida threw her arms around him, ran her tongue in his ear. When he reached for her, she stepped away.

"Wait until Saturday night, darling," she told him. "There'll be more than you can handle. Save yourself. And don't worry, I can get here by myself. Midnight . . . Bye, see you!" She blew him a kiss, unlocked the door, slipped out and was gone.

He went back to bed, still excited, unable to rid himself of her scent, her image. Christ no, it wasn't love; it was some kind of sorcery, a primitive rite. But his body called it love, even if his logical mind couldn't. He would count the days until they lay together again.

Did those men she mentioned really exist, or was she just playing with him? He couldn't imagine her spreading her favors that loosely, which made him realize that he already cared for her or he wouldn't be feeling pangs of jealousy.

He bathed, dressed slowly, turning alternately hot and cold as he relived every detail of their night together. He thought he would expire if she decided in some bitchy and capricious mood to deny him further access. He went to work in a stony mood, neither satiated by his adventure nor depressed, merely numb and dazed, in a state suspended excitement. He thought he was beginning to know what the word obsession meant.

Reb's ranch foreman Ramon came into town one day to visit the Sanderson Enterprises office on business. While talking with Robert he mentioned something offhand that immediately alerted Robert. Or perhaps it wasn't such a casual reference after all, Robert decided later.

Ramon said, "Reb looked fine when he came down the other day. It was good to see him. City life agrees."

Robert was under the impression that Reb hadn't been to the ranch in a fortnight. "Oh?" he said, "I didn't know he was down your way this week. What day was that?"

"Sunday, señor."

On Sunday Robert thought Reb was working at the city office. He had said he intended to be there most of the day, going over the purchasing accounts for the ranch.

"Yes, señor," Ramon went on, "he visited us with a very pretty young woman, an actress from the city."

"An actress?" While Pilar stayed at home, Robert reflected, immediately upset by Ramon's news but outwardly calm. "Reb has friends everywhere," he observed, and moved on to the business at hand.

Later in the day he told Reb, hard at work in his office, that he wanted to see him after business hours, not an uncommon occurrence. They used the quiet time in the building for a leisurely drink together and a chance to rehash without pressure the business of the day.

After discussing several business items concerning real estate holdings, leases, further investment potential, Robert pushed his papers aside, poured Reb another drink and settled into his chair, looking thoughtfully at his son, his adored and beloved child, now immensely mature in many respects, but still hot-blooded, still quite young.

"I don't want to sound like the stern patriarch," he told Reb, "but there's something of a highly personal nature I feel obliged to talk about with you. Do you mind?"

"I don't know until you tell me, father."

Already Robert found himself making allowances for Reb's possible infidelity with a beautiful woman whose name he didn't even know.

"Well," he began, "Ramon was in earlier today."

"Yes, I know. I saw him."

"You also saw him at the ranch last Sunday, I believe?"

Reb looked uncomfortable. "That's right, sir. I was there."

"And not alone? Ramon said you were in the company of a very lovely young woman. An actress, wasn't it?"

Reb nodded, frowning. "That's correct, sir.

Her name is Lida Ryan and she's playing in a new piece at the California. It's called *Lonely Hearts*."

"Is she—does she have ties?"

Reb grinned. "You mean, is she engaged or married? She's married, sir. Her husband's in New York. They have some kind of arrangement when they're apart."

"I see. And what's *your* arrangement with this lady?"

Reb's eyes opened wide. "Father, even when I was a boy you never did this to me. What's behind it?"

Robert throttled his mounting irritation.

"If you don't know," he said evenly, "then it's high time I told you. Pilar and Maria. You have responsibilities, in case you've forgotten."

"Sir, I've never shirked my responsibilities."

"You might have spent Sunday with your family."

"I wanted to visit the ranch, I wanted Lida to see it. That's all I can say."

"So, you are intimate with this woman?"

Reb locked eyes with his father. "Yes, I am," he admitted. "I'm rather fond of her. She's a friend."

"I think you ought to put this relationship aside before it claims you."

"Now you're playing God, father."

"There are two things I've never neglected—business and family. I don't expect you to default on them either."

"I'm neglecting no one," Rob protested.

"You are if you're having an affair with this woman," Robert declared.

"Sir, this is ridiculous," Reb said uncomfortably, but seeing Robert's point.

"It may seem that way to you, caught up in the heat of passion. But a line must be drawn somewhere, son. A casual moment's tolerable, but an affair . . ."

"You had Emily," Reb reminded him. "I'm just following in your footsteps."

Robert experienced a surge of intense anger.

"Dammit," he shouted, banging the heel of his hand on the desktop, "you know better than to twist this around for your convenience. Your mother was long dead by the time I met Emily; I was a man free to do as I liked. And at no time was I ever the gay young rake about town, as you've been since you were quite young—all of which I overlooked when you were growing up. I wanted you to spend your lust so that when you did settle down you'd do it with total commitment to family life. That worked for a while, but it's obviously not working now."

Robert paused, aware that imperious moralizing would only alienate Reb. And besides, he'd never used this tactic with his son before; he shouldn't start now.

"What am I supposed to do, father?" Reb asked with such a helpless tone that Robert instantly understood his dilemma. He was deeply infatuated with the actress, but that didn't alter the unseemliness of his actions.

"You will break off this relationship immediately," Robert said.

"Is that an order, sir?"

"I've never found it necessary to give you firm orders before, Reb. You're too intelligent not to recognize what must be done."

Reb was silent for a moment, then said, "I'll think about it, father."

"Is that your final word?" Robert demanded sharply.

"It's the way I feel right now in talking with you," Reb said stiffly. "May I be excused from this discussion, sir?"

Robert nodded without speaking, fearing that if he said anything more he would explode. He waved his hand at Reb in dismissal.

Reb stood up, a forced smile on his lips, his eyes anxious.

"You need to have Emily back, father—or to replace her memory."

On this note Reb departed, leaving Robert to brood darkly about his own life.

All at once the plans Robert had so carefully organized, like meticulously laid brickwork, now seemed no more than a house of cards, fragile and worthless. He wanted a grandson through Pilar. If anything should happen to his precious Reb along the trail of his womanizing, he would never have one. Robert had moved with extreme trepidation in his business ventures, at a time when San Francisco fortunes were made and lost in a day. He'd spread his money around between various good investments so as to insure against any possibility of ruin. He had refused to allow himself to speculate in business as he'd sometimes done at the gaming tables; bad luck could wipe out Reb's inheritance.

Ethan had been reckless sometimes. Money had come easily to Ethan and Flora, and disappeared as quickly. All Ethan could rely on now was the El Dorado Steamship Company partnership, and the Hotel Splendide, much out

of fashion these days, being transformed into a
boarding house of unglamorous atmosphere
catering to a range of shady losers. It had been
much more attractive as the bordello it was two
decades earlier.

Robert had constantly striven to maintain his
own life style apart from all class distinctions.
He prided himself on his detachment from business folk after hours, with the exception of
Ethan. Only after the birth of little Maria and
the sad death of his second grandchild had he
given serious thought to the condition of his
soul, and therefore religion. He wondered if this
lack of formal church affiliation had left him
and Reb spiritually undernourished. Maybe he
should have provided some kind of religious
education for the boy; the Baptist church school
didn't count. Pilar's faith sustained her, but
would it if she learned of Reb's infidelity? He
probably had no right to excoriate Reb for as-
sociating with this actress person; she must be
offering him something that Pilar couldn't.

At least, Reb hadn't denied having an affair
with the woman. Reb was no hypocrite, thank
God. He didn't sing hymns and dance to the
devil's tune simultaneously, as did the mealy-
mouthed psalm singers he met in business who
prayed ostentatiously on Sunday and then
cheated, lied and stole in the marketplace the
remainder of the week, as vicious, greedy and
ruthless a bunch as the lowest crib whores in
the city.

Reb might be right; he needed Emily, he
wished she were back. She had written from
time to time in the last year and some months.

He always answered her promptly at the various
forwarding addresses—London, Paris, Rome,
Athens, Istamboul. She'd gone everywhere, seen
everything. She told him about ruins and castles,
art galleries and museums, but little about herself, what her thoughts were. He missed her
more than he cared to admit, and he bitterly
regretted that she might never come back, lost
to him forever.

He opened his desk drawer. From it he drew
forth her last letter. It bore an English post-
mark. On the fine bond sheet was an engraved
family crest and a complicated country address.
He'd read it twenty times over, at least, and had
divulged its content to no one although it was
burning a hole in his mind. It read:

Dear Robert:

I suppose the best way to begin this letter
is to tell you right off that I am married. To
a man of fine family, a widower close to
your age, named Ronald Crimshaw. He's as
near to a title as I ever want to come and
has dukes and earls dangling from his family tree. You know me well enough to be
certain that titles don't impress me. I married Ronald because I love him and he's a
good man.

The engagement was a short one, but not
as short as Reb's and Pilar's was. I am confident that I made the right choice, Robert.
My only regret is that I may have dashed
your hopes. They were once my hopes too,
remember, but that time is past.

Should you ever need me for anything

that I can reasonably do, don't fail to get in touch. You can cable me here. Ronald will understand and not be jealous.

Well, that's about all I have to say. My love to you, to Reb, to Pilar. I am writing separately to Flora and Ethan.

Yours ever,
Emily

In the privacy of his office, with Reb gone and the great building tranquil in the early evening, he wanted to cry but couldn't. Dry-eyed he poured himself another drink, feeling very old, extremely mortal, and absolutely defeated, his life close to meaninglessness. The world was bitter brass on his tongue, the mockery of existence overwhelming.

Robert did not discuss Reb's affair with him again soon after their initial talk. Nor did he drop even the subtlest hint to Pilar that Reb was being unfaithful to her. Pilar's uncertain health was his main reason for refraining. But the news did reach Pilar eventually. After all, Reb was well-known about town as the good-looking, happy-go-lucky son of Robert Sanderson who did pretty much as he pleased. Since he was being seen in the frequent company of Lida Ryan, the toast of San Francisco, it was inevitable that Pilar should hear something.

The news was brought home by Maria's nurse. Pilar went first to Robert, in tears.

"I don't understand it," she told him. "He left my bed of his own accord, not my wish. And now he's taken up with this woman, in plain view of everyone. I could understand an occasional night on the town—I suppose most men do that. But Reb was so faithful—" She wiped her eyes with her kerchief.

"Left your bed?" Robert said. "I didn't know."

"Right after I lost my little girl."

Robert's anger started again; his face flushed and his forehead pulsed with pressure. He tried to get a grip on his nerves; it wouldn't do for both of them to become emotional.

"How do you feel about it?" he asked Pilar. "I mean, do you want a divorce?"

Pilar stared at him, incredulous. "I am still a Catholic in tradition, Robert, even if I no longer live in a Latin atmosphere. It would be unthinkable."

"Well then, what about a legal separation?"

Pilar drew herself up proudly, her tears under control. "We are still man and wife. Reb must be able to come and go as he wishes under his own roof. I would not banish him from Maria's life, too."

"What will we do then?"

"I think there is nothing we can do," Pilar declared, making one of those simple and pragmatic decisions that astonished Robert, considering her background, but one that also pleased his very American sense of efficiency. This time, however, he gained scant satisfaction from her words.

"I'll talk with him again. I'll forbid him once and for all to be seen in the company of this actress," he promised Pilar. "I wish I had your restraint; it's admirable, my dear."

Pilar smiled wryly. "Perhaps, but deep inside

I feel like killing him. I feel the way Manuel Domingo must have felt when he wanted us both dead."

"I'm moved by your honesty and spunk, my dear, and your self-control. I wouldn't blame you if you hit him over the head with a poker."

"That would solve nothing." Pilar looked closely at her father-in-law. "Tell me, is something else bothering you? You've been in many strange moods lately. I see it in your face when you come to play with Maria and we talk."

"I come to see you, my dear, as much as my granddaughter."

"That I know. But what is wrong? Is it any of your businesses?"

He hadn't intended to tell her about Emily until Ethan and Flora received word, but now he must. "I got a letter from Emily not long ago," he said.

"Oh? I hope it isn't bad news."

"Not good. She married an Englishman by the name of Crimshaw and will stay on in England."

"Dear Robert, I am so sorry for you!"

Pilar came over to him as he slumped down in the deep leather chair in Pilar's study.

"I know how you must feel." She knelt beside him and stroked his large cold hands with her small warm ones. Her touch pleased and soothed him. Once again he felt the imminence of tears but refused to let them pass his control.

"It's all right," he said in a dry, tight voice, "it's my fault, not hers. I was never any good at timing in my personal life, only in business. I let Emily go, really, which speaks worlds for my cold heart, doesn't it?"

"Don't scourge yourself," Pilar said sharply. "That's self-pity and it isn't your style. You're strong, sensitive and decent, Robert. No other man is quite like you."

He wanted to believe her statement but felt it was merely her method of reaching out, needing support for herself; she was in greater stress than he was.

"My dear," he said, "there is no woman quite like you in today's changing world. I have known two others in the past—my fiancée Sarah Calder, and Reb's mother, Jane, who had your kind of spiritual strength." He touched her cheek.

"We must give each other the courage to go on," Pilar said solemnly, and bent forward to kiss him lightly on the cheek, then stood up quickly and walked to the door that led into the outer hall. "I must see about Maria's supper. I am sorry about Emily; I liked her. Don't fret about Reb. It will work itself out. My only regret is that you may not have a male heir."

"I refuse to believe that," said Robert.

"But all the same, it might be true . . ."

Once the *Lonely Hearts* extravaganza at the California settled down for what appeared to be a long run, Lida Ryan decided to move from her hotel to a small apartment nearer the theatre. Reb found a place for her, had it furnished and spent as much time here as he did in his hotel suite and home combined. The lovers were seen billing and cooing at all the best restaurants and casinos. On clear Sundays they went out to the Cliff House for its exceptional French menu, getting there by horse-drawn omnibus from

Portsmouth Square, via Point Lobos Avenue.

Nob Hill society was not quite as friendly toward Reb as it had been, nor to Lida. She was not asked to the Flood mansion when another musicale was presented. This didn't bother Reb, however, who had never taken the snobberies and strategems of the *nouveau riche* nabobs very seriously anyway. And besides, the less social life that he and Lida had, the more time they could spend together, most of it in bed. Lida was sexually insatiable, Reb soon learned. She kept him at peak performance level with her demands.

Sometimes Reb wondered if he satisfied her, that she might sneak out on him; she had as easy an eye for good-looking men as he did for feminine beauty. But Lida saw to it that her interest was used only to pique Reb's appetite for more of her special variety of excitement. Reb's interest grew until his infatuation with the singing actress was beyond all good sense. He spent lavishly on her, bought her furs, dresses, jewelry.

Robert saw the bills come in and would have liked to stop them, but Reb was scrupulous about paying for these extravagances with his money from funds Robert couldn't touch.

These days the two men conversed only on business matters. They might have been rivals in commerce, their meetings became so cool and formal. Robert knew that Reb was as stubborn as he was and wouldn't give an inch until he made up his mind to change, which Robert prayed would be soon. Then the actress would be dropped like the proverbial hot potato. Until then, Robert intended to bide his time.

As a distraction and for reasons Robert

couldn't quite explain to himself, he took to attending mass with Pilar. He was impressed with the pageantry, less with the doctrine.

"It helps to have you accompany me," Pilar told him. "I am pleased that you wish to enquire into the nature of my religion."

Robert had no intention of becoming a Catholic. He enjoyed the ritual of the mass and found it soothing. St. Mary's Church at Grant Avenue and California had a rich tradition, a simple dignity that satisfied him. With Pilar sitting at his side, kneeling and praying with the congregation, which he did not do, Robert felt himself serene beyond words. Sometimes he wondered why he hadn't turned to religion when the earlier tragedies of Sarah's death and Jane's untimely passing had made his life almost unbearable. Instead of seeking God he had gone deeper into himself. He'd been younger and more resilient then; now he must draw sustenance from different values—attendance at mass and the staunch character that Pilar presented to society. Both were inspirational and comforting.

Still, strangely enough, he could understand Reb's defection from his marriage. Reb had remained a slave to his ebullient, open youth. The way the boy had been practically weaned on doting women had made him highly susceptible to their charms. Robert wished he could pray for Reb's soul, but Pilar did, he knew; she believed it would help.

Coming out of St. Mary's one Sunday morning with Pilar, he happened to glance up at the frontal dial of the church's bell tower clock and read: "Son, Observe the Time and Fly from Evil." He would of course never mouth anything that didactic to Reb, nor would he point out to Pilar that a specific moral could be drawn from Reb's situation. He worried probably more than he should about Reb. He was letting this preoccupation affect his concentration on Sanderson Enterprises. Reb would recover from whatever malaise presently possessed him. Then he would return to his wife and child. He had to.

During the second month of Lida Ryan's run at the California Theatre, her husband, stage director Arno Ryan, arrived in San Francisco unannounced. Ryan had purposely refrained from sending his wife a telegram. He was taking a month's vacation between theatrical assignments and was due in Chicago in three weeks to direct a play there.

A short, extremely volatile man, Ryan clung to the double standard in marriage. What was good for the husband was prohibited for the wife. He'd had countless romances with actresses and various society ladies previous to his two-year-old marriage to Lida. These did not cease after wedding her. Ryan's affairs were always ultra-discreet; he liked them that way. Skulking through midnight streets in dark, hooded capes, riding in curtained carriages, sending hand-printed, unsigned notes to his lady-loves. His system was designed to protect both himself and his ladies from all scandal, principally from their husbands' wrath, for he dallied only with married women. The one thing he could not forgive was blatant flagrancy in a love affair. Any public display was anathema to him; this truly offended his sensibilities; as a professional theater man he knew that such scandals in the case of theatrical folk might ultimately drive patrons away from the box office. It could even lead to the banning of a play or player. Therefore, Ryan considered discretion much better than valor; it was necessity's child.

Arno Ryan had two persuasive reasons for his unofficial visit to San Francisco. One, he wanted to see Lida in her first hit vehicle. Word had reached him since the California's opening night that the musical confection was almost good enough for New York, and that Lida was superb. If so, then he intended to see the show for himself and determine for himself the quality of her performance.

Two, Ryan had received a malicious letter from a fellow actor working in *Lonely Hearts*. The actor wrote that Lida was having a brazenly open affair with a young stud about town named Reb Sanderson. He had set her up in an apartment and was buying her expensive clothes and jewelry. The actor wrote that they were often seen huddled together in Sanderson's carriage on the way to Lida's apartment for a midnight snack after the evening performance.

On the night of Ryan's arrival, wearing a false moustache, he made his way to a downtown saloon where he checked his leather valise instead of checking into a hotel. Then he headed immediately for the California Theatre, anxious to catch the evening performance of Lonely Hearts.

Ryan was uncertain what he'd do if he found out Lida was unfaithful to him with Sanderson.

But making himself unidentifiable gave him a special sense of power and mobility; he could observe his wife's action undetected.

Ryan purchased a balcony ticket from the box office at the California an hour before the performance, then went to a nearby saloon to drink away some of the grit and weariness of the train ride West. He got into conversation with the Irish bartender and asked if he'd seen the California's *Lonely Hearts*.

"Sure I have," said the bartender. "Paid a big price, took the missus and meself. Worth every penny, sir, in particular the fair colleen with the red hair. A wicked beauty."

"Who would that be?" Ryan asked, stroking his fake moustache.

"Why, the prettiest lady in all of San Francisco. You must be a stranger in our fair city if you don't know the name of Lida Ryan?"

"She's good, eh?"

The bartender blew a kiss to the ceiling.

"More than good. A heavenly dish, an angel of mercy. I fell in love with her like every other lad in town. You owe it to yourself to see the show."

"Perhaps I shall."

"Here on business, sir?"

"I think so," said Ryan.

"What is your line, sir, if I may be so bold as to ask?"

"I'm looking into a deal," Ryan said with such heavy emphasis that the bartender nodded sagely at him.

"I understand how it is, sir. We don't talk about our dollars in San Francisco for fear some thief might cart 'em away." He poured Ryan another neat whiskey. "On the house," he said. Ryan downed his fourth and last drink, left a tip and went off to the theatre.

Twenty minutes later he was wedged into his seat in the airless balcony of the California, savoring the performance to the point of abandoning his surveillance and rushing backstage at intermission to greet and congratulate Lida, who was sensational. He was ready to accept her denial of the affair with this man Sanderson, and let bygones be bygones. Maybe he should be angry with the actor who wrote that letter. He hadn't quite worked out how he'd punish Lida if necessary. And if she were simply the victim of slander, he'd apologize. But he didn't budge from his seat at intermission, not leaving it until the final curtain fell amid bravos for all the cast, and especially for Lida Ryan.

Ryan filed out of the theatre with the audience and took up a position under the marquee near the stage door entrance, deciding to surprise Lida. She'd be changing into street clothes, removing make-up, and along soon. But minutes later she swept out of the stage door, still in make-up, on the arm of a handsome young man, clinging to him and gazing at him adoringly. Ryan had never seen his wife give a look like that to anyone. He was seized by a cold fury. But before he could move toward them the pair stepped gaily into a carriage and rode away.

Ryan ran for a waiting horse cab.

"Follow that vehicle," he ordered the driver, hoping the man wasn't good at remembering faces. He discharged the cab a few doors from the address where Lida's carriage stopped. He paid off the driver and added a most generous tip. As the cab departed, he watched a lamp come on upstairs in Lida's building, presumably in her apartment, for the rest of the building was dark.

He waited in a doorway across the street, nursing his growing fury, trying to decide what action he would take.

Should he force his way into the building? Bash down the apartment door, surprise the lover *in flagrante delicto*? Or should he walk down to a city hotel, get a good night's sleep to soothe his savage anger, come back in the morning and give Lida the good hiding she deserved, thus putting an end once and for all to her infamous behavior?

Ryan finally decided to wait and see what happened. Maybe the young blade would come right out, which would relieve his mind partially. The night was balmy; he sat down on the doorway steps.

In a few minutes the light went out in the upstairs window. Ryan was shaking with rage.

"You son of a bitch!" Ryan cursed to himself. "You'll pay for touching her." Then, for Lida, "Whore, devil woman!"

Clenching his fists between his knees, Ryan began his vigil. Nothing could drag him away now; he was a man possessed and would remain awake by sheer will power.

Several times his head dropped forward, chin on his chest from utter exhaustion. He hadn't slept properly in a bed for days. But each time his head sagged down he would snap awake with a start, then settle himself ramrod straight, start the process all over again, hoping that no one would walk down the silent street and see him huddled like a beggar, or a cutthroat, in the doorway.

As far as he was concerned, Ryan already had proof that Sanderson was making him a cuckold. Why else would the light go out? The actor's letter had said that Lida's lover was a married man who lived at home with his wife and child, so he would probably leave the apartment before dawn. Well, he could wait; he had all the time in the world. And when the scoundrel emerged from Lida's apartment house, he would confront the rotten scum . . .

Upstairs in Lida's apartment, the lovers were cozily entwined after satisfying their needs.

Lida took that moment to give Reb some news.

"Mr. Barrett told us just before tonight's performance that I'll be out of the San Francisco production," she announced. "The notice will be in tomorrow's papers."

Reb sat bolt upright and threw off the bedclothes.

"They can't do that to you! You're a big hit."

"I'll be leaving San Francisco."

"But you can't," Reb said in dismay. "Christ, what's going to happen to us?"

Lida prattled on as if she hadn't heard his question.

"*Lonely Hearts* will open in New York with a new cast, with me in my own role. They'll build new sets, make new costumes, entirely restage the show and present it to Manhattan audiences," she explained. "It's to be my very first Broadway appearance in a principal role. Just think of it, Reb! Aren't you excited? I'm thrilled to death."

"You're not going," Reb said emphatically. "You can't."

"Now darling, don't be tiresome. Of course I'm going. Do you think I intend to spend the rest of my life in this provincial town? I've done my stint here. And besides, there's my husband to think about. I'll join him in Chicago, now that I can—stay a week or two, then go on to New York for rehearsals."

"Forget about New York," Reb said in a commanding voice. "You're staying right here where I need you."

"Oh Reb, don't be difficult. This has been a marvelous interlude, we've had so much fun. But underneath this wanton exterior you like so much is a model wife. I am still very much married. I must return to that life, just as you have to resume your role of ideal husband and father. All this has just been a moment out of time for us. Now be practical, darling, and don't make a fuss, please. We were fated to part sooner or later."

"You've known about this for days, haven't you?"

"Well, maybe a few days."

"I thought so. Hasn't our time together meant anything serious to you?" Reb demanded.

"Of course, darling. But we have to be realistic. We both have our other lives. It's time to go back to them."

"Look, I've got money," Reb said, "plenty of it. My father's been very generous with me; the investments have paid off. We can leave San

Francisco and go away someplace. How'd you like to see the Hawaiian Islands?"

"What's there besides the natives?" Lida asked.

"Great natural beauty and one of the world's best climates."

"I'm not interested in climate, I'm interested in my career. But go ahead, tell me more. I'm listening."

"My father bought me a sugar cane plantation in Hawaii a few years ago, right after the whaling industry opened up the islands commercially. I've not seen the property but it's legally mine. We can settle down in Honolulu. They say it's a beautiful town. We'll live as man and wife. No one will ever have to know that we aren't married. It's another world."

"You're mad," Lida declared flatly. "I would never bury myself in such a remote, primitive place. Never! I am fond of you, Reb, or we wouldn't be together. But we have too much to lose to go running off to nowhere. You have your business interests, I have my theatrical career. And each of us has our marriage."

"So I don't mean anything to you, is that it?"

"Darling, you do," Lida insisted.

"I'm just a stage-door john who pays your bills," Reb said bitterly. "That's all I mean to you."

"You know that's not true," Lida protested, "you're very dear."

Reb knew that her words were not related to her actions; he should have known all along. "We're through, aren't we?"

"We'll part when I have to leave. Darling,

don't be so depressed. Everything has to end sometime. Put your arms around me, kiss me!"

Reb got out of bed. "I'll never touch you again, you whore," he said angrily. "I can't believe you'd turn out to be such a rotten, cold bitch. I was willing to give up my wife and child to go away with you. Break with my father, everything. But you're not even interested."

"Come back to bed, Reb."

He was standing in the darkened bedchamber nude, silhouetted against the clear window frame, his body illumined by the reflected glow of the street lamp two floors below.

Seeing him thus, savoring his attributes, she wondered if she weren't making a mistake. She hated to lose him; he was as beautiful as he was generous. But in the back of her mind she was aware and frightened of Arno's wrath, even at this distance from him. She must really break off the affair. And if she couldn't live without pleasure, next time she'd be more discreet. However, she had a certain tenderness for Reb; she didn't want to separate from him at quarrel's point.

"Come, darling. Don't be stubborn."

"No, Lida, I'm through with you."

The delicate, translucent lace curtains were wide open at the street window. He didn't bother to close them or the heavy opaque velvet draperies. He lit the oil lamp. As Lida watched wordlessly from the bed he began pulling on his clothes.

"If you go now," she said, thinking that perhaps it was best this way, after all, neat and quick, "you needn't bother to come back."

"Don't worry, you bitch, I won't. Your rent's

paid until the end of the month. You're on your own after that."

"Reb, please!"

"Go to hell," Reb muttered. "Good-bye and good riddance!" He slammed the apartment door as he left; the noise echoed along the silent corridor.

As he went downstairs he decided to go home for a change. He felt like throttling Lida but she wasn't worth the trouble. Perhaps it was all for the best, it would bring him to his senses. He'd been pretty much out of his mind with passion for her the past few weeks, no better than a rutting stag, crazy, obsessed. He had neglected Pilar and Maria shamefully, and his father. He'd humiliated them. What a bastard he was, he reflected, stepping out of the building into the night street.

He paused a moment on the sidewalk to look at his pocket watch; it said two in the morning. He could be home in fifteen minutes, creep inside, go to his room, back at last. In the morning he'd talk with Pilar, if she'd listen, and beg her forgiveness . . .

Downstairs in the doorway Arno Ryan watched the light come on in the upstairs apartment window. He saw the nude torso of the man named Sanderson framed against the lamplight. A few minutes later the front door of the apartment house opened. The man who emerged was the same one who had escorted Lida home, who had appeared upstairs in the window minutes earlier.

After pausing, the man began to walk slowly down the street away from him, hands plunged in his pockets, hunched over, absorbed in some reverie. Probably, thought Ryan, reliving the joys of Lida's sweet flesh.

Charged with the adrenalin of outrage, Ryan jumped up, loped across the street and caught up with Reb. Blocking his path, Ryan snarled, "You bastard, you've been sleeping with my wife!"

Startled, Reb stopped dead still, wondering if the man weren't confusing him with someone else. A head shorter than Reb, the stranger sported a luxuriant moustache, his features not clearly discernible beneath the slouch hat. No one he knew.

"I'm sorry," Reb said. "You've got me mixed up with somebody else."

"No, I haven't. I'm Lida Ryan's husband," he declared, "and I challenge you to defend yourself."

"I don't want her," Reb said. "The slut's all yours."

"I'll kill you!" Ryan shouted, and drove a furious fist into Reb's diaphragm, knocking him backwards against the railing of some basement steps.

Reb rallied, regained his balance, put up his fists and aimed a quick right at Ryan's face. The blow caught Ryan on his chin and caused him to stagger to one side. But Ryan was tougher, quicker and dirtier than Reb could ever be, driven on by his consuming anger. Suddenly he bent over. Using his head for a battering ram, he caught Reb a nasty blow in the belly.

Reb grunted, reeled back against the iron railing, toppled headfirst over it. He fell six feet to the brick passageway and lit on his neck. He lay quite still at the foot of the steps as Ryan peered anxiously over the rail at him, waiting for him to move and stand up.

Seconds passed. Reb did not alter his position. After a minute Ryan was clutched by a terrible premonition; the man could be dead, not just unconscious.

He heard a window open overhead and looked up. It was the same window where he had seen the half-naked man—Lida's window. She was leaning out and staring down at him as he stood on the sidewalk. He stood in a mellow circle of lamplight, but the slouch hat put his features in shadow.

As they stared at each other, a light came on in the basement windows near Reb's inert body. Ryan stepped back, deciding to run. He glanced quickly up at the window where Lida was still visible, and this time his face was in the light and his features distinguishable. He wanted to call out to Lida but didn't dare. If he lingered he'd be in dire trouble. He turned and fled down the street.

Lida watched him go. She knew it was Arno; she could tell by his build and his movements. She didn't know what had happened, but she'd heard two men arguing. If the man with Ryan happened to be Reb, where was he? She wanted to throw on some clothes and rush downstairs, find out what had gone on, but she was afraid.

If it had been Arno he didn't want her to know of his presence in San Francisco, which meant that he was spying on her. What had he seen? she wondered with a chill, and shut the window. He would tell her in his own good time, in his own way . . .

En route to the docks, Ryan stopped at the saloon to pick up his luggage before he started running for his life.

CHANGES

THE NEWS OF Reb Sanderson's untimely death was in all the newspapers that same day, for Reb's popularity as a young man about town and his position as the son of a respected, wealthy San Francisco businessman made his sudden death headline news.

The mystery of who killed Reb and why deepened as the police investigation into his death proceeded. It was assumed eventually by the authorities that Reb had met his death at the hands of one or more persons who bore him ill will. But no further identification, certainly no firm motive, could be linked to anyone.

The two pieces of evidence that might have described Arno Ryan as a stranger in the city lay at the bottom of San Francisco Bay. No one noticed Ryan as he jettisoned the prop moustache and the slouch hat. He took the eastbound train from Oakland Station as planned, fearful all the way to Chicago that at any moment someone might walk up to him, tap him on the shoulder and take him into custody for questioning.

At several points along the route, Ryan broke his journey to stay overnight in railroad hotels. He would buy all the available newspapers, scanning them for fresh news of the murder, hoping to learn more about the man he had accidentally killed. By the time he reached Chicago, the papers were saying that the murder was caused by a grudge fight. It seemed that recently on a visit to his ranch south of San Francisco, Reb Sanderson had been obliged to discharge a pair of young Mexican cowboys suspected of cattle rustling. That view appeared to concentrate the blame of the murder in the West. It was rumored that the Mexicans had threatened Reb's life at the time they were discharged and that subsequently they had fled south of the Mexican border, well beyond the reach of United States law.

Their news relieved Ryan, yet he worried about another aspect of the case, the ordeal that Lida must have undergone with the police interrogation. But he gave this no more than a day's worry, deciding that she had brought all of the unpleasantness upon herself by being such a wanton.

As Ryan's train changes took him nearer Chicago, he rationalized Reb's death and developed a plausible alibi. To account for his time between New York and his job, he planned to tell the theatrical company's producer in Chicago that he had stopped off in Philadelphia for a few days to visit friends and enjoy a short vacation. Since he often moved around to various Eastern cities directing theatrical productions, no one would question his story. He would, of course, never tell Lida anything about the San Francisco incident; it would be his secret forever, which it was to be. On the last leg of the journey in to Chicago, Ryan got drunk from a small hip flask he carried. While drinking in the train's vestibule, he attempted to close a window, opened the door instead, and fell from the moving train, killing himself. Since he was without identification, it was two days before the news of his death reached Chicago, longer before Lida learned of it.

Robert offered a five thousand dollar reward for information that might lead to the arrest of any person or persons involved in the murder of his son, Reb. The carriage driver who took Arno Ryan to Lida's apartment saw the notice but kept silent about the man in the slouch hat with the handlebar moustache. Much as he wanted the money and had an idea that this man might be the culprit, he was already in deep trouble with the police for collusion with prostitutes over robbing drunken clients and beating them afterwards. He couldn't risk the exposure.

The actor who had written the revealing letter to Arno Ryan also kept his mouth shut. He suspected Ryan of involvement in the death of Reb Sanderson, but he was married and wanted no publicity in that situation, nor did he want Ryan to wonder about his own brief affair with Lida shortly before she met Reb.

Robert hired a detective at one point to find out everything possible, but the man came up with nothing. Only that a stranger drifted into town, along with a thousand others, on the day of Reb's death, and must have drifted out again early the next morning.

Inconsolable, Robert went through the most distressing time of his life on the day of Reb's funeral. He stayed close to Pilar because her loss was as great as his, and because she begged him not to leave her alone. "I will break apart if you do," she said, and he didn't let her out of his sight all day long.

The funeral was a simple one. The burial south of San Francisco was an ordeal, with a Protestant minister muttering words of prayer over the open grave.

Pilar went through the formalities of the day in a state of pale blankness, holding up far better than Robert would have thought possible. She reinforced his suspicion that she harbored the strength of ten men in that small body of hers.

After the police had grilled Lida exhaustively on and off over a period of several days, Tom Barrett called her into his office and shut the door.

"You're out of here tomorrow, Lida," he told her.

"What about my replacement? You don't have an understudy even."

"That doesn't matter," the California's manager said. "We're closing the show for the time being. You'll be joining the company in New York, and when we reopen here there'll be a new principal in your place. If you could stay on you'd be excellent box office. But frankly, we don't think it advisable, or seemly. The prurient would all come to gaze and gape, of course, and that wouldn't do. I liked Reb Sanderson, and his father's a decent man. We're not running a circus here, although God knows this whole town is as bizarre as a carnival."

"You're saying I didn't behave correctly," Lida declared.

"Little lady, you're absolutely right. Bear that fact in mind as you make your way through life. And try to examine your conscience; you might learn a bitter lesson."

"You're being grossly unfair to me," Lida complained.

This was too much for Tom Barrett. "Get out," he barked, "before I slap that pretty face of yours! You disgust me!"

Lida left San Francisco, still in shock over Reb's death and blaming it on herself. If she hadn't driven him away in the middle of the night, he might be alive and well today. In brooding over his murder, she had put the pieces together fairly well. She wasn't for a minute taken in by the tale of the vindictive Mexican cowboys; she thought it was just a way for the police to justify their failure to find the murderer. Lida could only hazard a guess as to when Arno had arrived in San Francisco, but whenever, he had long since departed. He was probably now in Chicago.

She would just as soon never see Arno again. He terrified her. But for propriety's sake she would have to continue on with him, never letting him know what she suspected. Before she set off for Chicago she sent a telegram to the theatre where he would be rehearsing, saying she was on her way to New York and would visit him en route. She was greeted upon her arrival in Chicago by the news of Arno's death. She accompanied the body to New York for burial. Feeling a double guilt for both Reb's and Arno's deaths, the night before *Lonely Hearts* was to begin rehearsal she tried to kill herself with a massive dose of laundanum. Found in time by an actress friend and rushed to a hospital, she recovered. Feeling lucky to be alive, she continued her career.

The night of Reb's funeral was a somber one at Pilar's house. Robert and his daughter-in-law sat before a flickering fire in the study after dinner, each wrapped in separate moods. Robert was reluctant to return to his house on Russian Hill, and Pilar was indisposed to let him go. Little Maria was upstairs asleep. She had not yet been told of her father's death, but with a small child's awareness had realized that something was happening in the house. The servants tiptoed softly about; Maria's nurse, who had been fond of Reb, performed her duties with red, swollen eyes, unable to accept the master's death.

Out of a prolonged silence Robert finally said, "It's like a bad dream. I can't believe he's gone. He was the most vital person I've ever known, whatever else he may have been. I was never like that. I saw in him all my own faults, but so many other qualities that were remarkable."

Pilar nodded. "I tried not to be forgiving about that woman, but it's no good saying an eye for an eye. Now the world has stopped. If I didn't have you as a friend, Robert, I shudder to think what might happen."

"I feel the same way about you, my dear. Thank God we have one another."

"Yes, thank God," Pilar sighed, agreeing exactly with his sentiments.

"We could go on like this for the next year, you in mourning cloths, me talking about what might have been," Robert observed. "I think a change is indicated. Reb would want it."

"A change? I don't understand."

"Perhaps you should go away on a trip. To a different climate, meet some new people."

"I am in mourning, Robert," she felt obliged to say.

"We both are, my dear. Wear mourning clothes if you wish, but you're still alive, you have Maria."

"Who would look after her if I went away?"

"Her nurse Susan, of course. She's efficient and responsible, she loves Maria. The child won't be unhappy while you're gone, not with Susan around to pamper and entertain her all day. You're not deserting her."

"I suppose you're right. A change is indicated. But I don't feel up to a long journey."

"Who says it has to be very far away? Don't you have a cousin in Santa Barbara who's always been promising to come here for a visit?"

"Consuelo? Yes my spiritual twin. We haven't visited in several years. We write occasionally."

"Well then, get in touch with her, send her a telegram. I'll make arrangements for a suite at a Santa Barbara hotel, and see you off on the train. I'm sure that Consuelo will be delighted to see you. She'll relieve your burden."

"It's possible that you may be right," Pilar conceded. "I'm still hesitant to leave Maria. She thinks Reb is away, and if she asks too many questions, I'm afraid one of the servants might get careless and inadvertently tell her the truth."

"I'll brief them. No, I'll do better then that. I'll stay in the house while you're gone," Robert suggested. "Between Susan and me, Maria won't have a lonesome moment. . . . Think about, my dear."

"I shall."

They lapsed into silence again, more relaxed, warmed by the fire. Robert broke the quiet after a minute or so.

"Have you sent any word to Doña Maria about Reb?" he asked.

"None. What is the use? She will have read about it in the newspapers, or someone has told her."

"I wrote to her this morning," Robert admitted.

"You did?" Pilar's tone came close to recrimination. "But why Robert? She won't answer."

"Well, someone had to. I knew you wouldn't."

"You will only get silence from her."

"I hope not," said Robert. "I'd like to see the breach mended. This is the time you need her most. I know she's a very stubborn old woman, that's her heritage. But I believe she'll be sensitive to your loss."

"You should not have written, Robert. She will never, never forgive me."

Pilar stood up in a rustle of black moire silk

"I am very tired," she announced in a dry voice. "I may not be able to get to sleep, so much is on my mind, but at least I will go and lie down, rest. Why don't you take one of the guest rooms and stay here? I would feel much more relaxed if you were in the house tonight."

"That's a good idea," said Robert. "I'll take Reb's room."

Pilar nodded. "It is made up fresh." She held out her cold hands to him, took his, offered her cheek for him to kiss. At the foyer door she said, "I think you have the right idea about taking a journey. I'll send word to Consuelo in the morning. Thank you for being with me through everything. Without you I could not have faced today. Goodnight Robert."

"Nor I without you, my dear. Goodnight."

He sat by the fire untill it dwindled to embers He tried not to think about Reb, going back much further into time—to the death of his father, Lem, his first encounter with the passing of a loved one, that event now made benign by time. Then Sarah Calder, and his mother Caroline, his brother John, Jane's death.

He withstood many terrible losses; he would survive this one. It was not a particularly comforting thought, but he didn't feel he was defeated yet by life, nor that his days were numbered. He would grieve for his beloved Reb in a thousand different ways before the worst of the pain was gone, and for a long time afterwards the wound would refuse to heal. Reb's death in his mid-twenties was a tragic waste. It made no sense and couldn't be accounted for by any theological mumbo-jumbo. If Robert had thought seriously about the comforts of the church when he attended mass with Pilar, he knew now that such acceptance was impossible. A just God would not have taken Reb from him so brutally.

Bone-tired at last, he went upstairs to Reb's room with a heavy heart. As he passed Pilar's door he heard her muffled sobbing through the thick oaken panel. He paused a moment to listen. Curiously, the sobbing abruptly stopped; he went on.

As Robert lay in bed he thought about what he had failed to do for Reb. He had given his son everything except the assurance that he loved him. Maybe if he had conveyed that more fully, Reb might have grown more secure in himself and remained faithful to Pilar, and thus be alive today. But, he scolded himself, this was specious reasoning. He could pursue such ideas endlessly. That way lay madness, or at least an insurmountable guilt which he refused to put on his already overburdened shoulders.

At best, he had Pilar and Maria, he reflected. They were his family. Maria might be female, but he would raise her in a man's world, by man's standards, with Pilar's permission, of course. She would be his heir; the line would go on. Thus comforted, he fell asleep.

Three days after the funeral, Pilar took the new railroad line down through the San Joaquin Valley to Los Angeles. In October the great central valley was still hot and parched from the long, scorching summer of endless sunny days, but Pilar's mood was such that she was impervious to the climate. Under other circumstances she might have been elated by the open landscape, the desert and mountains, the change of scene, as Robert had suggested, but not now.

In Los Angeles she was to stay all night at a new hotel, then travel by coach early next morning from Los Angeles to Santa Barbara. Journeying alone did not intimidate Pilar. There were pleasent folk aboard the train who, when they saw her widow's black, made her as comfortable as they could. The train's conductor was solicitous, the railway coach was new and splendidly appointed, and a buffet car was attached where she could dine. All in all, it was a most agreeable passage.

Pilar was pleased upon arrival at Los Angeies to be greeted with kisses and tears by her cousin, Consuelo Moraga, who had journeyed down from Santa Barbara to meet her.

Consuelo was a distant descendant of Lt. José Joaquin Moraga who led the first Spanish settlers into California in 1776, one week before the American people declared themselves a nation. Consuelo was twenty-nine, aristocratic, with a fine ivory complexion, penetrating black eyes, quite large and a head taller than Pilar, and still single. This latter condition may have been because although Consuelo came from illustrious Spanish lineage, she possessed a razor sharp tongue men found unbecoming in a woman of position. Also she was no beauty. She was not ugly, but sharp-faced, which made her seem unfeminine, rather coarse.

The two cousins embraced each other warmly. Moments later Pilar was being whisked into a handsome black carriage, her luggage secured to the roof, and driven at breakneck pace through the sprawling, burgeoning pueblo of old Los Angeles toward the highway that led to Santa Barbara.

Consuelo fanned herself vigorously as they departed the dusty limits of Los Angeles. Pilar would have appreciated a more leisurely city traversal, having not seen Los Angeles in some years. But Consuelo was having none of it.

"We're out of that dust bowl at last," Consuelo said with relief as they passed the last of Los Angeles. "A dreadful place. Alongside it, I imagine San Francisco is like Paris." Consuelo sat back for the first time since they'd boarded the coach and with care appraised her small cousin in widow's weeds.

"Pilar, my darling, you look surprisingly well."

If there was one quality Pilar could always depend upon from Consuelo, it was her candor in getting directly to the point of a subject.

"I feel well," Pilar replied, waiting for the next observation.

"My condolances, of course," said Consuelo. "You received my telegram?"

"It was exactly right," Pilar said. "I gave it to my father-in-law to read. He asked me to thank you."

"It came from my heart," Consuelo said, and crossed herself vigorously. She took Pilar's hands. "Anyway, *querida*, I am so glad to see you again. We have much foolishness and gossip to discuss. Will you be staying long?"

"A week, at the most. I have little Maria to worry about back home, although her grandfather will be with her."

"You could have brought her along."

"It seemed unwise, staying at a hotel."

"Surely you have a reliable housekeeper?"

"A nurse," Pilar explained. "I'm the housekeeper. I need to keep busy. It's a large house but easy to care for."

"Appalling! With a nurse Maria will be badly spoiled," Consuelo pointed out.

Pilar smiled. "She is already. Her father began it and her grandfather will continue it while I am away."

"And how is Doña Maria?"

Consuelo knew of the old lady's bitterness over Pilar's elopement with Reb, and of the break that had existed since between the two women.

"She is alive," said Pilar. "I don't know the details. In other words, we have not spoken in a long time."

Consuelo laughed, not embarrassed in the least. "Stupid me! I just realized that of course you haven't seen her since your marriage."

"It doesn't appear that I'll see her again soon," said Pilar, "but I have other matters to worry about."

"Little Maria," said Consuelo, this time tactfully.

"Yes. How is your family?"

"Everyone is disgustingly healthy. Mama and papa are in excellent health, the *rancho* is running by itself, and our life is pleasant and uneventful, as you shall see."

"And José?"

José Alvarado was Consuelo's distant cousin by marriage. They had been engaged for nearly seven years. It was Pilar's private opinion that José intended to prolong the engagement another seven years if he could manage, or until he had sowed his wild oats and satisfied his curiosity about all the young women who caught his eye.

Meanwhile, Consuelo saw José as often as he came to visit at the *hacienda.* Not even Consuelo with full-time conniving could persuade José to surrender his bachelorhood for marriage until he was ready. The wedding had been announced and then postponed several times. First, José fractured an ankle while visiting at the Moraga estate. Another time it was a voyage to Peru on a proposed business venture that kept him away a year and failed to materialize. Another time it was because José took the train to New York and thence a ship to Málaga to collect a small legacy from a distant relative when the money could as easily have been transferred by post. The marriage was postponed a fourth time because José was simply too frightened of total commitment to go through with the ceremony. José was presently in residence at the Moraga estate and had made affirmative noises about marriage for some time next year, but no date had as yet been set. Pilar was confident that José would undoubtedly come up with another evasive tactic before the marriage. At this rate, Consuelo might never become a bride, at least not José's.

"José," said Consuelo, in a raspy, irritated tone, wrinkling her nose, "is still the single man that he has always been, if that isn't understating the case."

"I think perhaps it would be wise to look elsewhere for someone who will be more appreciative of your virtues than José," Pilar observed, feeling no reservation about speaking out to Consuelo. The two cousins had been frank with each other since Consuelo was in her teens and Pilar a small child.

"You're thinking in the right direction," Consuelo agreed. "But each year my chances grow slimmer for a marriage outside the family circle. I am certainly not beautiful, let us get that out of the way right off. And I am sometimes not even very civil toward men. Most of them want only one thing, will say anything to get it, and seldom say that with any panache. I am not the most seductive woman alive, need I add? So how can I reasonably expect to change my station in life by marrying anyone other than José? Beside, José is 38, I am all too close to 30. Yes, I think we were made for each other—our faults dovetail beautifully. But apparently only God sees it as a marriage made in heaven. Certainly not José. I think he cares for me as much as he can care for any woman, but marriage? I don't know anymore; I resign myself to fate."

Consuelo sighed dolorously, her large eyes glazed over at the probability of spinsterhood.

"Dear God," she said, shaking her head, "it's not as though I must force myself into a life of shame if José continues to be difficult. We Moragas are comfortable, as you know, and in the bosom of our family there is always room for a maiden aunt, especially if she excels at cooking, sewing and watching over the children of others, my sisters, for example."

"Now, now, Consuelo. Things aren't as grim as you paint them."

"Perhaps not. But they may become so as I move on toward my one hundredth year, and still remain single."

Pilar smiled, for the first time in many days. It was good that she had come down. Consuelo always made her feel a little light-headed.

Consuelo leaned toward her in the bouncing
coach and said in a tender voice, her hand on
Pilar's wrist, "My heart goes out to you, *querida*.
You had a brief, wonderful and romantic life
with Reb Sanderson. From the photographs you
sent to us I could easily imagine how handsome
he must have been."

"He was certainly that," Pilar confirmed. "He
was also quite brilliant. He enjoyed good times
and he was a good father." She refused to add
"good husband" to her appraisal, although until
the affair with Lida Ryan he had been that too.
She steeled herself against tears.

"You must have been gloriously happy in
your fine house," Consuelo ran on.

"Oh yes, we were indeed," said Pilar, wishing
she could turn back the clock, be in San Francisco with Reb as he was when they married.
Pride would never allow her to tell Consuelo of
the humility she suffered, of the anguished
nights she had spent weeping alone in the
house, with only little Maria to comfort her. In
due time she might be able to confide something of what she felt to Consuelo, as she had
to her father-in-law, but not yet. She was far
too raw and unhealed.

"Will I see José?" Pilar enquired in order to
change the subject.

"I doubt if you can miss him. He's gained
twenty kilos. He's very pleased that you're coming to visit us. He wanted to accompany me
down by carriage, but I knew we couldn't talk
about him if he did."

"You will marry soon, I hope," Pilar said.
"You're a good, large-hearted person, Consuelo.
You deserve a good life."

Consuelo snorted. "Ha! If we all got what we deserve!" She crossed herself ostentaciously. "Sometimes I wonder God doesn't strike me dead. I expect so much and have so little to give."

"Do I hear self-pity in your voice?"

"I suppose so, and I ought to be ashamed of it in your company. I hear none in yours. Tell me," Consuelo probed, prodding Pilar's knee with her fan, "do you think you'll marry again?"

From anyone else the question would have been insulting. Pilar shrugged. "I haven't given it a thought, cousin, but I would imagine not. I see no need."

"But you're still young, you're beautiful. I suppose you have money?"

"Some . . ." It wouldn't do to tell Consuelo how much; the news would spread throughout the Spanish-speaking families of southern California within a matter of days.

"I don't mean to pry." Consuelo's lustrous eyes glittered. "Good heavens, when I think of the opportunities for an unencumbered woman in San Francisco, my head starts reeling!"

"You have a vivid imagination. It's a city of distinct classes. One can't move about as freely as you might imagine. The lofty rich are a closed society, the middle class mercantiles float somewhere between the upper and the lower. A single woman, even a widow, is at the mercy of the town." Pilar said in an amused tone, "I think I'll speak to José and tell him to grab you before you whirl out of his life forever. You seem to be on the verge of an adventure."

"Now you're teasing me," Consuelo said, with a mock pout.

The stage coach pulled into the settlement of
Ventura on the Coast in late afternoon. The two
women spent the night at the mission convent,
on their way early in the morning. They reached
Santa Barbara around noon, in time for dinner,
welcomed with tears and laughter by the Moraga family. Pilar was not allowed to go to a hotel,
of course.

Within minutes Pilar understood that her new
role of widow was the way the Moragas would
view her from now on. She was determined to
be as relaxed as possible and play out her part.
Curiously enough, seeing the Moragas so confident in how to express their sincere sympathy
made it easier to deal with her grief.

After two days among the happy, easy-going
Moraga brood, her sharpest anguish had dissolved, Pilar was relieved to note. She knew
that by the time she departed for Los Angeles
to board the train for San Francisco and somehow take up her life again, without Reb, she
would be in excellent fettle and could start
remaking her life. This attitude was strongly reinforced by the knowledge that Robert was
there, and she could lean on him.

During Pilar's visit she had a strange conversation with José about Consuelo. She had
brought along her buckskins and was out riding
with José one afternoon when she saw the perfect opportunity to prod him about his forth-
coming marriage to Consuelo.

"I'm worried about Consuelo," she began.
"She is dispirited, she's lost much of her zest
for life."

"Ah yes," José replied, "she's getting older."

"It's not that. She's still quite young. José, may I presume upon your good nature, since we're old friends?"

"O course, dear Pilar."

"Are you and Consuelo going to marry?"

José frowned. "Did she send you riding with me to ask? It would be like her."

"No, her headache this afternoon was genuine."

José glanced obliquely at Pilar. All vestiges of his once youthful and dashing presence had gone in rich living. His features had coarsened; he had a paunch.

"Well?" probed Pilar. "Should Consuelo have hopes?"

"We all have them," José declared, "and dreams. One day we put them aside to face the bare truth."

"I'm having to do that now," said Pilar. "Then you mean you will mary Consuelo before long?"

José sighed. "I am nearly 40. I must decide soon about life, while you can take your time. You're young. My *caballero* days are nearly over. I must come to terms with the world or it will pass me by. I will have to sign a contract, making that for the best offer that I can get, which I suppose means I'll marry Consuelo."

"Is that prospect so disgusting?" Pilar said with ill-concealed contempt.

"Consuelo is a nice person, but the prospect of eternal bliss is, well—frankly, my dear Pilar, I find that the consequences look depressing."

"I'm surprised at you."

"Well, that's as I see things," José said morosely.

"You make marriage to Consuelo sound horrible," Pilar observed. "It won't be. She has reserves of joy and strength. She's a good person."

"Please, spare me the sermon, Pilar. There's no need to peddle me a bill of goods. I know what Consuelo is. I just wish she were more, much more, and myself too."

They rode back to the house in silence, and José said very little to Pilar during the remainder of her stay at the *hacienda*. She said nothing about her conversation with José to Consuelo. There was no need to depress her cousin. José would do what he wished, obviously.

Several days later Pilar departed for Los Angeles. Consuelo had planned to come with her and stay with relatives there, but she caught a cold and could not make the journey. José was planning to go to Los Angeles anyway in another week, so he volunteered to accompany Pilar, for which she was most grateful.

Pilar's farewell with the Moragas was again tearful and joyous. On the journey down José talked about every subject he could think of except Consuelo, and Pilar did not discuss his relationship with her cousin.

"You know," he said at one point, "you should get married. You are much too lovely to remain alone."

"That's beginning to be a familiar note in my life," Pilar said.

"It's true."

"I don't think I shall ever marry again."

"What a waste!" José murmured. "I would be your slave, as I suppose you know."

Pilar drew herself up. "I know nothing of the kind, José. Let's change the subject."

José saw his foolishness and obligingly went

on to talk about the crime rate in Los Angeles, which was soaring alarmingly. He saw Pilar to the night train and put her and her luggage aboard. Ceremoniously he kissed her hand and bade her a good journey.

Poor José, she thought, watching him disappear into the crowd. She suspected, but had no firm reason to believe it, that he was in love with some gloriously young, impossibly unattainable woman, probably not even Spanish, more likely an American. With his genteel impoverishment he had no chance of realizing his dream. He would soon have to make a decision about Consuelo, or lose even that sure thing.

As the train pulled out of Los Angeles, Pilar reflected with relief how glad she was to be northbound to San Francisco. She would probably never come this way again. The visit, however, had been salutary; it had done just what Robert predicted it would—dispelled a large measure of her gloom-filled bereavement. She felt that she was ready for a new phase in her existence, that life would open up for her, give her many rewards she was unable to find with Reb. She would, however, never love anyone in the way that she had loved him, with her whole being.

Somewhere on the journey back to San Francisco she began to relegate Reb's memory to the niche where it belonged, determined to retain only the happiness and joy of it as remembrance without pain.

"You have never looked better," Robert told her as they drove to Pilar's house from the ferry terminal. "I was right, a change of scene was just what you needed."

"I am not changed," Pilar said, meaning she was still in an official state of mourning, "only the scenery has changed."

"Well, whatever happened, your visit was the right medicine for you."

"It might have had something to do with my cousin and the family. Consuelo is always great fun. We laughed a lot, more than in a long time for me."

"When is she getting married?" Robert asked.

"That became funny, too; she made a joke of it. Poor Consuelo, she may end up being the family's favorite single aunt. Tell me, how did Maria behave?"

"Like an angel," said Robert.

"She didn't even miss me?"

"She accepted the fact that I was her good friend. We invented a number of games; I brought her a doll she's fallen in love with. Miss Hargrave was grateful for my relief brigade. Maria's a very demanding child."

"I have good reason to know."

Robert took Pilar's hand. "I thought about you constantly, wondering how you were getting along."

"Fine, Robert, really just fine. I know there's no way to wipe out the past, and I wouldn't want to. But I think I've found a way to live with it so that it doesn't affect Maria. Or you."

"And what is that?"

"I think I'd like to go into business one of these days."

"Oh?" Robert exclaimed in surprise. "You in enterprise?"

"Why not? I can't just sit around the house forever feeling sorry for myself. I have too much practical energy for that, and besides I've done it long enough already. And I'm not needed at my grandmother's side these days. So I thought on the train coming up that you might have some suggestions for me."

"There is a way in which you could be useful," Robert said. "You could take over some of Reb's responsibilities. I was thinking of hiring someone to assume the ranch's details at this end, to go down there and oversee the manager. There's no reason why a woman can't handle these duties as well as a man. Even on the ranch. No one knows the potential of the countryside down around Los Arboles better than you do."

"I daresay."

"And what it can produce. How would you like that obligation for starters?"

"I would indeed," Pilar said eagerly. "I'd be enthralled for the chance to see if the ranch can be made more productive."

"Very well then. You have a job. We'll talk about it in the morning. I imagine there'll be some men in business who'll take a dim view of your participation in a world that's dominated by males, but they're the ones who must adjust, not you and me."

"I'm excited at the prospect already," Pilar said. "How did you like staying in the house?"

"I liked it immensely. In fact, I enjoyed it far more than my own house. When I went back there several times for fresh linen, to see how it was, it seemed empty and gloomy, not really mine any longer. Unlived in, I should say. It's never really been much of a home to me since you and Reb moved into the new house."

"Why don't you sell it?" Pilar suggested.

"Sell it? I suppose I could. Any house with its location and size is in great demand on the market today. The only thing is, I'd have to move into an apartment, and that doesn't seem like a very domestic environment to me. I should be more adaptable. Do you suppose it's old age creeping up on me?"

"You're in your *mature* years, and hardly old," Pilar said rather severely, her words sounding like a reprimand for even suggesting that he wasn't her peer.

Pilar waited until dinner that night to discuss what she had in mind.

"I don't know quite how to approach this subject, Robert. I don't want to get your back up, as Reb used to say. But then, I don't care to shy around the matter either, so perhaps I'd best be as Consuelo always is, utterly candid. If and when you sell your house and furniture and you don't care to move into a furnished apartment, then why not come and live with us permanently? You could take Reb's room."

"Here, in your house?"

"Yes. It can be your home, too. I'm aware that you may wish to pursue a private life of your own that has nothing to do with me. That is your privilege—I would not interfere. Nor would you bring private matters here. Reb told me how discreet you are, and I can see, too."

Robert was deeply moved over Pilar's suggestion, flattered actually, although he had a horror of imposing himself upon her or anyone. He was nearing his mid-fifties, and while in good health, getting set in his ways. He knew that Pilar would expect him to come and go as he pleased, to entertain business friends occasionally at dinner, or to invite guests in for Sunday tea, or sherry. Pilar's house was large and comfortable, conveniently close to downtown San Francisco, to the highway that led toward the Sanderson ranch and Los Arboles. He would continue to be lonely as long as he lived by himself.

"You've opened up a tempting opportunity, my dear. I don't know quite what to say."

"Think about it, Robert. You can still take an apartment. Why not keep it for business friends who come to town and don't wish to stay in a hotel? You could use it sometimes as a refuge from me," she said, smiling. "You are my only family, since grandmother rejected me and Reb is gone. You are also my dearest friend. I welcome you to this house with open arms. If, of course, you meet someone and wish to pursue a relationship with her, you are free to go. I shan't sit in judgment on anyone who captures your fancy, should it happen."

"That seems an unlikely possibility," Robert observed.

"One never knows," Pilar countered. "Do think about what I've said."

Robert went home that evening for his first night's stay in the big house since he had used Reb's room. He found the house cold and impersonal, stifling and musty, unused. Even his cheery housekeeper who lived in basement rooms with her husband could not brighten up the place with her jovial smile at his arrival.

"Good to have you back," Molly Duggan told him. "Jim and me missed you greatly, sir."

Robert decided before retiring that he would get rid of the house. He spent a longer time reflecting on whether he should live with Pilar in the big house on Jefferson Square. He knew he would look forward joyfully to coming home there each evening and discussing the day's business events with Pilar, who would relish such conversation and have helpful suggestions. He would savor greeting little Maria when she'd rush in from the nursery to the study, smothering him with kisses as she always did. He owed it to Maria, if not to Pilar, to provide some kind of a paternal figure for the child, he told himself.

His only concern was that he might suppress Pilar's natural exuberance. She was still so young, she really ought to marry again. Many men Reb's age or older would find her attractive, even with a small daughter. He wouldn't mention such thoughts to Pilar; she would pooh-pooh the idea of another marriage as ridiculous, but the possibility was still there and bothered him somewhat. He fell asleep still unable to extract a decision from himself about moving into Pilar's house. He would of course take an apartment in any event.

On rising in the morning the first thing that came to mind was Pilar's offer. Reb would have approved highly of her offer, he knew, and in a way, if he moved to Jefferson Square, he would be closer to Reb's memory than if he lived alone. Putting flowers on Reb's grave at special holiday times was an empty ritual; graves had never drawn him. But living in Reb's house, sleeping in the bed that Reb had used for a time, meant that he was continuing the line, so to speak. But was it proper?

That evening he told Pilar, "I'm selling the house and taking an apartment."

Pilar could not mask her disappointment.

"But you'll be lonely there, Robert. Please come and live with Maria and me. Don't you want to?"

"Yes, very much. You know I've been called a maverick because I refused to have the ranch's cattle branded. Well, I'm a bit like that in life, an independent nonconformist. You have a long Spanish tradition of integrated family behind you. To you family is a clan arrangement, with relatives all over the place. My father and mother loved me and my brother John very much, but they urged us to leave the nest as soon as we were out of school. They wanted us to be on our own, and I've always held that view as the only one. I have decided that living here would be an imposition."

"But you are my family. I'm not just being gracious, or pitying. But anyway, Robert, the decision is entirely up to you. I shan't speak of it again . . ."

She bade him good-night and he left the house feeling that in some obscure way he had offended her deeply. He certainly hadn't intended to.

Instead of going directly to his empty house he stopped off at the Hotel Splendide, hoping that Ethan and Flora would be having coffee in their ground-floor apartment after one of their usual rich, late dinners.

Flora had retired early with a headache, but

Ethan was still up, reading a newspaper, with coffee and cognac at his elbow. He welcomed Robert warmly, sat him down, got him coffee and a glass of cognac. Robert settled back and told Ethan his problem.

"Move in now," Ethan urged him. "You've been dangling too lose since Reb died. Don't you realize that Pilar's offer is a desperate attempt to overcome her own feelings of emptiness? You're the nearest and dearest person to Reb and she needs you as a substitute."

"I suppose that could be the case."

"You suppose! Dammit, sometimes you're so thick I wonder how you've been so successful in business. You don't have to live in Pilar's house forever. Just a few months, maybe a year, until both of you find other interests and are on top of your sadness. Just because she hasn't told you in so many words doesn't mean that her heart's still not breaking."

"You could be right."

"I am right, lad."

"Pilar will be coming into the enterprises with me."

"Well now, that's a surprise," Ethan said. "What will she do?"

"Manage the ranch from the city, go down there as Reb did to oversee management and development."

"Not a bad idea. Yours or hers?"

"Mine, since she expressed a wish to enter the business world.'

"She'll do all right. Beneath that warm exterior beats a heart of iron-clad determination. What she wants she'll get."

"In that case I might as well move in."

"Now you're talking," said Ethan. "I'm glad you came along tonight. I've been thinking the last few days, why not sell El Dorado Steamship?"

"Sell it? Why? It's thriving."

"Just the point. More competitors are entering the business every month, as the railroads grow. Next year there'll be a new trans-Bay service. We're getting obsolete and the big boys are ready to buy us up. I know we can get two million for our equipment and facilities. Flora's making noises about buying a vineyard up in Napa Valley and raising varietals. I like the idea too. I'm fed up with the so-called cosmopolitan atmosphere of the city. What do you say?"

"Whatever you like. I'm not actively engaged in El Dorado anyway. You've done most of the work."

"Good lad," Ethan beamed. "The best thing that ever happened to me was you. I suppose you know that."

"We've been friends a long time."

"We have indeed. I worry about you, Bob. Flora and I both do. What you need is a woman, someone like Emily. Hell, someone a whole lot more stable. But a nice soft beautiful creature you can sink your sadness into and dally with."

"I'm past that age."

"You're crazy. Look around you at the customers Flora's entertained through the years. They weren't boys. Flora will find you somebody—she introduced you to Emily."

"I'm perfectly capable of making my own arrangements, thanks."

"Well, don't get huffy about it," Ethan retorted. "It's for your own good."

"I appreciate your concern, Ethan. It's just that I'm not ready for a liaison at present."

"You're still mourning Reb."

"And probably will for a long time."

"Yes. Well, drink up, have another."

The next morning Robert put the house up for sale. Three days later it was bought for cash, including all of its furnishings. Molly and Jim Duggan went to work for Pilar at her request, not losing a day. Simultaneously Robert found a three-room apartment that was tastefully furnished only a block from the flat Lida Ryan had occupied. Each day he had to pass the stairwell where his son had died. He stood this agony for a week, then told Pilar at dinner one night that he would accept her offer.

"I'll maintain the apartment for business purposes, as you suggested," he explained. "It'll be handy for entertaining out-of-towners who can't find hotel accommodations. That often happens."

"You know how pleased I am with your decision," Pilar said, clear delight in her eyes. "It cheers me up."

"But remember," Robert cautioned her gently, "if matters should ever get tense between us and you wish to be alone in the house, then let it be understood that I'll move out at once, so as not to cause you any further inconvenience."

"Fair enough," agreed Pilar, "although how could you inconvenience me? I'm happy to welcome you to this house!"

A TIME
TO LOVE

BOTH PILAR AND ROBERT were like different people after they began to share the house. The grief that they had been sustaining individually could now be brought to the light of scrutiny in small fragments, observed, analyzed, relegated to the attic of the past. While this should have interred Reb's memory, it did the opposite. It allowed father and daughter-in-law to relax in these roles, to seek a more common denominator than being in-laws. They became closer friends. And each went to work on projects with renewed vitality. There were even moments when Pilar felt a singing happiness she hadn't felt since she was a child free in the hills behind Los Arboles.

Pilar soon took over the general management of the Sanderson ranch property. The improvements Reb had been planning for some time in

311

advance of his death became Pilar's prime concern.

She supervised the building of a new abbatoir, a large pen for hog-raising, new poultry runs for the thousands of chickens, and newly-designed enclosed chicken roosts. She enriched the feed of the ranch's dairy cows and built underground beds for the culture of mushrooms, shipped at maturity to the better San Francisco restaurants and markets.

At every trip to the ranch, particularly when she donned her buckskins and rode out into the countryside that bordered on Los Arboles, she gazed with longing toward her grandmother's *hacienda,* sad that she could no longer see the old lady, and bitter that Doña Maria had not even deigned to acknowledge her loss of Reb.

She heard various rumors of Doña Maria's failing health. On one trip to the ranch she cinched up her determination to visit her grandmother, and rode over to Los Arboles by herself. She found it as she had left it, nestled like some exquisite jewel in its hillside cradle of giant oaks. She would have gone directly into the house, except that she encountered Antonio near the corral. After greeting him warmly she enquired about her grandmother.

"I'm going in to see her," she told Antonio.

Antonio shook his head. "She heard you were coming," he said. "One of the vaqueros raced in ten minutes ago to tell her he saw you were riding this way."

"Well, then, she knows that I am going to pay her a visit."

"I am sorry, *señora,*" said Antonio, "but I have strict orders to prevent you from entering the house." He sighed and blinked his rheumy eyes at her. "It is a sorrowful thing to have to say, but she will not see you." He clicked his tongue in disapproval, spread his hands in discomfort.

"She is a cold old woman," Pilar said without emotion. "Times have changed around her but she has stood still."

"She is unforgiving but there is still love in her heart for you, *señora*. I am sure of that."

"There is no love," Pilar maintained stoutly, and reined her mount about. "Tell her I was here, please. I shan't come again without being invited."

Two months after Pilar's unrewarding visit to Los Arboles, she sat one morning in her study, now converted into an office, working on the ranch accounts.

She heard the front doorbell ring but paid scant attention; Molly Duggan would answer it. Moments later Molly interrupted her concentration with a knock at the study door.

"Visitor, ma'am," she told Pilar. "A female of Latin persuasion who speaks very thick English. She says she's a relative."

Pilar went to the vestibule. There was Consuelo, slumped down in a chair by the front door, surrounded by leather cases, looking as forlorn as an abandoned waif. Her appearance was messy and she seemed indifferent to it.

The two women embraced and Consuelo immediately let loose a torrent of tears. When she calmed down a bit, Pilar led her into the living room, settled her on the sofa and sent Molly for coffee.

"Now, what in heaven's name happened to

bring you here so unexpectedly?" Pilar asked her cousin.

"Oh, *querida*, I am so miserable," Consuelo moaned. "It is a catastrophe."

"Why didn't you send me a telegram?" Pilar asked, and at this Consuelo shed further tears.

"It all happened so suddenly," Consuelo explained. "I went to Los Angeles on some business for my mother and father, and to meet José. Well, I met him all right, and he announced that he was marrying an eighteen-year-old of cheap family because they have money and he's a Moraga. Also because she will soon have his child. I am hurt and disgusted over his behavior."

"I can't believe that José would do that," Pilar said, but of course she could. José simply hadn't wanted to marry Consuelo; the benefits weren't great enough.

"You must believe it because it's true," replied Consuelo. "I was so ashamed and humiliated that I sent a message to my parents I was coming to see you."

"Well, I'm glad you did, but it isn't the end of the world."

"It's doomsday. The girl is no better than a prostitute and I'll be the laughing stock of all Santa Barbara. I just can't face the embarrassment of going to market or to mass, not right now anyway. So without thinking things through, I bought a ticket on the railroad and here I am."

Pilar's instant reaction to her cousin's arrival was one of irritation for dropping in on her unannounced. She had come to accept the American custom of signaling one's arrival in advance, especially if one intended to stay a while. There were domestic matters to adjust to a house guest, and in Pilar's case work schedules. A visitor should be expected.

"I hope I'm not intruding," Consuelo said, as if she sensed that she had been impulsive in coming.

"Nonsense, I'm happy to see you. We have plenty of room," Pilar told her. "There are only little Maria and my father-in-law, Robert. He is staying with us indefinitely."

"Oh? I thought you said he had a home of his own."

"He sold it recently after my return from Santa Barbara. He wasn't happy there, and Maria and I are glad to have him around. He cheers us up."

Molly brought the silver coffee service and the two women talked for a while. Pilar then took Consuelo upstairs to a small guest room at the rear of the house that overlooked the garden. Consuelo bathed, took a nap and was downstairs with Pilar and Maria when Robert arrived home late in the afternoon.

Consuelo was instantly impressed with Robert, who thought that Pilar's plump, garrulous cousin was amusing, but nevertheless rather a caricature of the standard Spanish spinster. Her English, while broken, was decoratively explicit. She had an endless fund of stories to tell them about life at the Santa Barbara *hacienda* and the scandals of the town, making the dinner hour different from the usual quiet time Robert spent with Pilar.

After dinner Robert soon excused himself and went to his room, pleading an early morning

appointment. Consuelo bade him good-night
with a flirtatious flutter of her heavy eyelids and
a wide flashing smile.

"Isn't he a lovely man!" Consuelo exclaimed
after Robert left. "So dignified, so handsome
with his full head of grey hair and his upright
figure."

"My father-in-law is one of the nicest, kindest
men I've ever known," Pilar declared. "He is
sincere and always a gentleman. I wish more
Spanish men were like him."

"You have my affirmative on that," said Consuelo. "Is Robert still leading an active life?"

"He oversees his enterprises: the ranch, the
distribution of mercantile supplies, the steamship company with his partner, Ethan Drew.
There's some real estate and other smaller interests."

"Very impressive, *querida*, but what I meant
was, does he have a preference in ladies?"

Pilar looked at Consuelo sharply. "What are
you suggesting?"

"Surely he has his lady friends, a man so
distinguished."

"As far as I know, this is his only life, living
here with us," said Pilar, beginning to understand what was in Consuelo's mind; she was
strongly attracted to Robert.

"What a shame," Consuelo observed, shaking
her head. "Robert should have a wife, and he
certainly appears healthy enough to sire another
family."

"I doubt if he'd want that," Pilar said abruptly. The conversation aws definitely not to her
taste. She glanced pointedly at the grandfather

clock by the foyer entarnce. "It's my bedtime, *querida*. You must excuse me."

"Good heavens, I hadn't imagined that you went to bed so early."

"We are working people, both of us," Pilar explained. "I have taken over some of Reb's former duties. I cannot be idle these days."

"I wish I had your determination," said Consuelo. "I shall remain unfit for such responsibilities. They are not my style, being an old-fashioned creature. In fact, I felt quite daring to consider the trip north by myself."

"Here there's no need for that kind of attitude," Pilar declared. "In San Francisco one is judged only as a person."

"I feel more comfortable with the traditional values."

"For some women that's not enough. Goodnight, my dear cousin. Sleep well!"

Lying awake in bed, Pilar wondered if perhaps she shouldn't discuss Consuelo's avid interest in Robert with her cousin. But then, Consuelo was a guest; she felt that it would exceed good taste. One didn't brief guests on how to behave. And as for Robert, he was a mature man without the slightest interest in Consuelo, so it appeared. Besides, she was probably making a big issue out of nothing. If Consuelo were short-sighted enough to act the fool over Robert, it was really none of Pilar's business. Let her.

Consuelo, however, did not make a fool of herself, at least not right away. Each evening she would regale Robert and Pilar with vivid tales of her life on the southern California Coast, focusing on herself and family.

After several days as a house guest, Consuelo suggested that she take Pilar and Robert out for supper, then to the theatre. For the occasion Consuelo chose a new French restaurant. At supper she drank too much wine, talked too much and too loudly, and was generally an embarrassment to Pilar who sat through the meal quiet and subdued.

With his stable disposition, Robert accepted Consuelo as a provincial person who had never been exposed to city life before, and was therefore bound to appear somewhat incongruous against the urbane San Francisco scene. He seemed eager to please her and was courteously deferential, Pilar noted, assuming that this was as much for her sake as for Consuelo's, considering Robert's natural sense of decorum. Pilar was relieved when supper was over.

As for the theatre, Robert tactfully pointed out that it was too late for a show by the time they'd finished supper, and Consuelo agreed. At home, Pilar left Robert and Consuelo to see about little Maria. From the nursery she went along to her room.

The following morning Consuelo made a breakfast announcement when she and Pilar were alone.

"Guess what, *querida!* I am having luncheon downtown today with Robert. He will show me his offices."

"That will be instructive," Pilar said evenly, experiencing a twinge of jealousy. Lunching with Robert in a restaurant was a luxury she had never considered, mainly because she knew that Robert often used that time to transact business with associates and she didn't wish to disturb his routine. "Did he invite you?" Pilar asked.

"I invited myself," said Consuelo, who came in around three that afternoon, filled with the details of her luncheon rendezvous with Robert.

"I think he's one of the finest men I have ever met," she gushed to Pilar, "an absolute angel of a man who knows how to please women. Beside him José is a pagan. You are very lucky to have him for a father-in-law."

"I think so, too," Pilar agreed. "But don't assume too much, Consuelo."

"What do you mean? I have the utmost respect for Robert. He is a true gentleman."

"I mean," Pilar said evenly, "you aren't thinking of Robert as a possible suitor, are you?"

Consuelo's bright eyes clouded. "Of course not! Don't be ridiculous. Why do you ask such a question?"

"Perhaps I'm not the one who is being ridiculous," Pilar said with a cool smile, and went about her household duties, leaving Consuelo to ponder the content of her words.

For the next few days Consuelo was more subdued and kept her opinions to herself. There was a marked diminution of the chatty intimacy that had formerly existed between the two cousins. Consuelo started taking longer *siestas* and at the evening meal had very little to say, in contrast to her former non-stop narratives. The main burden of the dinner conversations now rested heavily on Robert's shoulders, making him ill-at-ease. He began coming home only occasionally for dinner, pleading the excuse business friends to be entertained. This threw Consuelo and Pilar together for whole evenings of minimal and cheerless exchanges, which they were hard-put to maintain.

After having Consuelo as a house guest for two weeks, Pilar was looking forward to her cousin's departure. But Consuelo showed no signs yet of wanting to return to southern California, and Pilar felt that under no circumstances could she be ungracious enough to suggest even in a tactful way that Consuelo should go home.

Consuelo did, however, take a break from the San Francisco scene. One morning she announced to Pilar that se would go down to Los Arboles to visit with Doña Maria.

"Only overnight," she explained.

This decision did not decrease the subtle coolness between the cousins, but in fact Pilar welcomed Consuelo's brief absence, hoping that shortly thereafter Consuelo would decide to return to Santa Barbara.

Unaccompanied, Consuelo took the train down to the Los Arboles stop. She was met by Antonio in the old family carriage and driven to the Mendez *hacienda*. When she came back next day her news was not good.

"Doña Maria is very, very ill," she reported. "Her heart is much worse."

"Did you mention that you were visiting me?"

"Of course, *querida*. I said I was staying with you. I begged her to let me bring salutations to you. She said as far as she was concerned, you were no longer her granddaughter. I am sorry to tell you this, Pilar, but that's what she said."

"I'm not surprised," Pilar said, pained by her grandmother's adamant resistance.

"It's to be expected. She cannot adjust to your

not marrying Manuel Domingo. She thinks you betrayed her."

"Yes, yes. Well, at least I know now that there is no hope of a reconciliation. I am glad you saw her."

"She made a will and you are not in it."

"That doesn't matter. I'll survive."

"But all that land," said Consuelo. "It will be worth a fortune one day as San Francisco grows."

"It's already quite valuable."

"Without you as closest heir," Consuelo went on, "she will leave the estate to your Uncle Juan in Monterey. He is next of kin. She didn't mention Maria.*"

"That follows," said Pilar bitterly.

"Perhaps you should go and insist on seeing her," Consuelo suggested, "beg her forgiveness."

"Forgiveness for what?"

"For marrying Reb, of course."

"I shall never do that. Anyway, she doesn't want me in the house."

"She might relent if she saw you."

"I cannot eat humble pie, nor force my way in."

"Not even in exchange for Los Arboles?"

Pilar stared at her cousin with ill-controlled temper for sticking her long nose in where it didn't belong. "No, not even that," she said irritably.

"Then you're a foolish child," Consuelo said. "The real purpose of my Los Arboles visit was to try and reconcile the differences between you and Doña Maria. I didn't go there for my personal pleasure."

"Please allow me to handle my own affairs,"

Pilar said icily, and swept briskly out of the living room into her study, shutting the door behind her.

That evening Pilar sat through the beginning of dinner with Robert and Consuelo nursing a bad headache. Finally she was forced to excuse herself and took refuge in her room, hearing from time to time Consuelo's hearty laughter floating up the stairwell from the living room. She was probably regaling Robert with more of her *rancho* tales, Pilar imagined. Really, Consuelo was becoming quite tiresome. Wouldn't she *ever* decide to go home?

By ten-thirty the house was quiet, as Pilar lay in bed reading a book about viniculture that Robert had given her when she mentioned she knew nothing about the subject that had become a passion with Ethan and Flora.

Presently she heard muffled footsteps in the upstairs corridor. Someone was moving on tip-toe from one part of the house to another. She got up and went to her door, cracked it and peered out. She was just in time to see Consuelo in her dressing robe and nightgown disappearing into Robert's room.

She clung to her door in cold shock, which quickly turned to anger—anger, of course, that Consuelo would assume that she was desirable to Robert, and fury at Robert for daring to encourage her dumpy cousin. She had a brief second of even regretting that she had asked Robert to live in the house.

Making an instant decision, burning with indignation, Pilar slipped into her robe. Leaving her door ajar, she walked purposefully down

the hall to Robert's room. She knocked loudly
on the door.

"Come in," Robert called out.

Pilar threw open the door. The first object
she noted was the large canopied bed, completely made up. Next her gaze traveled to Robert,
sitting in a leather-upholstered chair beside a
table lamp, completely clothed beneath his ma-
roon satin dressing gown. The book he'd been
reading when Consuelo must have interrupted
him lay open on the table.

Consuelo stood uncertainly in the middle of
the room at the foot of the bed, half turned toward Pilar. Her robe was open and beneath it
was a lacy nightgown. Its severe neckline revealed all but the nipples of her large and
beautiful breasts, her best feature.

Pilar said, "I heard someone in the corridor.
I thought it might be you, Robert."

"It was *me*," said Consuelo, defiance in her
voice. "I came to visit Robert."

"This is not a whorehouse," Pilar said curtly.
Then she added, with mounting fury, "Consuelo,
you will leave my house in the morning." She
opened the door wide. "And now you will
please go back to your room," she commanded
her cousin, stepping aside as Consuelo hesitated, glanced briefly at Robert who gave her
no encouragement to remain, then gathered her
dressing gown across her bosom and swept past
Pilar without glancing at her. A moment later
Consuelo's bedroom door slammed shut.

"There was no need for that," Robert said
mildly.

Pilar stepped into the room, her eyes blazing,
arms akimbo.

"Do you want to sleep with her?" she demanded. "Go ahead then, take her to your apartment where you probably entertain a dozen women a month. But not in my house!"

Robert stood. "Pilar," he said softly, "I was just telling your impetuous cousin when you knocked on the door that she had made a miscalculation in coming to my room. I am not in the slightest bit interested in her—or in anyone else at the moment."

"Be that as it may, Consuelo is leaving in the morning. She is going if I have to buy her the ticket and personally put her on the train for Los Angeles."

"You're being over-emotional, making a mountain out of a molehill," Robert pointed out.

"You may think what you like. I will not tolerate treachery under my roof."

"My dear Pilar, that pitiful creature isn't treacherous, she's lonely and insecure. She's looking for a husband, any husband, in the only way she knows. Surely you can recognize that."

"Yes, and she's decided on you as the most likely game."

"She doesn't know anyone else in San Francisco besides the two of us."

"Well, in any case," said Pilar, slightly mollified, "she will be leaving this house tomorrow."

Robert nodded silently, and Pilar, feeling that there was nothing more to say, muttered goodnight, closed the door of Robert's room and marched down the hall to her own. She refused to analyze her explosion of wrath beyond the point of proper manners, but she did not make excuses to herself for her behavior. She sat up brooding in bed, unable to sleep, until the early hours of the morning, her lamp still burning, the viniculture book open in her lap and unread.

Consuelo departed by ferry for the Oakland train terminal the following evening, and Pilar accompanied her to the dock. The cousins had not discussed the previous night's incident, but a distinct coolness had settled between them, dampening their normal friendliness toward one another.

At the station Consuelo said, "I am going to speak my mind, *querida*. You're not as you once were. You've grown strange and bitter. You are trying to disregard everything in your blood and all the values we were taught to respect."

"Consuelo, don't go on like that, please," Pilar said impatiently.

"I have to point out that you are no longer a light-hearted person."

"I am a widow. That isn't a frivolous situation."

"Yes, and in five years if you keep on like this you'll be a grim, humorless person, dried up and soured on the world. When you go home tonight, do me a favor. Look at yourself in the mirror, really study what you see. You're not aware of the possibilities you're missing. Think about it."

"You're talking nonsense."

"No, I'm talking truth. I went to Robert's room with something on my mind. Why not? I'll never marry, and I found him attractive. I thought perhaps he would take pity on me. There, I've said it, whatever you may think of my actions. I had nothing to lose, and something to gain."

"What will happen to you without José?" Pilar asked her cousin.

Consuelo frowned and stuck out her lower lip, regarding the question ruefully.

"God alone knows. But I shall try to laugh a great deal. And if some small fragment of love should come my way, I shan't refuse it. I will *know* when it appears, too."

The ferryboat whistle blasted. Consuelo embraced Pilar quickly.

"Thank you for the introduction to San Francisco," she murmured. "We may never meet again, dear cousin, but I leave with a lesson learned. Robert convinced me that I am wasting my talents at home. So I shall try to seek employment as a governess. You know how much I love children. And I want to live a bit also, maybe even find a lover, if not a husband. We all waste too much time, *querida*, and I am through with that!"

Pilar was already regretting her unwarranted blunt behavior of last night, all the more embarrassing to her because of Consuelo's ability to rise so easily above it.

"I'm sorry about what happened," she confessed to Consuelo. "It was unforgivably rude of me. I misjudged you."

Consuelo grinned. "And I misjudged *you*, dear cousin. You have depths to explore," she said. "Now, don't forget to look in your mirror!"

She scurried aboard the boat just as the deckhands stepped forward to remove the ramp. On board she turned and waved good-bye rather gaily before she disappeared into the crowd of deck passengers. Unaccountably, Pilar started to cry . . .

That evening when Pilar got home she found Robert in the living room. "You know," he told her, "I miss Consuelo's idle chatter already."

"So do I," Pilar admitted. "Perhaps I was too hasty in ending the visit."

"You're under a strain."

"How so?"

"Doña Maria's situation."

"I suppose you're right. I was depressed by Consuelo's visit to Los Arboles, although I know she meant well by it. I almost hated her for seeing my grandmother."

"You should go and see her yourself," Robert urged. "Put aside your pride and go."

"It has gone beyond pride between us."

"No, Pilar, you're wrong. You have too much pride, you and Doña Maria. For all her foolishness, Consuelo was trying to put pride where it belongs, somewhere behind honesty."

"I hope Consuelo finds what she wants."

"I think she will," Robert said. "She has great determination. We could use more of it ourselves."

"I daresay," Pilar declared, and bid goodnight to him.

Upstairs in her room she undressed slowly, thinking about Consuelo's suggestion that she look into her mirror.

Nude, she opened the full-length three-paneled bird's-eye maple mirror that sat on casters in one corner of the room. Rarely had she inspected her body since Reb had left her bed. It was the part of her that was experiencing nothing and therefore had no meaning; she'd felt detached from it.

Now she lifted up her small pert breasts, weighing them in her hands. They were still firm and beautiful, like a very young girl's, she thought. Her hips were curving yet slender, her thighs rich and smooth, the delicate mound of her abdomen not an inch too thick.

She extended her arms, spreading them gracefully, and peered at her face. What did she see there? A young woman in her twenties with her whole life stretching ahead of her, slowly wasting away. Suddenly the present emptiness of her existence hit her. She experienced a blinding flash of desperation that left a residue of terror. Consuelo was right; she was willfully allowing herself to wither and die, she realized, bit by bit.

She turned away from her image in the mirror unable to bear more. With a muffled sob of despair she closed the mirrored panels. She grabbed her nightgown and stepped into it, buttoned it up quickly. She climbed into bed and blew out the oil lamp. She lay in the dark unable to give a name or a shape to her fear. Something must be done, and soon. But what, what? She prayed for an answer.

A week after Consuelo's departure, word came from Antonio at Los Arboles that Doña Maria was dying.

"You have to go, even if Doña Maria hasn't asked for you," Robert told Pilar, and she agreed with him. "If it will make things easier for you, I'll go along," he suggested.

They took the noon train down to the Los Arboles stop where Antonio met them with Doña Maria's ancient black carriage. Antonio advised them that the aged matriarch's condition was critical but unchanged. She could linger on for some time or be taken at any moment by a massive heart attack.

"She is almost dead," Antonio said sorrowfully, tears coursing down his furrowed cheeks.

Doña Maria was asleep when Pilar and Robert reached her bedside.

Pilar stood staring down at the bloodless, wasted frame of her grandmother, once so vital, so loving and dear to her, now someone she no longer seemed to know at all. The old lady was as Antonio had said, almost dead. Pilar had come prepared to wait out her grandmother's death. Together she and Robert settled down for the final vigil.

Toward evening Doña Maria awoke, saw Pilar sitting beside her, blinked at her, closed her eyes for a moment, then opened them in wide recognition.

With a small ghostly smile she whispered, "I didn't send for you . . ."

"I came anyway, grandmama."

"I am glad you did, child. It is good to see you. You haven't changed."

"Nor have you," said Pilar, tears in her eyes. Despite what she may have said to Robert and Consuelo about her grandmother, she had missed Doña Maria desperately and had never adjusted to their separation.

"Where is Uncle Juan?" Pilar asked. "I thought he would be here."

Doña Maria shook her head. "I didn't send for him either."

"But I thought he was to be your heir—"

"I know what Consuelo told you, and what you thought. I told it that way so as to bring you running. I wanted to know what you thought about Los Arboles going to Juan. You would probably fight that in the American courts and win, now that you are American."

"No, I wouldn't," said Pilar. "I would respect your wish."

"Well," said the old lady, with feeble emphasis. "My wish is that you come and live here once again. It is your home, beloved Pilar. You are the only one who loves Los Arboles the way I do. It must not go to anyone else after I am gone."

Doña Maria had slowly grown aware of Robert's presence in the room. She shifted her gaze and peered into the shadows where he sat unobtrusively, beyond the foot of the bed.

"Who is that?" the old lady asked Pilar. "Is it your . . . husband?"

"Reb is dead, grandmama," Pilar reminded her softly.

"Yes, yes. I should remember. Then who is it?"

"I am Reb's father, Doña Maria," said Robert. "I came with Pilar."

"I recognize your voice. Robert Sanderson."

Doña Maria closed her eyes for a moment, opened them and focused her gaze on Robert.

"Come closer," she murmured, and Robert rose and joined Pilar at bedside.

"When I am gone you must look after my little girl, Robert," she said softly. "You must see that she marries again, someone who will not cheat her of her inheritance which is only the land. He *should* be Spanish, but I have come to believe that it is not vital. Promise me you'll see that she marries an honorable man."

"I shall do my best," Robert promised.

"Good," Doña Maria nodded. "Now I am satisfied." She stared at the ceiling, exhausted.

The priest sent for by the housekeeper arrived. He heard Doña Maria's muttered confession and administered last rites.

An hour later the old lady sat upright in bed, out of what had seemed a coma. With the last of her vitality she reached out for Pilar's hand as a violent seizure began. Through painful convulsions she gasped out in a clear voice, "I have to go now!"

So saying, she closed her eyes for the last time, sank back on her pillow, lapsed into unconsciousness, and died . . .

Doña Maria's funeral was held the following day. All of the ranch hands attended, and several near neighbors, Spanish and American. The old lady was buried in a small family plot on the hillside some distance behind the *hacienda*. Pilar stood through the ceremony dry-eyed, leaning heavily on Robert's arm.

They returned to the city that same evening. They sat on the long, brocaded velvet sofa in the living room before a crackling fire. Both were exhausted from the ordeal of the past two days.

"What will you do with Los Arboles?" Robert asked Pilar. "You must decide soon."

"I haven't thought much about its development," she said. "But I am certain that in some manner it must be connected with the Sanderson ranch."

"We own the ranch together," Robert pointed out. "Los Arboles isn't part of it. You must preserve its identity. Your grandmother may have had the right idea, Pilar. You should probably marry a Spaniard."

"Never," Pilar said with spirited distaste. "Why should I marry someone as spineless as Manuel Domingo, or as fickle as José Moraga? I have little respect for the young men of Spanish blood that I have known, or even some of the older ones. They want only two things from a woman: her flesh and her will. They live to dominate women, to be masters of all they survey. The truth is, Robert, the mold has been broken for me. I could never love a Latino."

"It was your grandmother's wish."

"She said 'an honorable man,' not necessarily a Spanish one," Pilar reminded him. "All the same, she could only say what she was raised to believe, she didn't know any better. I do."

"Then what do you propose to do with your life?" Robert enquired.

"All at once you're asking the questions a parent would ask," Pilar observed. "Why is that?"

"I suppose only because I wonder what direction my life must take. Before we went down to Los Arboles a letter came from England. From Emily. She is divorcing her Englishman. Temperamental differences, she claims. She wants to return to California and suggested that if things work out, she is ready to marry me. After more than twenty years of knowing one another, she is willing to formalize our friendship."

Pilar did not look at Robert for some moments. She sat with her hands tightly compressed in her lap.

"Do you still want to marry Emily?" she asked in a dry, tight voice.

"No, my dear," said Robert, "I don't. That time has passed."

"Well then, why did you bring it up?"

"I hoped that it might move you to reveal your future plans."

"What plans?"

"We can't go on living together like this indefinitely. You will want something more than this sterile routine after a while."

"Such as what?" Pilar persisted. "We are good friends. We should say what's in our hearts."

"Friends," Robert mused. "My dear Pilar, I don't know how you'll react to this, but I am obliged to say it. As far as I'm concerned, we're more than friends. I love you. I think I've loved you since the very first day I met you in Emily's hotel room. How I wished that day for my years to roll away! I'd have given Reb some fierce competition had I been around his age."

Pilar said in a choked voice, "Why haven't you said anything until now?" as the blood throbbed in her temples.

"I couldn't have lived here with you if I had. It would have forced you to make a decision you might not have wished to make. But today the situation has changed. Doña Maria is gone, and your life will alter. I simply cannot contain my feelings any longer."

"What will you do now?" Pilar asked him.

"I'll move to the apartment temporarily, so as not to put you in an untenable position."

"There is no need to move," said Pilar. She took a deep breath and looked straight into his eyes. "I love you too, Robert. It began after Reb's death. I needed you and you were here to help. You've always been ready to give of yourself. Then Consuelo forced me to recognize what was happening. She told me to look into my mirror . . . I may not have wit, but I do have curiosity."

"And what did you see?"

"You, I think. I was too afraid to admit it, terrified that you didn't feel as I felt. It wasn't exactly like that," said Pilar, "but almost. Grandmama's words explained what I needed to know."

"Doesn't it seem strange to you that I'm old enough to be your father?" Robert said.

"That is the least consideration," Pilar replied. "I could never marry anyone else but you."

"It will cause quite a scandal in San Francisco."

"Yes, society will have some new gossip."

"We won't be accepted in the great houses," Robert pointed out.

"I am beyond that, as you are," said Pilar. "We are rich, we can lead the kind of private and self-sufficient lives we've always lived. We'll move to Los Arboles, modernize the *hacienda*, raise Maria there. Perhaps we can have a child or so of our own."

"There is one obstacle," Robert said.

"What is that?"

"What do we tell little Maria? Her grandfather and her stepfather will be one and the same man."

"It won't matter to her. She loves you for yourself. She would be terribly unhappy if you left us."

"I won't leave," Robert promised. He took Pilar's hand in his and drew her toward him, nestling her head against his shoulder. They kissed and clung to each other in a silent and impassioned embrace.

Finally Robert declared, "We'll be married tomorrow. There's no need to wait."

"But we will be wed tonight," Pilar whispered. "In God's eyes. A marriage made in heaven . . ."

Robert and Pilar were married the next afternoon in Robert's office by a justice of peace. Surprised but pleased, Ethan and Flora were their witnesses and the only friends present.

The pair spent a quiet honeymoon at Los Arboles, exploring their new relationship, filling the days with long rides in the hills, their nights rich with love. They made endless plans for the future development of Los Arboles, even talking of making it a township.

Less than a year later, Pilar gave birth to a healthy son, much to her delight, to Robert's intense joy and little Maria's wild excitement.

"Now I have a brother, now I have a brother," Maria chanted when she was first allowed to view the infant.

"Do you have a name for him?" Pilar asked her daughter, for she and Robert hadn't yet decided on one.

Maria thought hard for a moment, scratching

her tawny curls. "He's my half-brother so he needs a full name," she said. "Let me see . . ." She turned to Robert. "We could name him after you, grandpa."

Robert laughed. "I don't think so, Maria. Things are already mixed up enough around here. Why not call him John? That was my brother's name."

Little Maria clapped her hands together delightedly. "Then I can call him Juanito sometimes when he shows his Spanish side," she said.

"John is perfect," Pilar declared, and Robert confirmed her opinion.

"The Sanderson line appears like it might go on for a while," he observed to Pilar, both of them aware of the melancholy shadow behind his remark.

"Of course it will," Pilar assured him. "And the Mendez line, too. We are the happiest family in California and we haven't stopped growing with Juanito."

"We're just beginning," Robert said, feeling that his life had finally come full circle, the tragedies of the past put into their proper perspective, the joys of the future still to be experienced.

"May I hold Juanito?" Maria asked.

"If you're very careful," Pilar told her.

"We're lucky," said Robert, watching Maria as she cradled the baby. "We live in a beautiful, blessed land and we have a new family."

"There are wonderful years ahead," Pilar said.

"Yes," Robert added, with a smile, "with a world of time to love . . ."